Human Ecology

HEALTH AFFAIRS INFORMATION GUIDE SERIES

Series Editor: Winifred Sewell, Health Science Information Consultant, currently associated with the University of Maryland and the National Health Planning Information Center

Also in this series:

BIOETHICS—*Edited by Doris Goldstein*

CROSS-NATIONAL STUDY OF HEALTH SYSTEMS: CONCEPTS, METHODS, AND DATA SOURCES—*Edited by Ray H. Elling*

CROSS-NATIONAL STUDY OF HEALTH SYSTEMS: COUNTRIES, WORLD REGIONS, AND SPECIAL PROBLEMS—*Edited by Ray H. Elling*

HEALTH CARE ADMINISTRATION—*Edited by Dwight A. Morris and Lynne Darby Morris*

HEALTH CARE COSTS AND FINANCING—*Edited by Rita Keintz*

HEALTH MAINTENANCE THROUGH FOOD AND NUTRITION—*Edited by Helen D. Ullrich*

HEALTH STATISTICS—*Edited by Frieda O. Weise*

THE PROFESSIONAL AND SCIENTIFIC LITERATURE ON PATIENT EDUCATION— *Edited by Lawrence W. Green and Connie Cavanaugh Kansler*

EMERGENCY MEDICAL SERVICES SYSTEMS—*Edited by Carlos Fernandez-Caballero and Marianne Fernandez-Caballero*

The above series is part of the
GALE INFORMATION GUIDE LIBRARY

The Library consists of a number of separate series of guides covering major areas in the social sciences, humanities, and current affairs.

General Editor: Paul Wasserman, Professor and former Dean, School of Library and Information Services, University of Maryland

Managing Editor: Denise Allard Adzigian, Gale Research Company

Human Ecology

A GUIDE TO INFORMATION SOURCES

Volume 10 in the Health Affairs Information Guide Series

Frederick Sargent II, M.D.

Professor of Human Ecology
University of Texas School of Public Health
Houston

Gale Research Company
Book Tower, Detroit, Michigan 48226

Library of Congress Cataloging in Publication Data

Sargent, Frederick, 1920-80
   Human ecology.

      (Vol. 10 in the Health affairs information guide
series)
      Includes indexes.
      1. Human ecology—Bibliography.   2. Environmental
health—Bibliography.   3. Human ecology—Information
services.   4. Environmental health—Information services.
I. Title.   II. Series: Gale information guide library.
Health affairs information guide series ; v. 10
[DNLM: 1. Ecology—Bibliography.   ZW 84 AA1 H4 v. 10]
Z5861.S27   1983   016.3042   83-11571
[GF41]
ISBN 0-8103-1504-1

This book was in progress at the time of my husband's death. It was a project he worked hard on, but not alone. He had help along the way and that help has been extended to me. For all their patience, hard work, and encouragement, on Fred's behalf and my own, I wish to thank several people.

First of all, Stephanie Normann, the head librarian at the University of Texas School of Public Health in Houston, is a good friend as well as a never-failing source of all kinds of help. Next, thanks go to Mildred Hogan, an assistant librarian, and to Jean Blalock, who typed all of Fred's manuscripts, including this one. Last, but not least, is Winifred Sewell, the series editor, who also supplied me with the will to go on when it was hard to do so, and who did more than her share of the work.

This book should now be dedicated to Fred himself--who always gave so much of himself to anyone who asked for help. I know he viewed this volume as a useful tool for all those interested in human ecology and environmental science.

Lastly, I would like to dedicate this book to those people who use it, in the hope they will find it helpful as they continue to work to better the human condition and so see Fred's dream come a little closer to reality.

Anne V. Sargent

VITA

Frederick Sargent II was educated at Phillips Exeter Academy, Massachusetts Institute of Technology, Harvard University, and Boston University School of Medicine. He did his medical work at Presbyterian Hospital in Chicago and then joined the faculty at the University of Illinois. While at Illinois, he taught physiology, did research, and became head of the Center of Human Ecology. He was also involved in many national and international societies and consulted for the U.S. government in several fields. It was at Illinois that he carried out a program he thought important and hoped to see emulated elsewhere. Through the Committee on Institutional Cooperation in the Big Ten and the University of Chicago, he set up a "wandering scholar" program in biometeorology which was funded through the Department of Health, Education and Welfare and ran for eight years. This program allowed students to study at any or all of the eleven schools involved, to go where the professors and laboratories were, so that each school did not have to be all things to all people in the field.

During 1957-1958, Dr. Sargent had a Guggenheim Fellowship and studied at Oxford. In 1968 he became Dean of the College of Environmental Sciences at the University of Wisconsin-Green Bay, and in 1970 was the first provost at Western Washington University. In 1972 he decided to go back to teaching full time and came to the University of Texas School of Public Health in Houston, where he remained until his death.

He received several honors over his lifetime and wrote over two hundred articles on a variety of subjects. A really complete vita is being published in HIPPO-CRATIC HERITAGE: A HISTORY OF THE IDEAS OF WEATHER AND HUMAN HEALTH (Pergamon Press, 1982), his magnum opus.

CONTENTS

Contents

FOREWORD

Interest in health and the resources and activities that make it possible is not
new. However, the concepts of health as a national resource and as a human
right have emerged in the recent past. Legislation during the last two decades
has led from these concepts to a complex system with some unsurprising growing
pains.

Many people have come into the field, bringing a multiplicity of backgrounds
to supplement the traditional health sciences. In addition, today's laymen
must make decisions on health care at all levels--from voting for or against
legislators who will shape health laws, through serving on local health planning boards, to becoming participants in informed decisions on their own health
care. The new recruits and the laymen have in common the need for all kinds
of information on social, business, legal, ethical, and other aspects of medicine.

Much of this information has previously been unavailable and not readily understandable to the new audiences. Attempts to satisfy the need have resulted
in burgeoning publications on a variety of subjects, ranging from the broad to
the specific. These new publications are in many forms, from carefully edited,
important texts to poorly conceived and executed technical reports, with a vast
array in between. There are journals, newsletters, association and university
guidebooks and models, statistical reports, and audiovisuals--all with varying
quality and format.

Several problems have resulted. In the first place, there has not yet emerged
a major bibliographic resource, such as the National Library of Medicine and
Excerpta Medica provide for the clinical and research aspects of medicine.
Those who have access to MEDLINE services have recently been able to
find at least a part of the pertinent current periodical references through the
new data base, Health Planning and Administration, or FILE HEALTH. A
second problem is that some of the novices in the field are not accustomed
to using published literature in any form, let alone the complex of primary,
secondary, and tertiary publications with which their counterparts in clinical
medicine and research have become familiar.

Foreword

It is the purpose of the Health Affairs Series in the Gale Information Guide Library to provide guides for participants in the complex health care system to information on the system itself--on the process of the delivery of health care. We are concerned with the management of the system and with how researchers, educators, and practitioners assure the best health possible to each individual. We are not concerned with the content of the information with which researchers, educators, or practitioners deal, but rather with their mode of functioning in a real world of people with different racial, ethnic, sexual, financial, and geographic backgrounds. For example, we are not interested in how a surgical procedure is carried out, but we are concerned with its availability to those who need it. If one understands the social sciences broadly, then the Health Affairs Series deals with the social aspects of medicine.

Due to time constraints for completing the series, some of our original plans have been changed. However, we hope the volumes included will provide a useful picture of some of the areas where the need is greatest. Individual volumes cover: HEALTH STATISTICS, HUMAN ECOLOGY, HEALTH MAINTENANCE THROUGH FOOD AND NUTRITION, THE PROFESSIONAL AND SCIENTIFIC LITERATURE OF PATIENT EDUCATION, CROSS-NATIONAL STUDY OF HEALTH SYSTEMS, HEALTH CARE COSTS AND FINANCING, HEALTH CARE ADMINISTRATION, EMERGENCY MEDICAL SERVICES SYSTEMS, and BIOETHICS.

The user may ask, "Why another bibliography when there are already so many?" We agree, but the Health Affairs guides are much more than bibliographies. All contain a careful selection of materials for the intended audience, an evaluation of these materials in annotations and introductory paragraphs, and directions for finding further information. There are lists of many sources of information, such as information centers, schools, publishers, and audiovisuals. The journals which one should read regularly to keep up with the field are mentioned and annotated. In short, the reader will find specific resources for the present, and, for the future, methods of finding new sources as they are developed.

Because all of the social sciences dealing with health affairs are interrelated, it is both impossible and undesirable to prescribe strict limits for each individual volume, excluding from one anything included in another. Instead, each volume of the series is complete for the individual who is interested in only one specific subject. At the same time, other volumes serve as excellent supplements when the user wishes to go into related topics in greater depth. The series editor takes responsibility for the general organization and coverage of the series, but has left to the judgment of the volume editors decisions on individual items to be included or excluded. The series should be helpful to users not only for what they are able to find in the individual volumes, but for how it has been sifted to exclude those materials that would send them down blind alleys.

We hope that our audience for the series will consist of newcomers to the fields involved, as well as researchers and practitioners who have worked with health affairs in the past but need to renew their familiarity with resources in some aspect of their major current interests. We hope especially that the guides will be useful in the education of students who have chosen one or more of the fields covered for their future careers. And finally, we have tried to make the volumes simple and direct enough that they will provide the informed lay-person with access to the information resources needed to make decisions about future procedures and policies in assurance of the best match between national resources and the health care of the nation.

Dr. Sargent's unique qualifications for preparing this volume are discussed in my introduction. Here I should like to acknowledge the contributions of his friends, particularly Stephanie L. Normann, and his wife, Anne, in bringing the book to publication after his death. Anne Sargent was determined to get it published and to retain its original flair. Readers can be grateful to her and to Fred for what I feel is a major contribution to the bibliography of human ecology.

Winifred Sewell
Health Affairs Series Editor

ACKNOWLEDGMENTS

I would like to extend a personal note of thanks to the staff of the library at the University of Texas School of Public Health, Houston, and to Winifred Sewell, editor of the Health Affairs Information Guide Library.

Anne V. Sargent

INTRODUCTION

Frederick Sargent died in early 1980, in the midst of a productive life and many important projects. One of the projects outstanding but essentially complete was this annotated bibliography on human ecology. The major task which remained was to write introductions to each section, stating the definition of that particular part, the rationale behind organizing the material in the specified manner, and reasons for inclusion or exclusion of individual items.

After his death, there were several alternatives for our handling of his bibliography.

We could have abandoned the project. But that would have been unfortunate; it was virtually finished and it was one of those projects he had considered worth continuing in spite of cutting back some activities after an earlier illness. I never met Fred Sargent, though I feel I knew him well through correspondence and telephone conversations. I cannot tell his motivations in agreeing to do what to some might have seemed a pedestrian task--an annotated bibliography. But the final product suggests to me that Fred Sargent's respect for the literature, the written record of the creation of many minds, plus his need to pin down his very broad view of human ecology as it was drawn from a multiplicity of disciplines, compelled him to collect and organize this bibliography as a part of his own intellectual development and the continuing refinement of his concepts. This effort and its result seem to us too valuable to let disappear.

We could have had another ecologist take over the project, review the whole thing, determine final inclusions and exclusions, and write introductions to each component part. That would have insured that no item was left out that Dr. Sargent intended to include but simply didn't get to. However, it would have introduced another viewpoint. In a field so fluid as human ecology, we would then have had a different book and one that was only partially Fred Sargent's. It would quite possibly have lost the individual flavor he has given this volume.

We could have printed the book exactly as it existed in the notebooks left behind, without any introductions, letting the reader search out Dr. Sargent's philosophy from his inclusions or exclusions. But it seemed a pity to rely wholly on the implications of his selections from the works of others, when he was one of the most articulate authors in the field himself and has left us a valuable inventory of his own writings.

We have consequently opted to print the volume as he left it, except that we have selected excerpts from a number of his own writings to illustrate his philosophy about the topics under which he organized it. This decision was made partly to confrom more closely with other volumes in the Health Affairs Information Guide Series, all of which have contained introductory materials for each chapter or section. But it also provides the users of this bibliography with the viewpoint of a particularly brilliant and innovative mind in a fashion which is more explicit than can be shown merely by his selections and the annotations. In only one case have we quoted from others. In Section VI, on community health, we have used materials from Audy and Dunn which Dr. Sargent had included in his volume on HUMAN ECOLOGY (North-Holland, 1974), feeling that his selection of the authors for that volume indicates an agreement with their approach.

The only other part of the volume which Dr. Sargent did not create or review is the last chapter on sources of additional information. Stephanie L. Normann, director of library services, University of Texas Health Science Center in Houston, and a colleague of Sargent, had volunteered to prepare this section early in the project, but had not completed it before he died. She had, however, followed his outline carefully, and to the scope which he presents.

Any selection of quotations such as these is arbitrary. Just as individual papers annotated for this collection do not always fit neatly under a single rubric of its organization, so the quotations selected do not encompass the whole section and only the section which they introduce. Rather, they represent a major thrust of Dr. Sargent's thinking which appears to this editor to be pertinent to that section. I hope readers will agree that these quotations provide a continuum of his thought which adds to the volume. At least, we have not put words into Dr. Sargent's mouth. Ideally our selections will lead people back to the original works, where they will discover the dynamic thinking and breadth of perspective that makes it so difficult to limit any quotation from Dr. Sargent to a single category within this volume.

Winifred Sewell
Series Editor

Section I

NATURE AND SCOPE

In some unpublished remarks on September 27, 1979, Dr. Sargent describes the concept of human ecology held by workers in the field as follows:

"The most intriguing problems are identifying the origins and defining the scope and content of human ecology. When one calls himself a "human ecologist." Just what does he mean? What has been his heritage? What does he do?

"If you asked one of the members of the human ecology faculty for a definition, he might simply reply--without setting you down and explaining about adaptive capacity, adaptive strategy, and complex biosocial feedback--that human ecology was the study of man-environment interactions and interrelations. Probably that would not satisfy you, but the reason is that there is really no general agreement about scope and content, let alone origins.

"Origins:

1916 - Huntington coined term 'human ecology.'
1921 - The Chicago School of Sociology adapted the term to designate application of ecological principles and concepts to study of human communities.
1923 - Barrows claimed that human geography was really human ecology.
1936 - Bews wrote the first monograph entitled human ecology.
1938 - H.G. Wells suggested that sociology was really a branch of human ecology.

"With such diverse roots and viewpoints, it is not surprising that there was initially little agreement on nature and scope of this area of study. Over the years matters did not improve. When John Bruhn wrote of human ecology in 1974, he traced its roots in geography, anthropology, sociology, and psychology, but was not certain whether it as succeeding as a 'unifying science.'[1] It is curious that he omitted a root in medicine, for some of the most active human ecologists have been physi-

---

1. John G. Bruhn, "Human Ecology: a Unifying Science?" JOURNAL OF HUMAN ECOLOGY 2, no. 2 (1974): 105-25.

cians and physiologists.

"Recently I have been studying the literature that might be included under the title 'human ecology.' I have been rather amazed at the diversity of linkages between ecology and the sciences of man.

HEALTH EMPHASIS	BEHAVIORAL EMPHASIS	OTHER EMPHASIS
Ecological medical geography	Social ecology	Ecodevelopment
Epidemiology and human ecology	Behavioral ecology	Ecotoxicology
Occupational health as human ecology	Political ecology	Ecoscience
Environmental health as human ecology	Psychological ecology	
Clinical ecology	Ecological anthropology	
	Urban ecology	

Although this picture hardly suggests unification, if one allows for squabbles over the turf, it does suggest something of nature and scope. And if this range is not broad enough, René Dubos would add nutrition. Last year, at a NIH Conference on Biomedical and Behavioral Basis of Clinical Nutrition, he concluded a discussion of the intellectual basis of nutrition science and

> It seems reasonable to envisage a time when dietary regimens can be designed, not only for growth and health, but for certain functions and cultural values. Nutrition can contribute to a new science--as yet undeveloped--of human ecology.[2]

Even if undeveloped, there is now a journal and an international society."

In an earlier work, we find a more personal statement of Dr. Sargent's understanding of the nature and scope of human ecology.

> Life is the essence of a singular dynamic evolutionary process that characterizes the substance of this planet. Man is the most recent creation of this process. He is unique among free-living organisms, for he is endowed with capability of insight into his origins and into himself and he can control not only his own destiny, but also that of all other organisms. Man's abode is some five billion years old. The life-process emerged about 2.7 billion years ago, but man himself has an evolutionary history that extends back in time only two million years. It was the unusual configuration and properties of the earth's substances and the geophysical relationships among the planets of the solar system that provided the appropriate environment for that life-process.

2. René Dubos, "The Intellectual Basis of Research in Clinical Nutrition," in THE BIOMEDICAL AND BEHAVIORAL BASIS OF CLINICAL NUTRITION. A PROJECTION FOR THE 1980's, Report of a National Conference Sponsored by the Nutrition Coordinating Committee, National Institutes of Health, June 19-20, 1978 (Washington, D.C.: Superintendent of Documents, 1979), pp. 21-28.

With its emergence the bond between life-process and environment was forever sealed. Organism and environment became parts of an evolving interacting system. Organism shaped environment, environment shaped organism, organism shaped organism, and organism even shaped itself. Man, the youngest species of this system, is, in spite of his unique characteristics, no exception.

Human ecology studies this system. It explores the nature of man's place in this system. In essence, human ecology seeks to understand man and his problems by studying individuals and populations as biological entities profoundly modified by culture and by studying the effects of environment on man and those of man upon his environment. The environment in which man has his being is complex. It embraces physical, biological, and socioeconomic components. Human ecology observes man in these contexts in terms of his physiological and behavioral tolerances and the genetic and social mechanisms that provide continuities, feedback stabilities, and progressive adaptations of biological and cultural evolution.

As a biological organism man has both generic and unique features. Among the former, the phenomena of distinctiveness and of persistence over time are central. Here we deal with constancy and equilibrium. These are characteristics of all free-living organisms. They arise in part because organisms are in themselves systems of self-regulating processes but more fundamentally because free-living organisms exhibit direction. Direction is a characteristic of the organism in environment, for the survival of the organism depends upon its finding an environment which is adequate for it. To be successful in this search the organism must select from a diversity of environmental stimuli that act upon it only those events that are pertinent. These stimuli do not arise from a milieu which is unchanging, rather they arise from an environment that forms continuously as the organism grows, matures, and ages. Thus organism and environment are inseparable. It is this bond which gives rise to organismic behavior and to selection in evolution. . . .[3]

Barker, Robert G., and Wright, Herbert F. MIDWEST AND ITS CHILDREN: THE PSYCHOLOGICAL ECOLOGY OF AN AMERICAN TOWN. Evanston, Ill.: Row, Peterson and Co., [1954]. vii, 532 p.

Barker and Wright report a study made in the "Midwest." The objective was to examine and measure behavioral development within "its natural psychological habitat." Their results deal with the development of behavioral patterns in various natural and social settings and with social actions and interactions. The report

3. Frederick Sargent II, "Nature and Scope of Human Ecology," in his HUMAN ECOLOGY (Amsterdam: North Holland Publishing Co., 1974), pp. 1-2.

includes methodological details as well as some discussion of conducting a field study in psychological ecology.

Bates, Marston. MAN IN NATURE. Foundations of Modern Biology Series. Englewood Cliffs, N.J.: Prentice-Hall, 1961. xi, 116 p. Paperbound.

This is a survey of the ecology of man which considers human evolution, population structure, domestication and agriculture, health and disease, and resource management.

Bettmann, Otto L. THE GOOD OLD DAYS--THEY WERE TERRIBLE. New York: Random House, 1974. xiii, 207 p. Illus.

Bettmann demonstrates just how grim it was in the period between the Civil War and the early 1900s, the so-called Gilded Age or gay nineties. His story encompasses air, traffic housing, rural life, work, crime, food and drink, health, education, travel, and leisure.

Bews, J[ohn]. W[illiam]. HUMAN ECOLOGY. Introduction by J.C. Smuts. London: Oxford University Press, 1935. vii, 312 p.

This early monograph was written by a plant ecologist. The contents include discussions of environment; heredity, physiological and pathological responses to the environment; ecology of ancient man, food-gatherers, plant cultivators, and herdsmen and nomads; ecological classification of populations; and Bews's views on human ecology as a science. The philosophical theme of the book is the holism of J.C. Smuts.

_____. LIFE AS A WHOLE. London: Longmans, Green, and Co., 1937. ix, 347 p.

This work is an extension of holistic ideas first elaborated in Bews's HUMAN ECOLOGY (above). The objective is to focus attention on "methods of constructing wholes." The first part of the book is devoted to man's life history--childhood, adolescence, maturity, middle age, and old age. The second part comprises discussions of man's cultural history--discoveries and inventions, social institutions, history and philosophy, art, architecture, music, and literature. This work comprises an early attempt at systematic analysis of man-environment relationships.

Blau, Sheridan D., and Rodenbeck, John von B., eds. THE HOUSE WE LIVE IN; AN ENVIRONMENTAL READER. New York: Macmillan Co., 1971. xix, 515 p. Paperbound.

The editors have two objectives. First, the essays reprinted might provide provocative ideas for compositions for students in English composition. Second, the readings might be useful in interdisciplinary general studies courses in environmental problems.

Man's impact on his environment is depicted first as a set of dangers. Then these dangers are analyzed in terms of causes and solutions.

Boughey, Arthur S. MAN AND THE ENVIRONMENT; AN INTRODUCTION TO HUMAN ECOLOGY AND EVOLUTION. New York: Macmillan Co., 1971. viii, 472 p. Glossary.

In this introductory textbook on human ecology, the topics include the ecosystem concept, man's biological evolution, domestication and urban origins, population, environmental pollution, and environmental management. There is a list of governmental agencies involved in environmental problems.

Bowen-Jones, Howard, ed. HUMAN ECOLOGY IN THE COMMONWEALTH. Proceedings of the First Commonwealth Conference on Development and Human Ecology held in Malta, 18-24 October 1970. London: Charles Knight and Co., 1972. xiv, 192 p.

The sponsors were the government of Malta, the Royal University of Malta, and the Commonwealth Human Ecology Council. Four broad topics were considered by the representatives of Commonwealth countries. The first, the human predicament, included discussions of environmental quality; demography, education and development; environmental control; and planning. Under the second topic several papers reported an ongoing case study of Malta: historical review, nutritional status, natural food resources, and socioeconomic problems. Reports from Commonwealth countries comprised the third topic: ecological aspects of development in Africa, India, Singapore, Malaysia, Tristan du Cunha, and Australia. The final discussions revolved around plans for international action toward ecologically sensitive development.

Bresler, Jack B., ed. ENVIRONMENTS OF MAN. Reading, Mass.: Addison-Wesley Publishing Co., 1968. xi, 289 p. Paperbound. Appendixes.

Bresler suggests that the unifying theme for studies of man and environment is human ecology. The topics treated by the collected papers include man's ecosystem, adaptation to soils, adaptation to physical factors, human disease, food and water, reproduction, cycles, ecology and genetics, population and society, pollution and hereditary consequences, and the Martian environment. The volume contains a glossary and suggested supplementary readings. The book is intended as a supplementary text book for courses in biology, ecology, anthropology, and other sciences, or in general education.

_____. HUMAN ECOLOGY; COLLECTED READINGS. Addison-Wesley Series in the Life Sciences. Reading, Mass.: Addison-Wesley Publishing Co., 1966. viii, 472 p.

Part 1 is devoted to natural environments of man, both external (climate, land, altitude, and season and weather) and internal (fetal environment). Part 2 deals with man-made environments such as human populations, radiation, air pollution, and space. The editorial comment on the collection is minimal.

Bricker, Victoria Reifler, ed. "Special Issue: Human Ecology." AMERICAN ETHNOLOGIST 4 (February 1977): 1-198.

This group of articles deals with various human ecological topics: "Ecology and Human Ecology: A Comparison of Theories in the Biological and Social Sciences," by P.J. Richerson; "Ecological Niche Theory in Sociocultural Anthropology: A Conceptual Framework and an Application," T.F. Love; "Historical Perspectives on Frontier Agriculture as an Adaptive Strategy," M. Margolis; "Differential Risk Strategies as Cultural Style among Farmers in the Lower Chubat Valley, Patagonia," G. Williams; "Integration through Production: The Use of Zonation in Espinar," B.S. Orlove; "Traditional Agriculture, Central Places, and Postdisaster Urban Relocation in Peru," A. Oliver-Smith; "The Ecological Basis for Aztec Sacrifice," M. Harner; "The Process of State Formation in Madagascar," C.P. Kottak; "Individual Decisions and Functional Systems: Economic Rationality and Environmental Adaptation," H.J. Rutz; "Human Ecology and the Population Concept: The Yelnadu Reddi Population in India," E. Montgomery; "Knowledge and Power: Anthropology, Policy Research, and the Green Revolution," F.C. Miller.

Brierley, John K. A NATURAL HISTORY OF MAN. Rutherford, N.J.: Fairleigh Dickinson University Press, 1970. xv, 184 p. Tables; Figures.

Brierley has written this text for laymen or students. In the first part, the use of demographic data is introduced. In the second, the nature-nurture question and the role of homeostasis are discussed. In the third, the emergence and rise of biological and social man are sketched. The fourth part describes the roles of social progress and medical technology in the changing patterns of disease in different historical periods, regions, and age groups. The fifth deals with migration, and the sixth with war.

DeSanto, Robert S. CONCEPTS OF APPLIED ECOLOGY. New York: Springer-Verlag, 1978. ix, 310 p. Paperbound. Tables; Glossary.

DeSanto discusses concepts of ecology and demonstrates their application to current environmental problems. Major topics considered include ecosystem organization and human ecology, division of ecology (terrestrial, fresh water, and marine), the preparation of environmental impact statements, environmental stresses and pathways of related ecological factors (nutrients and toxic metals). The appendix contains numerous tables of conversion factors and a comprehensive glossary of terms used in applied ecology.

Dice, Lee R. MAN'S NATURE AND NATURE'S MAN: THE ECOLOGY OF HUMAN COMMUNITIES. Ann Arbor: University of Michigan Press, 1955. 329 p. Bibliog.

> Dice provides a general description of human communities, discussing their resources; the characteristics of their habitats; the human population and associated plants and animals, particularly those providing food and fiber; and the mechanisms regulating human communities. The emphasis is descriptive because practical methods for measuring quantitatively the ecological features of human communities were not generally available.

Dickinson, Robert E. CITY, REGION AND REGIONALISM: A GEOGRAPHICAL CONTRIBUTION TO HUMAN ECOLOGY. London: Kegan Paul, Trench, Trubner and Co., 1947. xv, 327 p.

> Dickinson develops the general theme that the nucleated settlement, whether it be village, town, city, or even city subcenter, is the focus of human activity and organization servicing the surrounding tributary area. This theme is human ecology in the United States and social morphology in Europe. He divides his presentation into four parts: (1) the urban settlement as a regional center, (2) the structure of the city, (3) the city region, and (4) regionalism and the region. His concepts should be useful in planning and he argues that one must be familiar with anatomy before recommending treatments.

Ehrlich, Paul R.; Ehrlich, Anne H.; and Holdren, John P. HUMAN ECOLOGY: PROBLEMS AND SOLUTIONS. San Francisco: W.H. Freeman and Co., 1973. xi, 304 p. Paperbound.

> The authors examine the problems that have emerged from the interactions of population, resources, and environment. The recent rapid growth of the population has led to itensified pressure on the carrying capacity of the earth: land, energy, mineral resources, food, and other renewable resources. The use and abuse of resources have consequences which affect society directly as environmental pollution and indirectly through the disruption of ecosystems. The solutions for these problems will depend upon population limitation and changing behavior toward environment.

Fosberg, Francis Raymond, ed. MAN'S PLACE IN THE ISLAND ECOSYSTEM. Honolulu: Bishop Museum Press, 1965. vii, 264 p. Paperbound.

> This volume contains papers included in a symposium held during the Tenth Pacific Science Congress, 1961. Topics include the concept of ecosystem, the physical and biological features of islands, the interactions between man and nature, and the modes of living, demographic pressures, and modifying influences of human activities in the islands of the Pacific.

Gutkind, Erwin Anton. COMMUNITY AND ENVIRONMENT; A DISCOURSE
ON SOCIAL ECOLOGY. London: Watts and Co., 1953. xiii, 81 p.

Gutkind calls for a new synthesis of studies by the social sciences.
The framework, social ecology, must examine man himself, man
in relation to the group, and man in relation to environment.
Man's relations both to his fellows and to his environment are
dynamic, always in transition. Four principal stages across human
history are recognized: a stage of fear and anxiety about unknown
nature, a stage of rational adaptation of environmental resources
to human needs, a stage of aggressive environmental exploitation
with loss of confidence, and a stage, only now emerging, of con-
scious planning for a balanced use of limited environmental resources for the common good. Social ecology should lead the
way toward better understanding mankind's relation to its whole
environment.

Hawley, Amos H. HUMAN ECOLOGY; A THEORY OF COMMUNITY STRUC-
TURE. New York: Ronald Press Co., 1950. xvi, 456 p.

As a logical extension of the general field of ecology, Hawley
views human ecology "as the study of the form and the development of the community in human populations." This concept places
human ecology among the branches of sociology. The present
book considers the human aggregate (where people live and growth
and composition of population), the organization of human communities in time and space, and the changes in the community as
a consequence of mobility and expansion.

Huxley, Julian, ed. THE HUMANIST FRAME. London: George Allen and
Unwin, 1961. 432 p.

Humanism is an idea-system based on an understanding of man as
an organism and his relation to environment. Huxley and his col-
leagues explore this idea-system in a series of essays: "Body,
Brain, Mind and Soul," by R. Brain; "The Human Animal," C.H.
Waddington; "Science is Human," J. Bronowski; "The Democratic
Challenge," F. Williams; "A Humanist View of Progress," M.
Ginsberg; "The Human Program," H.J. Blackham; "The Roots of
Virtue," E.H. Erickson; "Marginal Lands of the Mind," F. Huxley;
"Love in a Humanist Frame," M.M. Hunt; "The Shells of Society,"
W. Holford; "Towards the Condition of Music," M. Tippett; "So-
cial Purpose and the Integrity of the Artist," S. Spender; "The
Integration of Knowledge," O.L. Rieser; "The Frame of Humanist
Communication," P. Meridith; "An Education for Humanity," H.L.
Elvin; "Sociology and Public Policy," M. Young; "Humanist Eco-
nomics," R. Marris; "New Horizons for Under-developed Peoples,"
S. Sen; "Law, Science and Humanism," H. Kalven, Jr. and H.
Ziesel; "Humanism and Social Pathology," Baroness Wootton; "The
New Medicine and Its Responsibilities," R. Platt; "What are People
For?" G.C.L. Bertram; "The Place of Conservation," E.M. Nicholson;

"The Human Future," H.J. Muller; and "Human Potentialities,"
A. Huxley. The authors have an optimistic view of man's future.

Jones, J. Owen, and Jones, Elizabeth A. INDEX OF HUMAN ECOLOGY.
London: Europa Publications, 1974. ix, 169 p.

Since human ecology is a new focus on a very broad field in terms
of subjects and practices, there is a need for interdisciplinary
coordination of information among the specialized compartments
of knowledge. It is estimated that each year several million items
are published on subjects relevant to human ecology. Each subject
has its own literature with primary sources of information--articles,
papers, reports, books; some subjects have developed secondary
information services, such as abstract journals, bibliographies, and
information retrieval facilities. The present volume attempts to
provide a tertiary level by relating information services and their
secondary journals into a comprehensive reference system. Only
items meeting four criteria are included: coverage of world scientific and professional literature; output in the English language;
inclusion of abstracts of essential information as well as biblio-
graphical data; output published, readily available, self-contained,
and usable without further accessories. Thus this volume attempts
to provide a compact, convenient tool for locating research materials on all subjects relating to the question in hand.

Leroux, Robert. ÉCOLOGIE HUMAINE: SCIENCE DE L' HABITAT. Paris:
Editions Eyrolles, 1963. 318 p. Figures; Bibliog.

Leroux discusses theoretical and practical knowledge of the habitat
which is indispensible for professionals of the building industry.
In the first part he considers physiological matters important to
construction. The second part is devoted to discussions of habit-
ability, durability, economy, and exposure of buildings. In the
third part Leroux considers the application of concepts and principles of construction.

Levine, Norman D., ed. HUMAN ECOLOGY. North Scituate, Mass.: Duxbury
Press; Belmont, Calif.: Wadsworth Publishing Co., 1975. viii, 469 p. Glossary; Index.

Drawing upon experiences in teaching human ecology to undergraduates, Levine and his eight colleagues composed this introductory text. Part 1 is devoted to discussions of the physical and
biological aspects of man's environment. In part 2 the focus is
man's physical evolution (human adaptability, individuality, life
cycle, and homeostasis). Man's cultural evolution is considered
in part 3, in which demography and urbanization are discussed.
In part 4 the problems of food, disease, and pollution are considered. In a final chapter, the editor speculates about man's
future.

Martin, Geoffrey J. ELLSWORTH HUNTINGTON: HIS LIFE AND THOUGHT.
Hamden, Conn.: Archon Books; Shoe String Press, 1973. xx, 315 p. Bibliog.,
pp. 276-95.

> Ellsworth Huntington was a founding member of the Ecological
> Society of America. "He was a pioneer in the use of the term
> 'human ecology,' which he first adopted in 1916 to distinguish
> geographers' work from that of zoologists and biologists' who could
> not see beyond their big toe.'" (p. 143) He was the second
> president of Ecological Society of America, elected in 1917. His
> presidential address was "Climatic Change as a Factor in Organic
> Evolution."

Mills College. THREE PAPERS ON HUMAN ECOLOGY. Mills College As-
semble Series 1965-1966. Oakland, Calif.: 1966. 52 p. Paperbound.

> Three papers are "Man, Nature, and the Landscape: An Intro-
> duction to Human Ecology," by George Treichel; "A Glance into
> the Garden," John B. Calhoun; and "Adaptive Strategies: A
> Basic Problem in Human Ecology," Demetri B. Shimkin.

Park, Robert E., and Burgess, Ernest W. INTRODUCTION TO THE SCIENCE
OF SOCIOLOGY. 2d ed. Chicago: University of Chicago Press, 1924.
xxii, 1,040 p.

> This text is credited as one which introduces for the first time
> the term "human ecology." Chapter 3 (pp. 161-225) deals with
> society and the group; various societies, communities, and groups,
> including plant, animal, and human, are discussed. Selected
> materials from the writing of others are brought together "to
> show (1) the fundamental character of the relations which have
> been established between individuals through communication; (2)
> the gradual evolution of these relations in animal and human so-
> cieties" (pp. 164-65). Park and Burgess note: "The processes
> of competition, segregation, and accommodation brought out in
> the description of the plant community are quite comparable with
> the same processes in animal and human communities. A village,
> town, city, or nation may be studied from the standpoint of the
> adaptation, struggle for existence, and survival of its individual
> members in the environment created as a whole" (p. 166). The
> term "human ecology," however, does not appear until page 223
> in a list of "topics for written themes:" 3. Plant Communities;
> 4. Animal Societies: The Ant Colony, the Bee Hive; 5. Animal
> Communities, or Studies in Animal Ecology; 6. Human Communities
> Human Ecology, and Economics; 7. The Natural Areas of the City.
> The only citation of "human ecology" in the general index is to
> page 558, where the heading is "Competition and Human Ecology"
> and the statement is made that "The ecological conception of so-
> ciety is that of a society created by competitive cooperation."
> Nowhere do the authors explicitly and specifically define human
> ecology. The reader is left to infer it from contrasting discussions
> of plant, animal, and human communities.

Park, Robert E.; Burgess, Ernest W.; and McKenzie, R.D. THE CITY. Introduction by M. Janowitz. Chicago: University of Chicago Press, 1925.

> "The city has been studied, in recent times, from the point of view of its geography, and still more recently from the point of view of its ecology. There are forces at work within the limits of the urban community--within the limits of any natural area of human habitation, in fact--which tend to bring about an orderly and typical grouping of its population and institutions. The science which seeks to isolate these factors and to describe the typical constellations of persons and institutions which the co-operation of these forces produce is what we call human, as distinguished from plant and animal, ecology" (pp. 1-2).

> "Ecology has been defined as 'that phase of biology that considers plants and animals as they exist in nature, and studies their interdependence, and the relation of each kind and individual to its environment.' This definition is not sufficiently comprehensive to include all the elements that logically fall with the range of human ecology. In the absence of any precedent let us tentatively define human ecology as a study of the spatial and temporal relations of human beings as affected by the selective, distributive, and accommodative forces of the environment. Human ecology is fundamentally interested in the effect of position, in both time and space, upon human institutions and human behavior" (pp. 63-64).

Parsons, Howard L., ed. and comp. MARX AND ENGELS ON ECOLOGY. Westport, Conn.: Greenwood Press, 1977. xiv, 262 p. Bibliog.

> Parsons has brought together selections from the writings of Marx and Engels which demonstrate that these men had knowledge of ecological concepts and understood the nature and implications of ecological transformations produced by man. In the first part, there is a general discussion of the thoughts of these men and their relevance to current environmental problems. Selections from their writings comprise the second part.

Quinn, James A. HUMAN ECOLOGY. New York: Prentice-Hall, 1950. xii, 561 p. Bibliog.

> This is a textbook for students, particularly of sociology. Emphasizing that scientists of various disciplines are interested in man-environmental relations--sociologists, geographers, biologists, and economists--Quinn adopts the areal or regional approach and organizes his material around studies of spatial distributions of communities. The major sections of the book examine structure and planning of areas, processes underlying areal change, and various interpretations of spatial distribution.

Robertson, Thomas. HUMAN ECOLOGY; THE SCIENCE OF SOCIAL AD-
JUSTMENT. Glasgow: William Maclellan, 1948. xx, 534 p. Glossary;
Bibliog.

> Robertson treats reconstruction as a set of social phenomena and
> urges that the scientific method be applied vigorously to their
> study. There are seven basic processes operating in society--
> finance, industry, sanctions, administration, politics, education,
> and religion. Robertson explores the myths and real objectives
> of these processes. For him human ecology is the controlling
> science in a natural order of society which includes finance and
> religion in the operational matrix.

Rogers, Edward S. HUMAN ECOLOGY AND HEALTH; AN INTRODUCTION
FOR ADMINISTRATORS. New York: Macmillan Co., 1960. xviii, 334 p.
Tables; Bibliog.

> Written for students of public health, Rogers discusses three main
> topics: demography, vital statistics, and an ecological approach
> to concepts of health and illness.

Rogers, Paul, ed. THE EDUCATION OF HUMAN ECOLOGISTS. Proceedings
of a Symposium held at the Polytechnic, Huddersfield, 28-29 March 1972.
London: Charles Knight and Co., 1972. ix, 166 p. Appendix.

> The participants addressed three broad topics: human ecology and
> society, contributions of the principal disciplines, and course op-
> portunities. In the first, the scope of human ecology is described,
> including political implications, and employment opportunities are
> discussed. In the second, the contributions of ecology, economics,
> geography, anthropology, architecture, and medical science to
> human ecology are considered. In the third, several undergraduate
> programs available at English schools are described. The appendix
> contains a guide to multidisciplinary degree programs concerned
> with the human environment. The participants concluded that the
> courses in human ecology should be given at all levels of edu-
> cation, including continuing education.

Sargent, Frederick II, ed. HUMAN ECOLOGY. Amsterdam: North Holland
Publishing Co., 1974. xii, 475 p.

> This textbook for graduate students and postgraduate professionals
> seeks to identify the nature and scope of a not yet fully matured
> area of science--human ecology. In the twenty-one chapters,
> the editor and his colleagues examine ecosystems, man, man's use
> of resources, the human condition, and the management of en-
> vironmental quality. Individual chapters deal with nature and
> scope of human ecology; natural and human ecosystems; human
> biology and the uniqueness of man; biology of human variation;
> human individuality; human behavior; some biological and cul-
> tural determinants; human population and its control; agricultural

systems; energy; minerals; water; transportation and communication
systems; ecological dimensions of environmental hazards; shelter
and clothing in an ecological setting; planning for people, not
buildings; health and disease; community health; fitness of ecosystem; environmental health, environmental deterioration; environmental policy; environmental planning; and resource management
strategies.

Shepard, Paul, and McKinley, David, eds. THE SUBVERSIVE SCIENCE. ESSAYS
TOWARD AN ECOLOGY OF MAN. Boston: Houghton Mifflin Co., 1969.
x, 453 p. Paperbound.

The essays, collected from the published literature, have been
assembled into five parts. The first deals with men as populations; the second, environmental encounters; the third and fourth,
men's relation to other organisms and ecosystems, respectively;
and the fifth, ethical issues. The editors provide an introductory
essay and make editorial comments about most of the individual
articles so that a theme emerges.

Theodorson, George A., ed. STUDIES IN HUMAN ECOLOGY. New York:
Harper and Row, 1961. xiii, 626 p. Bibliog.

This anthropology brings together publications which deal with
human ecology as the study of human communities. Most of the
papers represent the work of geographers and sociologists. Part
1 comprises classical human ecology; the papers of section A discuss the classical position and those of section B are criticisms of
that position. Part 2 focuses on current theory and research; neo-
orthodox approach (section A), social area analysis (section B),
and sociocultural approach (section C). The papers of part 3 comprise cross-cultural studies, part 4, human ecology as human geography, and part 5, regional studies.

Thomas, Franklin. THE ENVIRONMENTAL BASIS OF HUMAN SOCIETY; A
STUDY IN THE HISTORY OF SOCIOLOGICAL THEORY. New York: Century,
1925. Reprint. New York: Johnson Reprint Corp., 1965. vii, 336 p. Bibliog.

Thomas expounds the anthrogeographical theories of society. Although he does not judge their scientific validity, he does review
and evaluate criticisms of the theories. He first discusses the importance of environmental theory for social science and the historical background of such doctrines. Three chapters are devoted
to theories of climatic influences dating from ancient to contemporary. Next he turns to the influences of natural resources and
to location and accessibility, direct psychological influence of
natural surroundings, the geography of history, man's control over
the physical environment, and finally critics of geographical determinism.

U.S. Department of Health, Education and Welfare. Consumer Protection and Environmental Health Service. PROCEEDINGS OF SYMPOSIUM ON HUMAN ECOLOGY. Public Health Service Publication, no. 1929. Washington, D.C.: 1969. vii, 123 p. Paperbound.

> The participants of the symposium held 24-27 November 1968 considered issues and formulated recommendations to assist the Consumer Protection and Environmental Health Service to deal with environmental and consumer problems. The issues were set out in several addresses: the crisis of man in his environment, some problems in economic analysis of environmental policy choices, centers of excellence for the study of human ecology, creation of public and professional awareness in the field of human ecology, and strategy for improvement of the status of man in his environment.

Watson, Richard A., and Watson, Patty Jo. MAN AND NATURE; AN ANTHROPOLOGICAL ESSAY IN HUMAN ECOLOGY. New York: Harcourt, Brace and World, 1969. ix, 172 p. Paperbound.

> The Watsons studied the sequential steps that primates and man have taken in controlling their environment. They suggest that the orderly development which they discern is a model which can be used for further studies in human ecology. In essence, they find cultural environments are increasingly substituted for the physical environment as primates and man have moved through various "ways of life": primate, protohuman, elemental man, hunter and gatherer, domesticator, food producer, industrial man, and atomic man. They emphasize, however, that no matter how important the culture environment might seem to be, man, nevertheless, will always be dependent upon nature. He cannot survive if he does not maintain an ecological balance.

Wells, H.G. THE WORK, WEALTH AND HAPPINESS OF MANKIND. 2 vols. Garden City, N.Y.: Doubleday, Doran and Co., 1931. xvi, 924 p. Reissued as OUTLINE OF MAN'S WORK AND WEALTH. 1 vol. Garden City, N.Y.: Garden City Publishing Co., 1936. xv, 760 p.

> In his SCIENCE OF LIFE, Wells writes of economics as a branch of ecology: "it is the ecology of the human species" (p. 35). "Economics is the science of the balance of human life and how it prospers or decays" (p. 35). Later in WORLD BRAIN (see below), Wells decides that the topics in WORK, WEALTH, AND HAPPINESS OF MANKIND really comprise human ecology. Here he has composed "a general conception of economic life, of industrial processes, trade and finance," and has provided first answers to how and why all men live and work as they do. The sixteen chapters treat how man became an economic animal; how he learned to think and capture energy and materials; how he conquered distance, hunger, climate; how goods are exchanged and work is organized; why people work, how work is paid and wealth acquired; the rich and the poor; the role of women; government; the numbers and qualities of mankind; the overflow-

ing of man's energy in leisure, sport, travel, and art; how
mankind is taught and disciplined; and man's outlook. The
treatment of economic history is realistic and the outlook for
the future is hopeful.

_____. WORLD BRAIN. London: Methuen and Co., 1938. xvi, 130 p.

This manuscript deals with constructive sociology, the science of
social organization. This science is a special subsection of human
ecology, which belongs to general ecology and the biological
sciences (p. 1). "Human ecology surveys the species of homo
sapiens as a whole in space and time; sociology is that part of
the survey which concerns itself with the interaction and interdependence of human groups and individuals" (p. v). "The human
individual is born now to live in a society for which his fundamental instincts are altogether inadequate. He has to be educated systematically for his social role. The social man is a
manufactured product of which the natural man is the raw nucleus"
(p. vii). Constructive sociology "seeks to detect and give definition to the trends and requirements of man's social circumstances
and to study the possibilities and methods of adapting the natural
man to them. It is the science of current adaptations. It has
therefore two reciprocal aspects; on the one hand it has to deal
with social organizations, laws, customs, and regulations, which
may either be actually operative or merely projected and potential, and on the other hand it has to examine the education these
real proposed social organizations require. These two aspects are
inseparable, they need to fit like hand and glove . . . " (p. vii).
The most effective way to bring about change, particularly social
change, is to create a "competent receiver." How to do that is
by education about the human situation (pp. vii-xii). The intelligence services of the world must undertake a gigantic, many-
sided educational renaissance (pp. xiii-xiv). This effort becomes
the world encyclopedia and the brain organization described in
various essays in the book. Wells made a first attempt along these
lines in his WORK, WEALTH AND HAPPINESS OF MANKIND
(above). He expresses disappointment that this work "remains--
practically uncriticized, unstudied and largely unread--the only
attempt to bring human ecology into one correlated survey" (p. 2).

White, C. Langdon, and Renner, George T. HUMAN GEOGRAPHY: AN
ECOLOGICAL STUDY OF SOCIETY. New York: Appleton-Century-Crofts,
1948. x, 692 p.

White and Renner state that geography is really human ecology,
the study of human society and its earth background. The first
part explains the nature and scope of geography; second, the
climatic factor; third, biotic factors; fourth, the physiographic
factor; fifth, the edaphic factor; sixth, mineral factors; seventh,
hydrographic factors; eighth, spatial factors; ninth, social factors;
and tenth, geographical theory. The principal theoretical topics
are geographic adjustment, the region as a unit of study, and
ecological succession in the region.

Section II
THE SETTING

The following two sections written for an unpublished syllabus by Dr. Sargent shortly before he died express the concepts of the abiotic and biotic environment of man. His view of man as a part of the setting are implicit here as well as in writings quoted later.

A. THE ABIOTIC ENVIRONMENT

Life's dependence upon energy for its very existence results in our concern for, and need to understand, the abiotic environment. Solar radiation supplies a continuous flow of radiant energy to the earth, other planets, and the entire solar system. Energy supplied to the earth permits water to be available; life as we know it can exist only with water in the 0-100 C temperature range. The solar energy supplied makes the earth unique among the planets in that with this energy, through interactions of the abiotic environment (the ocean-atmosphere and the solid earth systems), the earth is able to support a complex variety of living forms. Interactions between solar radiation and the ocean-atmosphere cause water to be circulated through the atmosphere to the continents. Interaction between the ocean-atmosphere system and the solid earth system leads to change in the solid earth which results in soil production. These complex, interacting systems comprise our abiotic or physical "environment."

The word "environment" literally designates surroundings. It includes the complex of climatic, edaphic, and biotic factors that act upon any thing, or group of things which ultimately determine the form and survival of that thing. The term is usually applied in terms of the surrounding factors which affect the human. These days "environment" is a much misused and abused word by those sophisticates who have become active in the so-called "environmental movement." Although frequently employed as a synonym for ecology, a scientific discipline, this context is assuredly wrong. For example, one frequently hears the statement, "The building of that plant or the construction of that highway will disturb the ecology." We are sure, however, that this illogic will be self-evident; we need not labor the point.

Environment can be divided by content into abiotic (material, physical), biotic (biological), and man-made environments and by scale into ambient, micro- , meso- and macro-environments. The divisions by content are more readily evident than those categories made according to scale. The limits for the spatial dimensions are never precise. For example, "ambient" suggests the immediate surroundings of an organism yet physiologists use the word to designate not only that milieu but also the conditions of a room or a factory area or even the weather conditions registered in a standard instrument shelter far removed from the subject under study. At the same time other environmental scientists use "ambient" to distinguish artificial conditions, for example, rooms or climate chambers, from natural conditions. The words micro-meteorology, meso-meteorology, and macro-meteorology may be precisely defined by one author, but there is considerable variation between different authors.

The abiotic environment comprises three components--atmosphere, hydrosphere, and lithosphere. Although each may be considered as a separate entity, it is the interactions of their physical and chemical ingredients, powered by solar energy, which we shall emphasize, for it is these dynamic processes which make life on earth possible. The adaptation to these interactions, as well as their utilization and manipulation, determine the effects of the abiotic environment on man's ecology and affect the biotic environment of man as well.

B. THE BIOTIC ENVIRONMENT

The environment of a man or any other organism can be said to include all factors external to him which affect his fitness or well-being. The biotic environment, like the abiotic environment, is controlled by the laws of chemistry and physics. But biology is the study of life and the ability of organisms to replicate and maintain themselves by gathering energy and nutrients from their environment. The biologist must understand not only the relevant physical and chemical laws but also the different ways in which individuals and species adapt to their changing environment, interact with one another, and transfer genetic and cultural information to the next generation. These are among the properties of life which make the distinction between man's biotic and abiotic environment useful and necessary. Laws of chemistry and physics set the boundaries for what is possible, but they offer little to explain the great variety of life on earth.

The properties of life can be reduced to and studied at the molecular level, but because the whole organism usually reacts to changes in its environment, the individual is the basic unit of study in ecology. Higher levels of organization are also of interest because of the expanded range of interactions that are possible. Populations have properties which individuals lack such as age structure and growth rate. The addition of other species to the realm of study adds new dimensions, thus only the biological community can be said to have a diversity of species, undergo succession, and consist of numerous trophic levels. The study of ecosystems incorporates the community and its abiotic (physical) environment, which on a global scale includes the entire biosphere. Biogeochemical cycles are best understood at this level of integration.

The Setting

The roots of ecology lie in natural history, human demography, biometry, agriculture, and medicine. Recognition of communities of living organisms and a sense of a natural balance are found in the writings of Herodotus and Plato, but careful studies of the interrelationships of organisms in communities did not begin until the mid 1800s. By about 1900 ecology was recognized as a distinct science, and a theoretical basis developed as ecologists began to note repeated patterns in the structure and function of biotic communities. These similarities suggest that natural processes control the patterns of nature that ecologists seek to explain. Their explanations, the principles of ecology, still lack the careful specifications and rigorous testing of chemistry and physics, but many ecological principles are ultimately based on laws from the hard sciences.

1. Environment (Abiotic [Physical], Biotic, and Human [Perception, Knowing, etc.])

Allaby, Michael. A DICTIONARY OF THE ENVIRONMENT. New York: Van Nostrand Reinhold Co., 1977. 532 p. Appendix.

> Allaby has drawn together many of the terms used by environmental scientists. There are omissions and one is economics. An appendix lists the principal organizations concerned with environment in the United Kingdom.

Bradshaw, Michael J. EARTH, THE LIVING PLANET. New York: John Wiley and Sons, 1977. 302 p. Bibliog.

> Bradshaw has produced a textbook on the environmental sciences designed as a reader for students in upper-level high school or college courses. The topics emphasized are weather, climate, ecosystems, and biomes.

Chicorel, Marietta, ed. CHICOREL INDEX TO ENVIRONMENT AND ECOLOGY. 2 vols. Chicorel Index Series, vols. 16, 16A. New York: Chicorel Library Publishing Corp., 1975. 745 p.

> The items in this bibliography are arranged in sixteen major categories, subdivided into 289 topics. There are no annotations.

Dansereau, Pierre. BIOGEOGRAPHY: AN ECOLOGICAL PERSPECTIVE. New York: Ronald Press Co., 1957. xii, 394 p. Glossary; Bibliog.

> Designed as a graduate text, this book attempts to synthesize information on environmental relations of all living organisms. The major topics covered include the history of biota, bioclimatology, synecology, autecology, and man's impact on the landscape.

Dworkin, Daniel M., ed. ENVIRONMENTAL SCIENCES IN DEVELOPING COUNTRIES. SCOPE Report 4. Indianapolis: Holcomb Research Institute, Butler University, 1974. xi, 70 p. Paperbound.

19

This report includes summaries of reports and recommendations produced at a symposium sponsored by the United Nations Environmental Program and the Scientific Committee on Problems of the Environment which was held in Nairobi, 11-23 February 1974. The topics addressed were agricultural development, cost control, river basin development, natural parks and reserves, environmental planning for industry and human settlement, population problems, environmental education, and institutional cooperation.

English, Paul Ward, and Mayfield, Robert C., eds. MAN, SPACE, AND ENVIRONMENT: CONCEPTS IN CONTEMPORARY HUMAN GEOGRAPHY. New York: Oxford University Press, 1972. 623 p. Paperbound. Bibliog.

This reader, intended for the beginning student of human geography, attempts to identify the major traditions in the discipline and those related conceptual frameworks which give coherence to contemporary human geography, focusing on the field as the study both of man-environment systems and of the spatial structure of human behavior. Included in the first topic are chapters on the cultural landscape, ecological perspectives, and environmental perception and behavior. The second topic covers spatial diffusion, the region, and spatial order.

Environmental Policy Division. ENVIRONMENTAL SCIENCE CENTERS AT INSTITUTIONS OF HIGHER EDUCATION. Series H. Washington, D.C.: Library of Congress, Legislative Reference Service, 1969. vii, 17 p. Paperbound. Committee Print available from Government Printing Office, Washington, D.C. Tables.

The survey was made by the Environmental Policy Division for the Subcommittee on Science, Research, and Development of the Committee on Science and Astronautics, U.S. House of Representatives, 91st Congress. Appended to the report are thirty-five tables summarizing information provided by 106 institutions of higher education which operated centers of environmental science.

Glacken, Clarence J. TRACES ON THE RHODIAN SHORE; NATURE AND CULTURE IN WESTERN THOUGHT FROM ANCIENT TIMES TO THE END OF THE EIGHTEENTH CENTURY. Berkeley and Los Angeles: University of California Press, 1967. xxvii, 763 p.

Glacken traces the history of Western man's thoughts on three basic questions. Is the earth, which is obviously a fit environment for man and other organic life, a purposefully made creation? Have its climates, its relief, the configuration of continents influenced the moral and social nature of individuals and have they had an influence in modeling the character and nature of human culture? In his long tenure of the earth, in what manner has man changed it from its hypothetical pristine condition? The four parts treat ideas of the ancient world, the Christian Middle Ages, early modern times, and the eighteenth century, respectively. Although what we view today as modern concerns were also problems for the earliest Greek thinkers, it was not until the seventeenth century that laws were first enacted to conserve natural resources.

Gribben, John R., ed. CLIMATIC CHANGE. Cambridge: University Press, 1978. xi, 280 p. Paperbound. Appendix; Indexes.

This monograph, written by fourteen contributors, comprises an examination of the evidence that the earth's climate changes over both geological and historical time. There are five sections: (1) climates of the past, (2) global heat budget, (3) astronomical influences, (4) modelling climatic change, and (5) climate and man. In the appendix there is a discussion of a geophysical model of the initiation of the next glaciation.

Grzimek, Bernhard, ed. GRZIMEK'S ENCYCLOPEDIA OF ECOLOGY. New York: Van Nostrand Reinhold Co., 1976. 705 p. Illus.; Appendix.

Translated from the original German, this volume supplements the thirteen-volume GRZIMEK'S ANIMAL LIFE ENCYCLOPEDIA. Part 1, on the environment of animals, describes the physical, chemical, and biological aspects of environment. Part 2 deals with the environment of man, stressing the threatening environmental crises.

Hammond, Kenneth A.; Macinko, George; and Fairchild, Wilma B., eds. SOURCEBOOK ON THE ENVIRONMENT: A GUIDE TO THE LITERATURE. Chicago: University of Chicago Press, 1978. x, 613 p. Bibliog.; Indexes.

Sponsored by the Association of American Geographers, twenty-six specialists present bibliographic essays. In part 1 the emphasis is on concepts, philosophies, and concerns. Case studies of human environmental modification are the subject of part 2. The chapters of part 3 examine the major environmental elements, for example, air, water, land, plants and animals. Part 4 contains three appendixes on research aids: selected periodicals, review of federal environmental legislation, and selected list of environmental organizations.

HISTORY OF AMERICAN ECOLOGY. New York: Aronpress, 1977. Unpaged.

This anthology reprints nine articles which describe the history of ecology in America: "Ecological Studies and Observations before 1900," by F.N. Egerton; "Ecology since 1900," R.P. McIntosh; "Trends in Fishery Research," J.L. McHugh; "Wisconsin: The Birge-Juday Era," D.G. Frey; "The Development of Association and Climax Concepts: The Use in Interpretation of the Deciduous Forest," E.L. Braun; "Recent Evolution of Ecological Concepts in Relation to the Eastern Forests of North America," R.H. Whittaker; "H.A. Gleason: Individualistic Ecologist, 1882-1975," R.P.

McIntosh; "History of the Ecological Society of America," R.L. Burgess; and "American Grassland Ecology, 1895-1955: The Life Cycle of a Professional Research Community," R. Tobey.

Jeffers, John Norman Richards. AN INTRODUCTION TO SYSTEMS ANALYSIS WITH ECOLOGICAL APPLICATIONS. Student Texts in Contemporary Biology. Baltimore: University Park Press, 1978. x, 198 p. Tables; Figures; References.

Jeffers discusses models and mathematics; dynamic, matrix, stochastic, and multivariate models; optimization; the modelling process; and computers.

Kopec, Richard J., ed. ATMOSPHERIC QUALITY AND CLIMATIC CHANGE. Studies in Geography, no. 9. Chapel Hill: University of North Carolina, 1976. 167 p.

The volume contains papers presented at the Second Carolina Geographical Symposium, Chapel Hill, North Carolina, 1975. They are: "Do Recent Climatic Trends Portend an Imminent Ice Age?" by Hurd C. Willett; "Some Lessons of Climatic History," Reid A. Bryson; "The Definition and Determination of Climatic Changes, Fluctuations and Outlooks," Helmut E. Landsberg; "Physical Causes and Possibilities of Climatic Change," George D. Robinson; "Climatic Non-Limits to Growth," William W. Kellogg; "Future Climate and Decision-Making," Gordon A. McKay; "Is There Really a Food-Climate Crisis?" Stephen S. Schneider; "Policy and Management Implications of Climatic Change," F. Kenneth Hare; "Possible Effects of Climate Changes on Natural Vegetation," Helmut H. Leith; and "What Can We Say about Future Trends in Our Climate?" J. Murray Mitchell, Jr.

McGRAW-HILL ENCYCLOPEDIA OF ENVIRONMENTAL SCIENCE. New York: McGraw-Hill Book Co., 1974. 754 p. References; Index.

This volume treats in brief nontechnical language the present state of knowledge in all fields of study of the external conditions that influence life--meteorology, climatology, conservation, ecology, oceanography, soil science, pollution, sewage treatment, nuclear engineering, agriculture, mining, and petroleum engineering. The three-hundred signed articles were selected by a board of consultants and written by authorities in their respective fields. Almost every article opens with a definition of the subject and ends with a bibliography for further reading.

Miller, David H. WATER AT THE SURFACE OF THE EARTH; AN INTRODUCTION TO ECOSYSTEM HYDRODYNAMICS. International Geophysics Series, vol. 21. New York: Academic Press, 1977. xii, 557 p.

Because water is an essential factor in biological, physical, urban, and cultural processes, Miller discusses water's dynamic role in ecosystems. The first five chapters deal with atmospheric processes.

Chapters 6-9 focus on the input of water to ecosystems. Chapters
10-17 examine outputs, such as evaporation, groundwater, and
surface runoff. Water budgets is the subject of chapter 18.

Miller, G. Tyler, Jr. LIVING IN THE ENVIRONMENT: CONCEPTS, PROB-
LEMS, AND ALTERNATIVES. Belmont, Calif.: Wadsworth Publishing Co.,
1975. 380 p. Addenda; Bibliog.; Glossary.

This introductory college textbook contains two parts: a basic text
of twenty chapters covering general ecological principles and their
applications to major environmental problems; and twenty enrich-
ment studies useful to expand topics covered or to add new topics.
Thus are provided both a balanced overview of environmental concepts, problems, and alternatives and the means of emphasizing
particular areas of interest. There is a list of periodicals and
environmental organizations.

Monteith, John L., ed. VEGETATION AND THE ATMOSPHERE. Vol. 1:
PRINCIPLES. London: Academic Press, 1975. xx, 278 p.

This volume depicts the state of knowledge of plant-atmospheric
interrelations. The several authors demonstrate the integration of
biological and physical sciences. There are seven chapters: (1)
"Micrometeorology and Ecology," by J. Elston and J.L. Monteith;
(2) "Radiative Transfer in Plant Communities," J. Ross; (3) "Mo-
mentum, Mass and Heat Exchange of Plant Communities," A.S.
Thom; (4) "The Hydrological Cycle in Vegetation," A.J. Rutter;
(5) "The Movement of Particles in Plant Communities," A.C.
Chamberlin; (6) "Micrometeorological Methods," P.E. Waggoner;
and (7) "Instruments and Their Exposure," G. Szeicz. The authors adopt a set of symbols for their equations. Although there
are occasional departures, the set is generally consistent with ac-
cepted practice.

_____. VEGETATION AND THE ATMOSPHERE. Vol. 2: CASE STUDIES.
London: Academic Press, 1976. xix, 439 p.

The volume comprises thirteen case studies illustrating the principles discussed in volume 1. The first five chapters deal with
agricultural crops--wheat, maize, rice, sugarbeets, sunflowers,
and cotton. Townsville Stylo growing in a mixed pasture is the
subject of chapter 6. The authors of chapters 7 to 9 discuss
forests--coniferous, deciduous, and tropical rain forests. Citrus
orchards are the subject of chapter 10. The last three chapters
describe micrometeorological studies in whole ecosystems such as
swamps, prairie grassland, and tundra.

Moore, Gary T., and Golledge, Reginald G., eds. ENVIRONMENTAL
KNOWING: THEORIES, RESEARCH, AND METHODS. Community Development

Series, no. 23. Stroudsburg, Pa.: Dowden, Hutchinson and Ross, 1976.
xxii, 442 p.

> Knowing how people perceive their environment and behave in
> response to those perceptions is of fundamental interest as well as
> practical value in formulating design and policy about the sur-
> roundings. This volume, emphasizing theory and research method-
> ology, grew out of national discussions of environmental design
> convened in 1972 and 1973. Participants in those conferences
> are the authors of the thirty-five chapters. There are three parts,
> each introduced by the editors. The chapters of part 1 deal with
> (1) information-processing theory, (2) personal construct theory,
> and (3) environmental learning theory. Part 2 is devoted to case
> studies grouped under three perspectives: (1) sociological, (2)
> cross-cultural, and (3) theoretical and phenomenological. The
> final part contains methodological chapters which deal with (1)
> psychophysical scales, (2) maps and models, and (3) linguistic
> and semantic constructs.

Moran, Joseph M.; Morgan, Michael D.; and Wiersma, James H. AN IN-
TRODUCTION TO ENVIRONMENTAL SCIENCES. Boston: Little, Brown and
Co., 1973. x, 389 p. Appendixes.

> This introductory textbook provides an integrated understanding of
> the ecosystem. Successive chapters treat the ecosystem itself and
> then its major components--hydrosphere, lithosphere, atmosphere,
> and biosphere. Considerable attention is focused on man's impact
> on these components through exploitation to sustain a growing
> population and through pollution from man and his technology.

National Research Council. U.S. Committee for the Global Atmospheric Program.
Panel on Climatic Variation. UNDERSTANDING CLIMATIC CHANGE: A
PROGRAM FOR ACTION. Washington, D.C.: National Academy of Sciences,
1975. xv, 239 p. Paperbound. Appendixes; References.

> The members of the panel present a critical review of information
> on paleoclimatology, identify research needs for formulating models
> to forecast future climatic trends, and propose a program to meet
> those needs. They discuss the physical basis of climate and cli-
> matic change, summarize past climatic variations and projections
> for the future, and document current research on paleoclimatology.

National Science Foundation. National Science Board. ENVIRONMENTAL
SCIENCE: CHALLENGE FOR THE SEVENTIES. Washington, D.C.: The
Foundation, 1971. xvii, 50 p. Paperbound.

> This is an annual report to the president, focusing on environ-
> mental science.

_____. PATTERNS AND PERSPECTIVES IN ENVIRONMENTAL SCIENCE.
Washington, D.C.: Government Printing Office, 1972. xiii, 426 p. References.

This volume provides a detailed supplement to ENVIRONMENTAL
SCIENCE: CHALLENGE FOR THE SEVENTIES (above). Here
are assembled the views and opinions of many scientists concerning the scope and nature of environmental sciences. The extensive material is arranged into several sections: (1) solar-terrestrial
environment, (2) dynamic of the solid earth, (3) climatic change,
(4) dynamics of the atmosphere-ocean system, (5) severe storms,
(6) precipitation and regional weather phenomena, (7) water resources, forestry, and agriculture, (8) aquatic ecosystems, (9)
terrestrial ecosystems, and (10) environmental contaminants and
human adaptation to environmental stress.

Owings, Loren C., ed. ENVIRONMENTAL VALUES, 1860-1972: A GUIDE
TO INFORMATION SOURCES. Man and the Environment Information Guide
Series, vol. 4. Detroit: Gale Research Co., 1976. xii, 324 p.

The theme of this selective annotated bibliography is the historical
development of attitudes toward, and concern for, nature in the
United States. Emphasis is on the general concepts underlying
the work of conservationists, nature-lovers, and ecologically
oriented citizens. Books, articles, documents, pamphlets, bibliographies, and reference works are included; fiction, poetry,
and unpublished theses and dissertations are excluded. The chapters
cover the following topics: "Man and Nature in America"; Travel
Reports"; "American Landscape Painting"; "Conservation and the
Preservation of Natural Beauty"; "Conservation and the Idea of
Wilderness"; "Conservation and the Ecological Ethic"; "American
Nature Writing"; "Nature Study"; "Camping and Outdoor Life";
"Back to Nature"; "General Reference Works."

Press, Frank, and Siever, Raymond. EARTH. 2d ed. San Francisco: W.H.
Freeman and Co., 1978. xiii, 649 p. Glossary; Illus.

Although brought up to date since the first edition of 1974, this
second edition of a general introduction to the science of geology
follows a similar format. In the first part, Press and Siever discuss
how the earth evolved and how its processes and materials are
measured. The second part is devoted to surface processes such
as weather, erosion, and the water cycle; and the third to internal processes such as volcanoes and earthquakes. There are
five appendixes which provide technical information on conservation
factors, data relating to the earth, properties of most common
minerals, and geological maps. There is also a glossary.

Quigg, Philip W. WORLD DIRECTORY OF ENVIRONMENTAL EDUCATION
PROGRAMS. New York: R.R. Bowker Co., 1973. 289 p.

This work, prepared by the International Institute for Environmental
Affairs in cooperation with the Institute of International Education,
describes post-secondary study and training programs in seventy

countries. The annotated listings are given geographically, but
indexes provide ready access to them by fields of emphasis or
specialization, degree programs, cooperative programs, teaching
programs and short-term programs.

Rosswall, Thomas, ed. MODERN METHODS IN THE STUDY OF MICROBIAL
ECOLOGY. Ecological Research Committee Bulletin, no. 17. Stockholm:
Swedish Natural Science Research Council, 1973. 508 p. Paperbound.

Sponsored by the Swedish National Committee for the International
Biological Program, the Ecological Research Committee of the
Swedish Natural Science Research Council, and IAMS Commission
of Microbial Ecology, a symposium on the study of the ecology
of micro-organisms in soil and water was held at the Agricultural
College, Uppsala, 19-23 June 1972. Seven sessions were devoted
to technical papers: (1) introductory considerations, (2) observa-
tional techniques, (3) isolation and characterization, (4) measurement techniques in ecological investigations, (5) growth rates
under natural conditions, (6) model systems, and (7) mathematical
modelling. There were three panel discussions: (1) plate count
techniques, (2) effect of pollutants on micro-organisms, and (3)
detection of extraterrestrial life.

Seddon, Brian. INTRODUCTION TO BIOGEOGRAPHY. New York: Barnes
and Noble, 1971. viii, 220 p. Appendix.

This book attempts to explain in layman language the forces that
have shaped the territories of living things and the problems posed
by their geographical distribution. It is based on work published
in the past twenty years in many branches of biology, ecology,
and geology; it attempts to build a bridge between the biological
and the geographical sciences, adopting an areal approach to the
history of biological species on earth and to their present and
future roles.

Shaw, Robert H., ed. GROUND LEVEL CLIMATOLOGY. AAAS Publication,
no. 86. Washington, D.C.: American Association for the Advancement of
Science, 1967, xii, 395 p.

These are papers from a symposium held in December 1965 during
the annual meeting of the association. The general topics addressed were effects of ground level climate on plants and animals
and weather modification technology as a means of altering the
climate and its effects.

Stapp, William B., and Liston, Mary Dawn, eds. ENVIRONMENTAL EDU-
CATION: A GUIDE TO INFORMATION SOURCES. Man and the Environment
Information Guide Series, vol. 1. Detroit: Gale Research Co., 1975. xii,
225 p.

This is an annotated guide to learning resources in the field of
environmental education from kindergarten through college, plus
sources for adult education and teacher education, for government
officials, and for industrial information officers. The eight sections of the book are devoted to "Instructional Aids"; "Reference
Materials"; "Governmental Services"; "Organizations and Asso-
ciations"; "Magazines, Journals, and Newsletters"; "Preservice
and Inservice Education"; "Programs and Centers"; and "Funding."

Strahler, Arthur N., and Strahler, Alan H. ENVIRONMENTAL GEOSCIENCE:
INTERACTION BETWEEN NATURAL SYSTEMS AND MAN. Santa Barbara,
Calif.: Hamilton Publishing Co., 1973. ix, 511 p. Bibliog.

This textbook stresses the understanding of the natural systems and
processes of the earth and their implications for and impact on
man. Related subjects are omitted: noise pollution, nuclear warfare, the technologies of materials processing and pollution control, and consumerism. Since the interactions of man
with natural systems occur in two areas--those within the realm
of physical phenomena (geoscience) and those within the realm
of biological phenomena (ecoscience)--this book concentrates on
the former. Special attention is given to nonrenewable natural
resources such as fossil fuels, and an energy systems approach is
used throughout, examining and analyzing flows of energy and
matter within and between open energy systems. An epilogue
concerns the relationships between society and environment.

_____. GEOGRAPHY AND MAN'S ENVIRONMENT. New York: John
Wiley and Sons, 1977. xi, 525 p. Bibliog.

The authors provide the scientific background for understanding
man's environmental problems. In order to interweave current
environmental problems and scientific principles, the material is
arranged by study units. Each unit contains an introductory essay
on a specific environmental problem or issue and a discussion of
the scientific concepts, factual information, and case histories
which serve to elucidate the particular problem or issue. The
text is organized into eight parts, each part containing five to
twelve study units: (1) atmosphere, (2) water resources, (3) lithosphere, (4) geomorphic processes, (5) ecosystems, (6) soils and
climate, (7) the wilderness resource, and (8) energy resources.
Problems of environmental management are briefly discussed in an
epilogue.

_____. INTRODUCTION TO ENVIRONMENTAL SCIENCE. Santa Barbara,
Calif.: Hamilton Publishing Co., 1974. ix, 633 p. Appendixes; Bibliog.

This introductory textbook stresses the natural systems and processes
of the earth and their implications for and impact on man. The
authors recognize two areas of interaction between natural systems
and man: the first, geoscience, is in the realm of physical phenomena

and concerns the components and processes of the lithosphere, atmosphere, and hydrosphere; the second, ecoscience, is in the realm of biological phenomena, including the structure and functions of the biosphere. Throughout, an energy systems approach is used, analyzing flows of energy and matter within and between open energy systems.

Tuan, Yi-Fu. TOPOPHILIA: A STUDY OF ENVIRONMENTAL PERCEPTION, ATTITUDES, AND VALUES. Englewood Cliffs, N.J.: Prentice-Hall, 1974. x, 260 p. Illus.; References.

Tuan undertakes a general survey of environmental perception, attitudes, and values so that, with a better understanding of themselves, men may more effectively solve environmental problems. His central theme is topophilia, "the affective bond between people and place or setting." He discusses environmental psychology, cultural influences, interrelations between topophilia and environment, and values regarding landscapes, including gardens, suburbs, and cities. His survey is both historical and modern.

Turk, Amos; Turk, Jonathan; Wittes, Janet T.; and Wittes, Robert. ENVIRONMENTAL SCIENCE. Philadelphia: W.B. Saunders Co., 1974. xii, 563 p. Bibliog.; Tables.

This textbook brings together a body of concepts and facts which can be identified as environmental science. The topics included are natural systems, human adaptability, species extinction, the human population, resources, agricultural systems, pest and weed control, pollution, and socioeconomic and legal aspects of environmental degradation.

Watkins, Joel S.; Bottino, Michael L.; and Morisawa, Marie. OUR GEOLOGICAL ENVIRONMENT. Philadelphia: W.B. Saunders Co., 1975. xi, 519 p. Paperbound. Bibliog.

This introductory text covers three broad areas of geology: earth processes, earth resources, and role of geologist in policy and planning.

Watt, Kenneth E.F. PRINCIPLES OF ENVIRONMENTAL SCIENCE. New York: McGraw-Hill Book Co., 1973. xiv, 319 p.

This is an advanced textbook which demonstrates that ecology, along with such other disciplines as urban and regional planning, economic geography, epidemiology, community medicine, and meteorology, is an integral part of environmental science. Fourteen principles of environmental science are stated and discussed. The ecological variables--matter, energy, space, time and diversity-- and the mechanisms of self-regulation in ecosystems are considered. A number of examples of organism-environment interactions are examined in terms of these concepts and principles: weather perturbations of biological systems; pollution; exploitation of lakes, forests, watersheds and range and grasslands; agroecosystems; biological control; infectious diseases; and urban, regional, and national planning. In the concluding chapter, a global strategy for mankind is proposed. Accompanying each chapter, suggestions are provided for individual and group projects.

Wheeler, David L., ed. THE HUMAN HABITAT. CONTEMPORARY READINGS. New York: Van Nostrand Reinhold Co., 1971. xii, 275 p.

Wheeler's anthology of papers is intended for courses on physical and cultural geography. The papers, which deal with man and environmental quality, are grouped under three general headings: weather, climate and water; land and conservation; and population.

Winton, Harry N.M., comp. and ed. MAN AND THE ENVIRONMENT: A BIBLIOGRAPHY OF SELECTED PUBLICATIONS OF THE UNITED NATIONS SYSTEM 1946-1971. New York: Unipub; R.R. Bowker Co., 1972. xxi, 305 p.

This bibliography calls attention to the valuable information and publications issued by the United Nations and its seventeen related but autonomous agencies, such as the International Atomic Energy Agency, the Food and Agriculture Organization, the World Health Organization, and the World Meteorological Organization. Over twelve hundred entries are arranged by subject, with a descriptive annotation for each. Separate lists are included for filmstrips and other visual aids; dictionaries and glossaries; bibliographies; and periodicals. There are four indexes: author, series and serials, title, and subject.

World Meteorological Organization. METEOROLOGY AS RELATED TO THE HUMAN ENVIRONMENT. Special Environmental Report, no. 2. WMO, no. 312. Geneva: 1971. xv, 151 p. Paperbound.

Containing papers from both the World Meteorological Congress of 1971 and the United Nations Conference on the Human Environment, Stockholm, 1972, this report consists of three chapters. These deal with modifications of the atmospheric environment; meteorology, human settlements, and natural resources; and the hydrosphere.

World Meteorological Organization. Commission for Climatology. CLIMATIC CHANGE. Technical Note, no. 79. WMO, no. 195.TP.100. Geneva: 1966. xvi, 79 p. Paperbound. Appendixes; Glossaries; References.

This study examines the measurement and statistical interpretation of climatic fluctuations. The most suitable statistical methods are indicated, with consideration of additional techniques useful in advancing understanding of variations in climate, and suggestions for standardizing definitions of terms used in this field.

The Setting

2. Man

a. MAN'S BIOLOGY

Behnke, John A.; Finch, Caleb Ellicott; and Moment, Gairdner Bostwick, eds. THE BIOLOGY OF AGING. Publication of the American Institute of Biological Sciences. New York: Plenum Press, 1978. xi, 388 p. Bibliog.

> This volume summarizes major research developments in the study of the aging process. There are six groups of essays: (1) introduction; (2) aging in cells and their molecules; (3) aging in plants and lower animals; (4) aging in humans and other mammals; (5) hormones and aging; and (6) aging in perspective, especially its evolutionary biology.

Bodmer, Walter L., and Cavalli-Sforza, Luigi Luca. GENETICS, EVOLUTION, AND MAN. San Francisco: W.H. Freeman and Co., 1976. xvi, 782 p. Appendix; References; Glossary.

> This textbook contains four parts. In the first, there is a discussion of the mechanisms of inheritance. The second part deals with population genetics. In the third, the authors discuss those traits which have a complex inheritance, particularly behavioral traits. The fourth part focuses on genetics in human evolution and the significance of genetics for medicine and society.

Brady, John. BIOLOGICAL CLOCKS. Institute of Biology's Studies in Biology, no. 104. Baltimore: University Park Press, 1979. 69 p. Paperbound. References.

> In this introductory text on chronobiology, Brady surveys the observations on daily, tidal, lunar, and annual rhythms; their relation to exogenous and endogenous events, circadian rhythms, celestial navigation, photoperiodism, and clock mechanisms.

Damon, Albert. HUMAN BIOLOGY AND ECOLOGY. New York: W.W. Norton and Co., 1977. xii, 367 p. Paperbound. Glossary; Index.

> This was published after Damon's death in 1973 by W.W. Howells. Together with five collaborators, Damon put together a broad introduction to the fields of human biology and human ecology. The principal topics addressed include genetics and evolution, age, sex, race, and constitution, human adaptability, the man-made environment and the biology of urban man, and populations.

Dobzhansky, Theodosius. MANKIND EVOLVING: THE EVOLUTION OF THE HUMAN SPECIES. New Haven, Conn.: Yale University Press, 1971. xiii, 381 p. Paperbound.

> Dobzhansky provides an overview of human evolution and genetics.

He deals with the roles of biology, heredity, and culture in evolution, the relative significance of heredity and environment; human variation; heredity in health and disease; natural selection and the evolutionary process; the emergence of man, his mental facilities and their antecedents; and man's future and the biological and social problems with which he must cope.

Dubos, Rene. SO HUMAN AN ANIMAL. New York: Charles Scribner's Sons, 1968. xiv, 300 p. Paperbound.

Dubos develops the theme that all experiences leave an imprint on man's physical and mental characteristics. He examines evidence for this idea from both historical and contemporaneous life. From this evidence, he suggests that a science of humanity might be able to use such knowledge to shape man's future.

Farb, Peter. HUMANKIND. Boston: Houghton Mifflin Co., 1978. xiii, 528 p.

Farb describes and characterizes the human species. His story includes man's ascent, his adaptations (for example, domestication of plants and animals, urbanization, and modernization), his diversity (for example, males and females, constitutions, and races), his intelligence, and social organization and institutions. Farb concludes that man will survive some difficult periods and enjoy a future.

Finch, Caleb Ellicott, and Hayflick, Leonard, eds. HANDBOOK OF THE BIOLOGY OF AGING. New York: Van Nostrand Reinhold Co., 1977. xvi, 771 p. Tables; Bibliog.

The editors review the status of the basic biological knowledge of gerontology hierarchically. In part 1, the focus is comparative. Part 2 contains reviews of aging at the molecular level; part 3, the cellular level; part 4, the tissue and organ level; and part 5, the whole organism level.

Friedlaender, Jonathan Scott. PATTERNS OF HUMAN VARIATION: THE DEMOGRAPHY, GENETICS, AND PHENETICS OF BOUGAINVILLE ISLANDERS. Cambridge, Mass.: Harvard University Press, 1975. xxvii, 252 p. Tables; Figures; Appendix.

Friedlaender reports field studies of over two thousand persons living on Bougainville and Buka Islands. Following a general discussion of modern evolutionary theory and a description of the islands and their inhabitants, he presents details on their demography, blood genetics, anthropometry, finger- and hand-prints, and dental variation.

Gould, Stephen Hay. ONTOGENY AND PHYLOGENY. Cambridge, Mass.:

Belknap Press of Harvard University Press, 1977. xiv, 501 p. Notes; Bibliog.; Glossary.

> Gould examines the history and scientific bases of Ernst Haekel's doctrine that ontogeny recapitulates phylogeny. In part 1, Gould traces the idea of recapitulation from Greek science through Haekel, up to the present day. In part 2, he discusses heterochrony and paedomorphosis. Of particular interest to human ecology, chapter 10 is devoted to retardation and neoteny in human evolution. Gould concludes that the slow progress of his life's course is essential for the human organism.

Harrison, G. Ainsworth; Weiner, J.S.; Tanner, J.M.; and Barnicott, N.A. HUMAN BIOLOGY: AN INTRODUCTION TO HUMAN EVOLUTION, VARIATION, GROWTH AND ECOLOGY. 2d ed. London: Oxford University Press, 1977. xiv, 499 p. Paperbound. Illus.; References; Indexes.

> The material is arranged in five parts: (1) human evolution; (2) human genetics; (3) biological variation in modern populations; (4) human growth and constitution; and (5) human ecology.

Huxley, Julian S. MAN STANDS ALONE. 2d ed. New York: Harper and Brothers, 1941. x, 297 p.

> This collection of previously published essays reflects Huxley's humanistic views on some aspects of the biology of man. He examines the uniqueness of man, eugenics, climate and human history, and the concept of race. He discusses the idea-system of humanism. Several essays deal with biological topics concerning birds and other animals. He stresses the fact that in the future man's problems will demand an increasingly social outlook.

International Commission on Radiological Protection. Task Group on Reference Man. REPORT OF THE TASK GROUP ON REFERENCE MAN. ICRP Publication, no. 23. Oxford, Engl.: Pergamon Press, 1975. xix, 480 p. Tables; Figures; Appendixes.

> To make possible the estimation of maximum permissible annual intake of radioactive substances, the task group assembled information about the biological characteristics of the "reference man," who was defined as "being between 20-30 years of age, weighing 70 kg, is 170 cm in height, and lives in a climate with an average temperature of from 10 to 20 C. He is Caucasian and is Western European or North American in habitat and custom." Chapter 1 provides information on the anatomical characteristics of reference man drawn from 931 references; chapter 2, on the gross and elemental content from ninety-seven references; and chapter 3, physiological data from 625 references. Data on growth, development, and aging are included. Appendix 1 considers specific absorbed fractions of photon energies for reference man; appendix 2 lists signs and symbols used.

Swanson, Carl P. THE NATURAL HISTORY OF MAN. Englewood Cliffs, N.J.: Prentice-Hall, 1973. xii, 402 p. Illus.; Bibliog.

Swanson discusses man's biology and the effect which scientific discoveries have had on man's view of himself. These he identifies as natural history, but there is much that can be labeled history of biology also. Among the topics discussed are historical geology and evolution, primate and human evolution, uniqueness of man and of the individual, cultural evolution, and the present-day problems of man, such as population, food, and resources.

Williams, Bobby Joe. EVOLUTION AND HUMAN ORIGINS: AN INTRO-DUCTION TO PHYSICAL ANTHROPOLOGY. New York: Harper and Row, 1973. ix, 276 p.

This text on human biology deals primarily with population genetics, methods of studying primate fossils, human evolution, human variation, climatic adaptation, and evidence for on-going human evolution.

Young, John Zackazy. AN INTRODUCTION TO THE STUDY OF MAN. Oxford, Engl.: Clarendon Press; London: Oxford University Press, 1971. xxv, 719 p. Tables; Glossary; Bibliog.; Indexes.

Young introduces human biology. He discusses the chemical composition of man; his molecular, cellular, and organ organization; functional regulations and adaptations; individuality, consciousness; growth, maintenance and repair ot tissue; reproduction; human growth, development, and aging; fertility and mortality; origin of life; human populations; human evolution; cultural evolution; the diversity of modern man; and human behavior.

b. MAN'S BEHAVIOR (COMMUNICATION, CULTURE)

Allman, Lawrence R., and Jaffee, Dennis T., eds. ABNORMAL PSYCHOLOGY IN THE LIFE CYCLE. New York: Harper and Row, 1978. xxiii, 600 p. References; Glossary; Indexes.

Together with several contributing authors, Allman and Jaffee have written a discussion of abnormal behavior and mental illness which treats these human difficulties in the context of the life cycle and from the perspective of development-family systems. The four parts deal with (1) basic concepts, (2) the life cycle, (3) drugs, and (4) theory and therapy for changing human behavior.

Arnott, Margaret L., ed. GASTRONOMY: THE ANTHROPOLOGY OF FOOD AND FOOD HABITS. The Hague: Moulton Publishers, 1975. xv, 354 p.

The papers were presented at the ninth International Congress of Anthropological and Ethnological Sciences, Chicago, 1973. Six broad topics were discussed: ethnobotanic change, dietary change, tropical foods, cooking utensils, American Indian food, and food in tradition.

Binstock, Robert H., and Shanas, Ethel, eds. HANDBOOK OF AGING AND THE SOCIAL SCIENCES. New York: Van Nostrand Reinhold Co., 1976. xvi, 684 p. Indexes.

> Containing twenty-chapters prepared by authorities in the social sciences, this handbook comprises a reference on the social aspects of aging. The text is arranged in five parts: (1) social aspects of aging, (2) aging and the social structure, (3) aging and social systems, (4) aging and interpersonal behavior, and (5) aging and social intervention. Each chapter is extensively documented.

Gambino, Richard. A GUIDE TO ETHNIC STUDIES PROGRAMS IN AMERICAN COLLEGES, UNIVERSITIES AND SCHOOLS. Working Papers, Rockefeller Foundation. New York: Rockefeller Foundation, May 1975. xi, 39 p. Paperbound. Bibliog.

> Gambino views programs of ethnic studies as creating an integrative pluralism, adding to the humanistic aspect of human ecology. He gives some examples of academic programs, and lists several resource centers for information on ethnic studies.

Greene, Lawrence S., ed. MALNUTRITION, BEHAVIOR, AND SOCIAL ORGANIZATION. New York: Academic Press, 1977. xv, 298 p.

> At a symposium held at the annual meeting of the American Association for the Advancement of Science, February 1978, the fourteen contributors marshal evidence that malnutrition significantly influences both human behavior and social organization. Malnutrition is depicted as one of the components of environmental impoverishment. The first five chapters summarize the interrelations between malnutrition and human behavior. Chapters 6 and 7 examine the concept of nutritional stress. Chapters 8, 9, and 10 focus on the general relations among malnutrition, behavior, and social organization. The final three chapters bring together and emphasize salient points made in earlier chapters. The general inference is that the conceptualization of social organization must include a broader biological perspective.

Hardesty, Donald L. ECOLOGICAL ANTHROPOLOGY. New York: John Wiley and Sons, 1977. ix, 310 p. Glossary.

> Hardesty has prepared an anthropological textbook for advanced undergraduate and graduate students, which has an ecological perspective. Part 1 treats ecological systems and emphasizes energy and adaptability. In part 2, the ecology of human populations is discussed. Part 3 deals with ethnoecology and human paleoecology.

Hardin, Garrett [James]. STALKING THE WILD TABOO. 2d ed. Los Altos, Calif.: William Kaufmann, 1978. ix, 284 p.

Previously published essays by the author are grouped under subjects: abortion, religion, technology, competition, and "need" as superstition.

Landy, David, ed. CULTURE, DISEASE, AND HEALING: STUDIES IN MEDICAL ANTHROPOLOGY. New York: Macmillan Publishing Co., 1977. xv, 559 p.

This is an anthology of articles dealing with health and disease in human societies. The selections are arranged under fourteen groups: (1) the field of medical anthropology; (2) paleopathology; (3) ecology and epidemiology of disease; (4) medical systems and theories of disease and healing; (5) divination and diagnosis; (6) sorcery and witchcraft in sickness and in health; (7) public health and preventive medicine; (8) anatomy, surgery, and the medical knowledge of preindustrial peoples; (9) obstetrics and population control; (10) pain, stress, and death; (11) emotional states and cultural constraints; (12) the patient: status and role; (13) the healers: statuses and roles; and (14) healers and medical systems in social cultural change. Each group of selections is preceded by an introductory essay.

Osborne, Robert Travis; Noble, Clyde E.; and Weyl, Nathaniel, eds. HUMAN VARIATION: THE BIOPSYCHOLOGY OF AGE, RACE, AND SEX. New York: Academic Press, 1978. xvii, 392 p. Tables; Graphs; References.

The commissioned contributors to this volume have written broad surveys of relationships between organismic factors (age, race, and sex) and human performance: (1) "Fallacies in Arguments on Human Difference," D.J. Ingle; (2) "Genes and Melting Pots," D.C. Rife; (3) "Genetic and Behavioral Effects of Nonrandom Mating," A.D. Jensen; (4) "The Nature and Development of Intellectual Abilities," J.L. Horn; (5) "Race and Sex Differences in Heritability of Mental Test Performance: A Study of Negroid and Caucasoid Twins," R.T. Osborne; (6) "Sex Lineage: A Biological Basis for Greater Male Variability in Intelligence," R.G. Lehrke; (7) "Own-Race Preference and Self-Esteem in Young Negroid and Caucasoid Children," S.M. Shuey; (8) "Ethnic and Racial Differences in Intelligence: International Comparisons," R. Lynn; (9) "Age, Race and Sex in the Learning and Performance of Psychomotor Skills," C.E. Noble; and (10) "Epilogue: The Evolution and Variation of Human Intelligence," D.C. Darlington.

Platt, John R., ed. NEW VIEWS OF THE NATURE OF MAN. Chicago: University of Chicago Press, 1965. 152 p.

The volume is a collection of lectures, dealing with the questions: Where did man come from? Who is he? Where is he going? The six lectures are: (1) "Man's Place in the Physical Universe," W.F. Libby; (2) "Determinacy, Individuality, and the Problem Free Will," G. Wald; (3) "The Science of Science," D.J. de Solla Price; (4) "Mind, Brain, and Humanist Values," R.W. Sperry;

(5) "The Impact of the Concept of Culture on the Concept of Man,"
C. Geertz; and (6) "The Sense of Crisis," J.M. Redfield.

Spicer, Edward H., ed. ETHNIC MEDICINE IN THE SOUTHWEST. Tucson:
University of Arizona Press, 1977. xiii, 291 p.

Informs medical practitioners trained according to Western traditions
about the basis and nature of medical beliefs of other peoples
whom they may encounter in their practice. E.H. Spicer discusses
"Southwestern Healing Traditions in the 1970s." There are four
essays dealing with specific cultures: (1) "Popular Medicine in a
Black Neighborhood," Loudell F. Snow; (2) "Health and Illness in a
Mexican American Barrio," Margarita Artschwager Kay; (3) "Disease
and Curing in a Yaqui Community," Mary Elizabeth Shutler; and (4)
"Medical Beliefs and Practices among Lower-Income Anglos," Eleanor
Bauwens. Spicer suggests that these other medical systems must be taken
into account in training if Western medicine is to survive.

Turney-High, Harry Holbert. MAN AND SYSTEM: FOUNDATIONS FOR THE
STUDY OF HUMAN RELATIONS. New York: Appleton-Century-Crofts, 1968.
viii, 635 p.

Turney-High deals with man's physical work, his biological and
behavioral characteristics, social systems, frustrations and anxieties,
and personal and social inadequacies.

Wallace, Bruce, ed. PEOPLE, THEIR NEEDS, ENVIRONMENT, ECOLOGY: ES-
SAYS IN SOCIAL BIOLOGY. Vol. 1. Englewood Cliffs, N.J.: Prentice-
Hall, 1972. xviii, 265 p. Paperbound.

Wallace has collected writings of others and has prepared some
essays of his own to provide the beginning student of biology with
a range of views about biology and man's social problems. Essays
relate to population and resources, the quality of the environment,
and aspects of the biotic environment.

_____. GENETICS, EVOLUTION, RACE, RADIATION BIOLOGY: ESSAYS
IN SOCIAL BIOLOGY. Vol. 2. Englewood Cliffs, N.J.: Prentice-Hall,
1972. xvii, 221 p. Paperbound.

These essays deal with genetics and genetic disorders, ideas about
evolution, some biological problems of race, and biological impacts of nuclear radiation.

_____. DISEASE, SEX, COMMUNICATION, BEHAVIOR: ESSAYS IN SO-
CIAL BIOLOGY. Vol. 3. Englewood Cliffs, N.J.: Prentice-Hall, 1972.
xviii, 313 p. Paperbound.

Essays relate to the changing patterns of epidemic diseases over
time; venereal disease, blood marriage, and population control;
problems of social communication; and behavior and social conformity.

Watanabe, Hitoshi, ed. HUMAN ACTIVITY SYSTEM. ITS SPATIOTEMPORAL STRUCTURE. Tokyo: University of Tokyo Press, 1977. xi, 260 p.

The concept developed by the authors is that the human ecosystem is an integration of man's activity system and the environmental system. The several contributions, reprints of previous publications, explore human subsistence activities--hunting, gathering, fishing--among Japanese communities. The authors discuss allocation of tasks according to sex and age and wide individual variations in subsistence skills and success.

Weisz, Paul B., ed. THE CONTEMPORARY SCENE. READINGS ON HUMAN NATURE, RACE, BEHAVIOR, SOCIETY, AND ENVIRONMENT. New York: McGraw-Hill Book Co., 1970. xxi, 349 p. Paperbound.

This anthology seeks to enable the reader to find his own identity and better understand the changing contemporary scene. The scene is presented as ideas of persons who had a wide-ranging interdisciplinary viewpoint. The editor arranges his selections in five parts: man's nature, man's diversity, man's behavior, man's society, and man's environment. There is a minimum of editorial comment. The reader may draw his own conclusions.

Zipf, George Kingsley. HUMAN BEHAVIOR AND THE PRINCIPLE OF LEAST EFFORT; AN INTRODUCTION TO HUMAN BEHAVIOR. Cambridge, Mass.: Addison-Wesley Press, 1949. xi, 573 p.

This book, bringing together some twenty-five years of research, comprises a natural science of human behavior. The organizing concept is the principle of least effort, which states that individuals behave so as to minimize the work they must expend to solve not only immediate problems but also probable future problems. The supporting evidence derives from studies of words, speech, and communication and of human relations.

c. POPULATIONS OF MAN

Brass, William, ed. BIOLOGICAL ASPECTS OF DEMOGRAPHY. Symposia of Society for Study of Human Biology, vol. 10. London: Taylor and Francis; New York: Barnes and Noble, 1971. vii, 167 p.

Most of the papers in this volume were first presented at a symposium held in November 1967 but since revised: "Population Structure and Movement Patterns," A.J. Boyce, C.F. Kuchemann, and G.A. Harrison; "A Monte Carlo Simulation of Reproduction," J.C. Barrett; "Milling Masses and Open Spaces;" J.L. Clark; "Some Aspects of Theories of Mortality, Causes of Death Analysis, Forecasting and Stochastic Processes," R.E. Beard; "On the Scale of Mortality," W. Brass; "Palaeodemography," D.R. Brothwell; "Human Population Dynamics Considered from an Ecological Standpoint," J.G. Skellam; and "Intrauterine Growth: A Discussion of

Some of the Problems Besetting Its Measurement," P.M. Dunn and
R.N. Butler.

Cox, Peter R. DEMOGRAPHY. 5th ed. Cambridge: University Press, 1976.
xi, 393 p. Bibliog.

This textbook on demography discusses the nature and sources of
demographic data and the mathematical procedures for analyzing
those data. Although much of the illustrative material comes
from Great Britain, data from other countries are included. There
are chapters dealing with population and resources, issues of population policy, and the population outlook.

Ford, Thomas R., and DeJong, Gordon F., eds. SOCIAL DEMOGRAPHY.
Englewood Cliffs, N.J.: Prentice-Hall, 1970. x, 690 p. References.

The focus of social demography is the analysis of relations between
general social and cultural factors and population structure and
process. The readings illustrate various aspects of these relations
and are arranged into four parts, each introduced with a brief
essay: (1) explorations in social demographic theory; (2) social
action systems and demographic structure and processes (for example,
informal groups, marriage and family, religious, economic and
political groups, health, education and educational institutions);
(3) social aggregate systems and demographic structure and process
(for example, racial and ethnic groups, social differentiation, attitudes, values, and beliefs); and (4) demographic transition and
the socioeconomic development of societies. The final chapter is
on systems analysis.

Hardin, Garrett [James], comp. POPULATION, EVOLUTION, AND BIRTH
CONTROL. 2d ed. San Francisco: W.H. Freeman and Co., 1969. xvi, 386 p.

Hardin has drawn together "a collage of controversial ideas" about
population, evolution, and birth control. The collage comprises
both brief and lengthy extracts from writings of many authors, ancient as well as modern. The objective is to increase awareness
of the serious nature of the population problem.

Hollingsworth, Thomas Henry. HISTORICAL DEMOGRAPHY. Sources of History:
Studies in the Uses of History. Ithaca, N.Y.: Cornell University Press, 1969.
448 p. Appendixes.

Historical demography studies the changes in populations of people
in times and place with a view to achieving accurate estimates of
human numbers. Hollingsworth describes the nature of the data
available and the analytical procedures for arriving at estimates
of numbers of people: population counts; taxation returns and surveys; vital registration data; closed populations; other written evidence and nonwritten sources; and discusses the limits and implications of demographic research in history. Three appendixes provide

case studies of historical demography: (1) stable populations, (2) an approach to the demography of plague, and (3) replacement rates in medieval England. There is a selected reading list of some four-hundred references classified into twenty aspects of historical demography.

Section III

MAN-ENVIRONMENT INTERACTIONS:
HUMAN ADAPTABILITY

Again, we have selected two of Dr. Sargent's writings to provide a concise view of his thinking in the area of man-environment interactions. As a physician, Dr. Sargent found human adaptability among the most fascinating of his areas of exploration. Anyone interested in this subject will find it worthwhile to pursue Dr. Sargent's own writings intensively, as well as the other books he cites.

The rise in the diversity of organisms provided a mechanism for stabilizing the life-support system. During the course of evolution complex hierarchical dependencies of one species on another emerged. Although these interdependencies are sometimes identified as food chains, they are more precisely depicted as webs. Energy and nutrient flow from the environment through complex linkages among organisms and back to the environment. These linkages provide for both the metabolism of the ecosystem and the regulation of numbers or organisms in the biosphere. The linkages become metabolic options for flows of energy and nutrients. The stabilizing action of these metabolic options allows for an adaptability of the system toward environmental change. When environmental change seriously disturbs the system, a gradual recovery is accomplished through succession.[1]

Adaptability within the biosphere derives not only from system processes but also from organismic regulations. Insofar as individual organisms are concerned, this adaptability has been achieved through genetic variation and natural selection acting over a span of time measured in millions of years. As Henderson[2] observes, 'the fitness of organic beings for their life in the world has been won by an almost infinite series of adaptations of life to its en-

1. E.J. Kormondy, CONCEPTS OF ECOLOGY (Englewood Cliffs, N.J.: Prentice-Hall, 1969).

2. L.J. Henderson, THE FITNESS OF THE ENVIRONMENT (New York: Macmillan, 1913), p. 5.

vironment, whereby, through a correspondence series of transformations, present day complexity has grown out of former simplicity.'
This adaptability is largely past-oriented. Organisms carry within
their genetic structure the capacity to adapt to environmental conditions and circumstances that prevailed during their evolutionary
history. It is on this evolutionary history that the constraints of
environment have acted; they have in a sense directed evolution.
At least these constraints served to reduce considerably alternate
pathways available for developing life systems to follow. This
adaptability does not necessarily include anticipatory reactions,
reactions that function to allow organisms to adjust successfully to
environmental circumstances never before experienced by the species.

Organismic adaptability is expressed as morphological, biochemical,
physiological, and behavioral plasticity. This plasticity is an out-
ward expression of the hereditary constitution of the organism. In
man, for example, we find that the capacity of the skin to tan
when exposed to sunlight is inherited. Whether the skin is actually
tanned depends upon exposure to sunlight. That pale skin becomes
tan when irradiated is evidence of phenotypic plasticity. Among
other expressions of this phenotypic plasticity in man are acclimatization to heat, the increase in stature with improved nutriture,
and the obesity that is the consequence of overeating.

The limits within which this plasticity functions are inherited. These
limits are set by the evolutionary history of the species. During
its evolution each species experienced environmental change. Some
species survived, others perished. Those that survived carry within
their genetic structure varying degrees of adaptability. For all
organisms, the plasticity is past-oriented; i.e., conditioned by their
evolutionary history.[3]

If serial measurements are made on a single living organism, no
matter whether the determinations relate to the chemical properties
of the blood, functions of important organs and systems, or to
overt behavior, the values obtained vary, i.e., the measurements
are not identical from one time to the next. The variability derives fundamentally, from two sources: errors made in the measurements themselves and real changes in the organism which are
sufficiently great to be detected in spite of instrumental or ob-
servational errors. The variability attributable to real changes in
the organism might be thought of as organismic variability.

Now the statement that the organism exhibits temporal variability
is certainly nothing new to a biologist. What is not so obvious
to him are the complex causes of this variability. Perhaps they
are spontaneous. Maybe they are 'biological rhythms.' On the
other hand, they may reflect meteorological changes, seasonal

3. Frederick Sargent II, Chapter 17. "Fitness of Ecosystem. 4. Adaptability within
the Biosphere," in his HUMAN ECOLOGY (Amsterdam: North Holland Publishing
Co., 1974), pp. 370-71.

variations, or cosmic events. Variations in activity or in eating habits may provoke them. Thus, the nature of organismic variability should be of primary concern to the bioclimatologist, for a basic assumption which he makes is that the temporal variability detected in an organism is caused by weather changes. In other words, he postulates that changes in the atmospheric environment condition the organism. To be able to justify or validate this assumption the bioclimatologist must be able to control all other factors which might cause organismic variability. To achieve this refinement of experimental control, he must possess expertness on the nature of all variations which living organisms exhibit.

Few investigators have concerned themselves with a systematic study of the variability of organisms. Those who have contributed most notably to the subject are H. Monod, E. Schreider, and R. J. Williams. Three fundamental facts stand out from their investigations. (1) Organisms are biochemical, functional, and behavioral individuals. That is, inter-individual variability is greater than intra-individual or temporal variability. (2) There is a significant rank-order correlation between inter-individual variability and intra-individual variability. (3) Whether one studies the individual organism or a group of organisms, there is an hierarchy of variability. In a general way, for example, the variability of the chemical composition of the blood is less than the variability of the functioning of homeostatic mechanisms (Sargent, Johnson, Wogan, Pandazi, KLIN. WOCHENSCHR. 37, 889, 1959).[4]

Bennett, John W. THE ECOLOGICAL TRANSITION: CULTURAL ANTHROPOLOGY AND HUMAN ADAPTATION. Frontiers of Anthropology Series. Elmsford, N.Y.: Pergamon Press, 1976. ix, 378 p.

The author discusses changes that have occurred in concepts held by anthropologists concerning man and nature. He proposes that human adaptability, both biological and behavioral, should be the new integrating focus. He also stresses the importance of cultural anthropology or human ecology in the formulation of social policy. It is Bennett's view that social policy should move to a philosophy of sustained yield of resources so that man can survive at a reasonable level of security.

Cohen, Yehudi A., ed. MAN IN ADAPTATION: THE BIOSOCIAL BACKGROUND. 2d ed. Chicago: Aldine Publishing Co., 1974. xi, 522 p.

The forty-four selections emphasize the concept of human adaptation arranged topically. The first section deals with issues and concepts; the second, adaptations in primates; the third, natural history of human adaptations; the fourth, adaptations in local popu-

---

4. Fred Sargent II, "Importance of Physical Environment in Conditioning the Organism," in INTERNATIONAL BIOCLIMATOLOGICAL CONGRESS, 1960. BIOMETEREOLOGY (Oxford, Engl.: Pergamon Press, 1962), p. 655.

lations; the fifth, speech; and the sixth, cultural adaptations. Each
section has an introductory essay and each chapter is preceded by
a bibliographic note prepared by the editor.

Dubos, Rene. A GOD WITHIN. New York: Charles Scribner's Sons, 1972.
ix, 326 p. Paperbound.

Dubos discusses the changes that have occurred in man's environmental relation over time and the resultant mutual interactions,
both destructive and beneficial. With the development of an understanding of environment, man developed first an environmental
awareness and more recently an environmental ethic, suggesting
that man and environment might eventually become reconciled.

Frisancho, A. Roberto. HUMAN ADAPTATION: A FUNCTIONAL INTERPRE-
TATION. St. Louis, Mo.: C.V. Mosby Co., 1979. xi, 209 p. Illus.;
References.

Frisancho uses adaptation broadly to encompass genetic, physiological, and cultural processes which permit individuals and populations to adjust to the environments in which they live. He
proposes that the good of these adaptive responses is to preserve
homeostatis both within the organism and between organisms and
their environment. With these concepts in mind he then discusses
acclimatization and habituation of man to heat, cold, solar
radiation, and mountain-altitude hypoxia as well as cross-
acclimatization. Finally he considers the influence of protein-
calorie malnutrition on human development and the effects of the
Westernized diet on disease.

Moran, Emilio F. HUMAN ADAPTABILITY: AN INTRODUCTION TO ECO-
LOGICAL ANTHROPOLOGY. Series in Anthropology. North Scituate, Mass.:
Duxbury Press, 1979. xii, 404 p. Bibliog.; Glossary; Indexes.

Moran discusses human adaptability as an ensemble of biological
and sociocultural responses to problems posed by human habitats.
Part 1 is devoted to history, theory, and methodology of ecological anthropology. The several chapters in part 2 deal with
human adaptability according to habitat: arctic, mountain, arid,
grassland, and humid tropics. In part 3, Moran discusses new
directions for research and comments on urban ecology. Each
chapter presents recommended readings as bibliographic notes.

PROGRESS IN HUMAN NUTRITION. Vol. 2. Edited by Sheldon Margen
and Richard A. Ogar. Westbury, Conn.: AVI Publishing Co., 1978. xiii,
313 p.

This volume contains updated papers originally presented at a symposium on "The Biological and Cultural Sources of Variability in
Human Nutrition" sponsored by the U.S.-Japan Malnutrition Panel

of the U.S.-Japan Cooperative Medical Sciences Program and held at Berkeley, California, 3-5 December 1975. Five general topics were considered: (1) man's historical and sociocultural evolution and the effect of nutrition; (2) effects of man's cultural and biological interactions and variability on nutrition; (3) biological variables in human nutrition: human adaptability to nutritional variables; (4) limits of tolerance of man's biological variability; and (5) man's complex culture of today and tomorrow: can man's biological adaptation cope with culture change, especially as regards nutrition?

Watts, Elizabeth S.; Johnston, Francis E.; and Lasker, Gabriel W., eds. BIO-SOCIAL INTERRELATIONS IN POPULATION ADAPTATIONS. The Hague: Mouton Publishers, 1975. xi, 412 p.

The papers stem from a symposium on "Biosocial Interrelations in Population Adaptations" held at Wayne State University, Detroit, 29-31 August 1973. The papers are grouped according to four themes: (1) adaptation and adaptive strategies; (2) genetics, society, and population dynamics; (3) nutrition, health, and disease; and (4) growth and development.

A. BIOLOGICAL

Ali, Mohamed Ather. SENSORY ECOLOGY: REVIEW AND PERSPECTIVES. New York: Plenum Press, 1978. x, 597 p.

Most of this material was originally presented at a NATO Advanced Study Institute on Perspectives in Sensory Ecology held at Bishop's University, Lennoxville, Quebec, 10-22 July 1977. The objective of the conference was to provide for an interface between sensory physiology and ecology. Two broad topics were considered: eco-sensory functions in various groups of animals and adaptive radiations of various sensory modalities.

Baker, Paul T., and Weiner, J.S., eds. THE BIOLOGY OF HUMAN ADAPTABILITY. Oxford: Clarendon Press, 1967. viii, 573 p. References; Index.

This volume originated in a symposium organized jointly by the International Biological Programme and the Wenner-Gren Foundation for Anthropological Research, held in Burg Wartenstein in 1964. Its main purpose is to review the present state of knowledge in the field covered by the studies on human adaptability under the aegis of the International Biological Programme. The nineteen papers represent a collaboration of scientists from nine countries and six disciplines: genetics, anthropology, anatomy, pediatrics, medicine, and physiology.

Boyden, Stephen V., ed. THE IMPACT OF CIVILIZATION ON THE BIOLOGY OF MAN. Toronto: University of Toronto Press, 1970. xx, 233 p.

The papers were presented and discussed at length at a symposium sponsored by the Australian Academy of Science, Canberra, 11-12 September 1968. The topics included "Chairman's Opening Remarks," F.M. Burnet; "The Biology of Pre-Neolithic Man," F. Barnes; "The Time Scale of Genetic Change," J.M. Rendel; "The Effects of Changing Social Organization on the Infectious Diseases of Man," F.Fenner; "Changes in Non-Infectious Diseases Associated with the Processes of Civilization; Some Effects of Different Diets," F.W. Clements; "Social Adaptation to Crowding in Animals and Man," G. McBride; "Stress in Relation to the Processes of Civilization," C. Mims; Cultural Adaptation to Biological Maladjustment," S. Boyden; and "The Biology of Civilization--with Emphasis on Prenatal Influences," R. Dubos.

Burnet, Macfarlane. ENDURANCE OF LIFE: THE IMPLICATIONS OF GENETICS FOR HUMAN LIFE. Cambridge: University Press, 1978. 230 p.

Burnet discusses his ideas about genetics of aging, disease, power, and behavior, with particular reference to man. In his concluding chapter he compares his ideas about the next million years for man with those of Charles Darwin.

Cohen, Bernice H.; Lilienfeld, Abraham M.; and Huang, P.C., eds. GENETIC ISSUES IN PUBLIC HEALTH AND MEDICINE. Introduction by Bentley Glass. Springfield, Ill.: Charles C Thomas, 1978. xxv, 486 p. Bibliog.

The authors examine not only the scientific problems of human genetics but also social, political, legal, and moral-ethical issues. In addition they address "eco-genetics," which deals with genetic changes caused by extrinsic agents such as drugs and pollutants. Contributions are arranged into six sections: (1) genetic material and its interrelationship with the environment; (2) prenatal diagnosis of genetic disorders; (3) population screening and surveillance; (4) investigations and programs in special population segments; (5) genetic counseling and intervention; and (6) present capabilities and future possibilities.

"Discussion of Human Adaptability in Ethiopia." PROCEEDINGS OF THE ROYAL SOCIETY OF LONDON, B 194 (1976): 1-98. Paperbound.

The discussion, organized by the Society for the Study of Human Biology, was held 20 June 1975. Among the topics considered were peoples and their cultures; genetics of high and low altitude populations; Ethiopia applied nutrition project; medicine; thermogenesis at high and low altitudes; blood pressure at high and low altitudes; and growth and development of children living at high altitude in Ethiopia, Peru, and Nepal.

Edholm, Otto G. MAN--HOT AND COLD. Institute of Biology's Studies in Biology, no. 97. London: Edward Arnold, 1978. 60 p. Paperbound. Bibliog.

This monograph, designed to present recent research findings in nontechnical language, discusses the physiology of thermoregulation in man, man in the heat, and problems of the built environment. Edholm outlines several practical experiments that can be done on one's self.

Folinsbee, Lawrence J.; Wagner, Jeames A.; Borgia, Julian F.; Drinkwater, Barbara L.; Gliner, Jeffrey A.; and Bedi, John F., eds. ENVIRONMENTAL STRESS: INDIVIDUAL HUMAN ADAPTATIONS. New York: Academic Press, 1978. xiv, 393 p. Figures; Tables; References.

Folinsbee and his colleagues have brought together papers from a conference held at the University of California, Berkeley, 31 August-3 September 1977. The environmental stresses considered were heat, air pollution, physical work, cold, and altitude. The participants emphasized adaptive processes and variability arising from age, sex, and genetic heritage.

Halsey, Albert Henry, ed. HEREDITY AND ENVIRONMENT. New York: Free Press; Macmillan Publishing Co., 1977. vii, 337 p.

The theme is the nature-nurture question. Halsey has assembled articles which represent the methodological approach to the question and substantive issues stemming from current research. The readings are assembled in four parts: (1) approaches; (2) population; (3) IQ and social stratification; and (4) IQ, genetics, and race.

Ingram, Douglas Leslie, and Mount, Laurence Edward. MAN AND ANIMALS IN HOT ENVIRONMENTS. New York: Springer-Verlag, 1975. xi, 185 p. Bibliog.

Ingram and Mount discuss the physiological reactions of man and animals to hot environments. Two chapters are devoted to physical principles of heat exchange. Five chapters focus on physiological mechanisms, for example, sweating, cardiovascular and endocrine systems, behavior, and thermoregulation. In the last two chapters, there is a discussion of adaptive mechanisms.

Kerslake, David McK. THE STRESS OF HOT ENVIRONMENTS. Cambridge: University Press, 1972. x, 316 p. Appendixes; Bibliog.

Kerslake examines the biophysical aspects of the effects of environmental heat on the human body. The first four chapters deal with mechanisms of heat exchange between the environment and the body. In the next three chapters, he discusses clothing, respiration and insensible water loss, and physiological responses. In the last three chapters, he reviews various indexes of heat stress. There are nine appendixes with tables on psychrometry, heat exchange, and body surface area; conversion factors; and important symbols.

Landsberg, Helmut Erich. THE ASSESSMENT OF HUMAN BIOCLIMATE: A LIMITED REVIEW OF PHYSICAL PARAMETERS. Technical Note, no. 123. WMO, no. 331. Geneva: World Meteorological Organization, 1972. 36 p. Paperbound. Tables; Charts; References.

> Originally prepared for the World Meteorological Commission for Climatology in 1969, this report has been revised as a comprehensive survey on physical bioclimatology dealing with the expression in physical laws of the thermal influences of climate.

Lee, Douglas H.K., and Minard, David, eds. PHYSIOLOGY, ENVIRONMENT, AND MAN. Environmental Sciences Series. New York: Academic Press, 1970. xv, 239 p.

> This book is based on a symposium conducted by the National Academy of Sciences-National Research Council in August 1966 at Bretton Woods, New Hampshire. Among the participants were authorities on disciplines ranging from molecular biology to human ecology, and including toxicology, biochemistry, oncology, pathology, human genetics, and several subspecialties of physiology. The symposium sessions concentrated on effects of environmental agents acting on mechanisms at various levels of biological organization: the molecular and subcellular level; that of cells and organ systems; the level of the intact human organism; and finally the level of populations. The resulting papers were intended as a step in establishing a sound scientific and conceptual foundation for the science of environmental health.

Nutrition Reviews. PRESENT KNOWLEDGE IN NUTRITION. 4th ed. New York: Nutrition Foundation, 1976. xxii, 605 p. Paperbound.

> This is an overview of the current state of the art concerning the nutrients, nutrition and disease, and nutritional therapy. There is a chapter devoted to historical landmarks in nutrition. The concluding chapter provides "A Bedside Library for Nutrition Scholars."

Slonim, N. Balfour, ed. ENVIRONMENTAL PHYSIOLOGY. St. Louis: C.V. Mosby Co., 1974. xviii, 573 p. Glossary; Bibliog.; Illus.; Tables.

> Intended as a text for advanced undergraduate and early postgraduate students of the biological sciences, this book focuses on the environment-organism interface, especially the interaction of environmental stimuli with biological systems that produce a physiological response in the human being. The twenty-two contributors represent many fields of science and medicine. Chapter headings include: biorhythmicity; biometeorology; temperature and humidity; sound, vibration, and impact; acceleration, gravity, and weightlessness; radiant energy; magnetobiology; aerospace environments; marine environments; environmental pollution; and artificial closed ecological systems.

Yousef, Mohamed K.; Horvath, Steven M.; and Bullard, Robert W., eds.
PHYSIOLOGICAL ADAPTATIONS: DESERT AND MOUNTAIN. New York:
Academic Press, 1972. xiv, 258 p. Indexes.

> The papers were presented at a symposium honoring Dr. David B.
> Dill, held in Boulder City, Nevada, 19-20 April 1971. Among
> the topics discussed were concepts of physiological adaptation,
> acclimatization to heat, partitional calorimetry, sweat mechanisms,
> cardiovascular and respiratory reactions to heat, nutritional phys-
> iology in heat, desert mammals, principles of altitude adaptation,
> psychological reactions to altitude, work at altitude, respiration
> at altitude, mountain vertebrates, and metabolic adaptations to
> high altitude.

B. BEHAVIORAL

Auliciens, Andris. THE ATMOSPHERIC ENVIRONMENT: A STUDY OF COM-
FORT AND PERFORMANCE. Department of Geography Research Publication,
no. 8. Toronto: University of Toronto Press, 1972. xvi, 166 p. Paperbound.
Appendixes; Bibliog.

> Auliciens studied school children in Reading, England. He mea-
> sured external and classroom atmospheric conditions, sensation of
> comfort, and mental performance. Comfort and performance were
> then correlated with the meteorological measurements. He dis-
> cusses the significant relations found and compares them with re-
> ports from the literature.

Chagnon, Napoleon A. YANOMAMO: THE FIERCE PEOPLE. New York:
Holt, Rinehart and Winston, 1968. xiv, 142 p. Paperbound. Glossary;
Bibliog.

> This is a case study in cultural anthropology based on fieldwork
> by the author between 1964 and 1967. Chagnon discusses the
> adaptations these people have made to their physical and social
> environments, their social organization, their political alliances,
> trading, and feasting, and their warfare.

Cohen, Yehudi A., ed. MAN IN ADAPTATION: THE CULTURAL PRESENT.
2d ed. Chicago: Aldine Publishing Co., 1974. xiii, 602 p. Bibliog.

> This anthology contains thirty-nine selections containing the theme
> of culture as an adaptive process. There is greater emphasis on
> the sociopolitical aspects of adaptation than in the first edition
> (1968). The selections are arranged in three parts: a prologue
> on the concept of culture: evolution and adaptation; stateless
> societies, which includes chapters on hunting-gathering, culti-
> vating and pastoralism; and state societies, which brings together
> chapters on cultivating and industrialism. Each part contains an
> introductory essay by the editor, and editorial comments precede
> each chapter.

_____. MAN IN ADAPTATION: THE INSTITUTIONAL FRAMEWORK. Chicago: Aldine Atherton, 1971. xii, 478 p.

This anthology is a companion volume for MAN IN ADAPTATION: THE BIOSOCIAL BACKGROUND (p. 43) and MAN IN ADAPTA-TION: THE CULTURAL PRESENT (p. 49). Cohen brings together selections which illustrate the institutional, psychological, and ideological dimensions of man's adaptive strategies. The selected papers are arranged in six groups: (1) marriage and the family; (2) law and social control; (3) religion and magic; (4) values and ideologies; (5) the individual; and (6) the arts. Each group and selection is preceded by an essay by the editor.

Goldschmidt, Walter. CULTURE AND BEHAVIOR OF THE SEBEI: A STUDY IN CONTINUITY AND ADAPTATION. Berkeley and Los Angeles: University of California Press, 1976. xvi, 395 p. Maps; Figures; Photos.; Tables; Glossary; Bibliog.

This book is a general ethnography of the Sebei, a southern Nilotic people of Uganda, with special attention to their adaptive process to altered economic conditions in institutionalized behavior, in customary procedures of life, in cultural values, and in patterns of individual behavior. Contents include discussion of the Sebei culture and polity; clan kin, and age-set; the roles of agriculture and livestock; compensation, craftsmanship, and the cash economy; women and men; infancy and childhood; the ritual transformation from child to adult; Sebei metaphysics; continuities and adaptation.

Kates, Robert W., and Wohlwill, Joachim F., eds. "Man's Response to the Physical Environment." JOURNAL OF SOCIAL ISSUES 22 (October 1966): 1-140. Paperbound. Appendix.

This issue contains eleven papers: "Stimulus and Symbol: The View from the Bridge," R. W. Kates; "The Physical Environ-ment: A Problem for a Psychology of Stimulation," J.F. Wohlwill; "Psychological Aspects of Urbanology," A.E. Parr; "The Role of Space in Animal Sociology," John B. Calhoun; "Man's Proximate Environment," Robert Sommer; "Variable Values in Space Land-scape: An Inquiry into the Nature of Environmental Necessity," Joseph Sonnenfeld; "The Role of Attitude in Response to Environ-mental Stress," Douglas H.K. Lee; "Migration as an Adjustment to Environmental Stress," Julian Wolpert; "Site Planning and So-cial Behavior," Robert Gutman; "The Contribution of Environmental Research to Wilderness Policy Decisions," Robert Lucas; and "Ar-chitectural Programming and Human Behavior," Raymond Studer and David Stea.

Landsberg, Helmut Erich. WEATHER, CLIMATE, AND HUMAN SETTLEMENTS. Special Environmental Report, no. 7. WMO, no. 448. Geneva: World Meteorological Organization, 1976. 45 p. Paperbound. Maps; Charts.

This paper, prepared for the United Nations Conference on Human

Settlements held in Vancouver in June 1976, deals with the impact of weather and climate on human settlements. Its chapters are devoted to weather disasters; climate and energy use; climate and building construction; air pollution; climate and land use; climate and recreation; and effects of urbanization on climate.

LaRuffa, A.L.; Freed, Ruth S.; Saunders, Lucie Wood; Hansen, Edward C.; and Benet, Sula, eds. "City and Peasant: A Study in Sociocultural Dynamics." ANNALS OF THE NEW YORK ACADEMY OF SCIENCES 220 (11 March 1974): 347-568. Paperbound.

The papers were originally presented at monthly meetings of the Anthropology Section of the New York Academy of Sciences during 1971. The population groups studied resided in India, Southeast Asia, the Middle East, the European Mediterranean, and Western and Eastern Europe. The several papers reported studies of socialization, urbanization, and modernization.

Leff, Herbert L. EXPERIENCE, ENVIRONMENT, AND HUMAN POTENTIALS. New York: Oxford University Press, 1978. ix, 523 p. References; Indexes.

Leff makes proposals to enhance human experience with a view to making the quality of life more fulfilling and more ecologically sound. He examines his proposals with theory and research in psychology and social sciences. He discusses environment and motivation, cognition and affect, attitude and values, and design, as well as ecological consciousness and utopia and change.

Moos, Rudolf H. THE HUMAN CONTEXT: ENVIRONMENTAL DETERMINANTS OF BEHAVIOR. New York: John Wiley and Sons, 1976. xiv, 444 p.

This book deals with what might be identified as social ecology. The author first examines various environmental perspectives (e.g., human ecology, gestalt theory, environmental psychology, and social ecology) and concepts such as determinism, possibilism, and free will. Then he examines in some detail the influence of physical factors--weather, architecture, population density, and noise and air pollution--on human behavior, the impact of social environment on behavior, and ideas regarding the optimum human milieu. He concludes that ideas about limiting environmental factors described by utopian thinkers and environmentalists are surprisingly congruent.

National Research Council. Division of Earth Sciences. Committee on the Alaska Earthquake. THE GREAT ALASKA EARTHQUAKE OF 1964: HUMAN ECOLOGY. Washington, D.C.: National Academy of Sciences, 1970. xvii, 510 p.

This volume is one of a series of eight reports on the 1964 Alaska earthquake. A panel of experts representing geography, sociology, economics, anthropology, law, public administration, and business investigated human behavioral responses to this natural disaster.

The results are presented in four parts: implications of the earthquake experience, selected studies of impacts and behavior, public
administration aspects, and human responses in selected communities.
The conclusions and recommendations stress the need for more research on natural hazards and for planning for effective strategies
for coping with such hazards.

Salaman, Redcliffe N. THE HISTORY AND SOCIAL INFLUENCE OF THE
POTATO. Cambridge: University Press, 1949. xxiv, 685 p.

Salaman traces the domestication of the potato (Solanum) by the
Amerindians inhabiting the Andes of Peru and Chile and attempts
to unravel its dispersion to Europe following the Spanish Conquests.
The potato was probably established in Ireland late in the sixteenth
century. Over the subsequent three centuries the tuber became
so bound to the life-way of the Irish that the rural economy became a single-crop subsistence economy. This fact made the
blight of 1845-1846 and the famine of 1846-47 all the more tragic.
Salaman examines the complex political, social, and economic
forces that set the stage for this catastrophe and the long time
that was required afterwards to begin to move toward improvement
in Irish social conditions. Other chapters examine the role of
the potato in the political economy of the British Isles (Scotland,
Wales, and Great Britain) as well as Tristan da Cunha, St. Helena,
and Jersey. There is a discussion of industrial uses of the potato
(written by W.G. Burton), the potato in war-time, devices used
in production, and the potato in art.

Sorokin, Pitirim A. HUNGER AS A FACTOR IN HUMAN AFFAIRS. Translated
by Elena P. Sorokin. Edited by T. Lynn Smith. Gainesville: University of
Florida Press, 1975. xxxix, 319 p.

Drawing upon personal experience in the Russian famine of 1918-
1922, Sorokin discusses first the biological and behavioral impacts
of hunger on the individual and then the effects of hunger on
communities and nations: social impacts, international food ex-
changes, emigration, war, criminality, and riots, insurrections,
and revolutions.

Stokols, Daniel, ed. PERSPECTIVES ON ENVIRONMENT AND BEHAVIOR:
THEORY, RESEARCH, AND APPLICATIONS. New York: Plenum Press, 1977.
xiv, 360 p. Bibliog.; Indexes.

Following an introductory chapter on the history of environment-
behavior research by the editor, the individual contributions focus
on four general areas: (1) ecological psychology (behavioral ecology),
(2) environmental psychology, (3) applications of behavioral research to environmental design, and (4) directions of research on
environment and behavior.

Vayda, Andrew Peter. WAR IN ECOLOGICAL PERSPECTIVE: PERSISTENCE, CHANGE, AND ADAPTIVE PROCESSES IN THREE OCEANIAN SOCIETIES. New York: Plenum Press, 1976. xiv, 129 p. Notes; Bibliog.

Vayda writes of warfare as a ecological process and examines it as a means by which people respond to environmental problems. He builds his arguments around the study of three Oceanian societies: warfare as a reaction to population pressure among the Maring people of New Guinea; headhunting by Iban people of Sarawak; and disruptive effects of the musket on warfare among the Maoris of New Zealand.

_____, ed. ENVIRONMENT AND CULTURAL BEHAVIOR: ECOLOGICAL STUDIES IN CULTURAL ANTHROPOLOGY. Garden City, N.Y.: Natural History Press, 1969. xvii, 485 p.

In this anthology there are twenty-three studies of human behavioral interactions with the environment. In the first part, "Systems in Operation," the studies deal with cultural practices in specific environments. The articles in the second part, "Origins and Development," deal with origin, development, and spread of different types of subsistence and with other cultural practices conditioned by climate, air pollution, and epidemic disease.

Walcher, Dwain N.; Kretchmer, Norman; and Barnett, Henry L., eds. FOOD, MAN, AND SOCIETY. New York: Plenum Press, 1976. xv, 288 p.

The chapters comprise papers presented at the third meeting of the International Organization for the Study of Human Development, held in Madrid, 21-24 September 1975. A. Kornberg introduces nutritional science. L. White, Jr. and F.J. Simoons discuss variations in food habits over time and space. E.J. Ojala and J.E. Austin look at the demographic and economic aspects of the food crisis. E.M. DeMaeyer and C.A. Canosa consider how to assess the status of a community's nutriture and intervention strategies. J. Tremoliers reviews the modes of human behavior toward foods which satisfy emotional and physical needs and I. de Garine focuses on cultural determinants of prestige foods. W.J. Darby discusses benefit-risk decisions in food safety. F.J. Stare examines trends in food faddism. H.D. Cremer reviews recent efforts to improve the nutrition education of health professionals. The final six chapters focus on nutrition and individual human development: combinations of protein which provide optimal intakes of amino acids (H.E. Aebi); interactions between food and genes controlling development (J. Frezal); food and psychological development (H. Papousek); malnutrition and brain development (J. Dobbing); nutrition and somatic growth (E. Rossi); and nutritional requirements for low-birth-weight infants.

Watanabe, Hitoshi. THE AINU ECOSYSTEM: ENVIRONMENT AND GROUP

STRUCTURE. Rev. ed. Tokyo: University of Tokyo Press, 1972. ix, 170 p. Notes; Bibliog.

This monograph, originally published in 1964 in the JOURNAL OF THE FACULTY OF SCIENCE, UNIVERSITY OF TOKYO, addresses the difficult problem of reconstructing the traditional functions of the Ainu society. The topics treated are group structure, food-getting activities, cooperation and division of labor, territories and gathering areas, and the system of social solidarity between man and nature.

Yudkin, John, ed. DIET OF MAN: NEEDS AND WANTS. London: Applied Science Publishers, 1978. ix, 358 p.

This volume comprises the proceedings of an international symposium organized by the Rank Prize Funds and held in England, 17-22 April 1977. The purpose of the discussions was to examine the health implications of man's wants for foods as contrasted to his nutrient requirements. Topics discussed were variations in national statements of nutrient needs; dietary factors in coronary heart disease, diabetes mellitus, intestinal disease, and obesity; comparative nutrition; changing patterns of food consumption and nutritional status in relation to anthropology, physiology, and economics; constraints on agriculture expansion; and planning to meet needs and wants.

Section IV

MAN-ENVIRONMENT MANIPULATIONS:
USE OF RESOURCES

To deal effectively with (the topic of human habitat and health)
we must conceptualize 'man,' 'habitat,' and 'health,' and we
must inquire into the relationships among these concepts. From
among the various viewpoints that one could adopt to develop this
topic, I have chosen to consider it in the context of Dansereau's
Law of the Inoptimum.[1] According to this law, 'No species encounters in any given habitat the optimum conditions for all of its
functions.' All organisms act to modify their habitats with a view
to achieving more nearly optimal conditions for their various functions. Man is no exception. His evolution has been anagenetic;
that is, he has increasingly exploited his habitat for his own ends,
and his mind has played an increasingly important role in his development.[2]

Man emerged into the terrestrial habitat some 2 million years ago.
Recent evidence suggests that the human species might even be 4
or 5 million years old. For most of that vast span of time, man
subsisted as a predator by hunting and gathering within the food
chain. His impact on his habitat was relatively inconsequential.
His capacity to effect change was limited to living in caves,
erecting simple huts, manufacturing crude stone implements, and
establishing rudimentary social organization. It was only 500,000
years ago that he first harnessed fire. This discovery greatly increased his capacity for change. With fire, man gained in power
to optimize habitat, to begin the transformation of the natural
ecosystem into the human ecosystem.

---

1. P. Dansereau, "Ecological Impact and Human Ecology," in FUTURE EN-
VIRONMENTS OF NORTH AMERICA, eds. F.F. Darling and J.P. Milton
(Garden City, N.Y.: Natural History Press, 1966), p. 459.

2. C.H. Waddington, "The Human Animal," in THE HUMANIST FRAME, ed.
J. Huxley (New York: Harper and Brothers, 1966), pp. 67-80.

THE EMERGING HUMAN HABITAT

We can mark the steps in this transformation of ecosystem as anthroposeres. Let us follow Dansereau in tracing the evolution of this ongoing transformation.

Gathering comprised the first seral stage. At this sere, primitive groups engage in collecting vegetable materials for sustenance, clothing, and shelter. Here man's impact on habitat was negligible.

The second seral stage was hunting and fishing. Man's role became that of a predator. Although he did introduce sensible modification of habitat, the exploitation did not upset balances.

Herding identifies the third anthroposere. At this sere, the human impact is significant. Fire and grazing led to plant communities which could not maintain themselves without human intervention. At this sere, domestication of animals begins.

The fourth anthroposere is agriculture. Now domesticated plants are introduced. Domestication of animals continues to be limited. Widespread animal husbandry requires stable human communities and cultivated fields. Early in this sere, there is an active and symbiotic partnership between man and plants, and conditions are good for their continuing development. Subsequently the human impact on habitat becomes considerable, for with the pressures of a growing population, the strategy is one of preventing natural succession. Man begins to create the 'domesticated landscape,' that panorama of domesticated plants and animals, cultivated fields, and single species reforestation.[3] Now this domesticated landscape comprises a series of man-made ecosystems designed to assure plentiful food and raw materials to meet domestic and industrial requirements.

Industry comprises the fifth anthroposere. Additional substitutions for natural ecosystems take place. For example, damming streams creates artificial waterways and lakes, the water levels of which are out of phase with natural precipitation processes. Wide expanses of landscape are allocated to exploitation of resources by mining industry. This exploitation disrupts natural processes by changing soil profiles and introducing wastes into streams and rivers.

The sixth anthroposere is urbanization. At this stage, all natural elements are replaced by man-made ones. There is an interlocking web of subsystems each of which includes the city, its satellite towns and villages, a diversity of cultural traditions, a complex of communication links to areas of agricultural production, pools of wild plants and animal genes, natural resources, depots for wastes, and recreational sites.

---

3. E. Rostlund, "Taming Trees," BULLETIN OF ATOMIC SCIENCE 17 (1961): 326-30.

Man now stands at this sixth anthroposere. The city is a key
element. It may be conceptualized as an empirical allocation of
the landscape to accommodate high population densities in functional configurations of structures, spaces, institutions, and processes. Although the city gives the appearance of an independent
existence, it is inexorably bound to a wide environs. The city
is a specialized consumer of resources, and it is wholly dependent
for its existence upon a continuing inflow of foodstuffs, fuels, and
raw materials.

Over the entire globe, there is a shifting of the population from
rural areas to the city. This shifting has accentuated the de-
pendency of high density areas on the efficient management of
the domesticated landscape, the sources of natural resources, and
the communication links between the city and surroundings.[4]

Forrester, Jay W. WORLD DYNAMICS. Cambridge, Mass.: Wright-Allen
Press, 1971. xiii, 142 p. Appendixes.

In connection with THE LIMITS TO GROWTH (see p. 58) the
present book contains a dynamic computer model of world interactions to form a basis for the project. The system structure includes five variables: population, capital investment, natural resources, fraction of capital devoted to agriculture, and pollution.
All of these interact in multiple ways. An epilogue foresees the
future development of the new profession of social dynamics as
the world moves toward a global equilibrium. Three appendixes
supply equation notation, equations of the world model, and definitions of terms.

Kamarck, Andrew M. THE TROPICS AND ECONOMIC DEVELOPMENT. Baltimore: Johns Hopkins University Press, 1976. xiv, 113 p.

Kamarck discusses the constraints to economic development which
are peculiar to the tropics: climate, soils, weeds and insects as
agricultural enemies, minerals, and health hazards. He concludes
that these constraints cannot easily be overcome by transfer of
technology from developed countries and recommends agricultural
and health research to overcome the special obstacles to economic
development.

McCabe, Robert H., and Mines, R.F., eds. MAN AND ENVIRONMENT.
Englewood Cliffs, N.J.: Prentice-Hall, 1972. 414 p. Paperbound.

This book, produced at two workshops attended by representatives
from twenty-five colleges is intended for college-level courses on
man and environment. Topics deal with environmental imperatives,

---

4. Frederick Sargent II, "The Human Habitat: From Inoptimum to Optimum?"
ARCHIVES OF ENVIRONMENTAL HEALTH 25 (1972): 229-33.

man's nature and values, natural resources, population problems, environmental pollution, and man's responsibilities for environmental management.

McHale, John. THE ECOLOGICAL CONTEXT. New York: George Braziller, 1970. vii, 188 p.

The author examines man's use of resources, energy and materials, from an ecological perspective. The chief topics are man in the biosphere, population and food, energy, and materials. He urges that man establish firm limits for these resources and redesign their use, for example, by recycling materials more efficiently.

Meadows, Donella H.; Meadows, Dennis L.; Randers, Jorgen; and Behrens, William W. III. THE LIMITS TO GROWTH: A REPORT ON THE CLUB OF ROME'S PROJECT ON THE PREDICAMENT OF MANKIND. New York: Universe Books, 1972. 205 p. Paperbound. Tables; Figures.

Formed to consider the major problems of mankind in all their interrelated complexities, the Club of Rome is an informal organization of about seventy persons representing many different nations and backgrounds. This report covers in a brief, nontechnical way its first project, conducted chiefly at the Massachusetts Institute of Technology, where experts in the field of system dynamics analyzed the components of the problems involved. The conclusions are that if present growth trends in world population, industrialization, food production, and resource depletion continue unchanged, the limits to growth on this planet will be reached within one-hundred years; that it is possible to alter these trends and to establish a condition of ecological and economic stability; and that work to achieve the second outcome must begin at once.

Montgomery, Edward; Bennett, John W.; and Scudder, Thayer. "The Impact of Human Activities on the Physical and Social Environments: New Directions in Anthropological Ecology." ANNUAL REVIEW OF ANTHROPOLOGY 2 (1973): 27-61.

The authors examine problems of modern society which increasingly involve research by anthropologists concerned with the environmental effects of industry and commerce. Montgomery focuses on "Ecological Aspects of Health and Disease in Local Populations," Bennett on "Ecosystemic Effects of Extensive Agriculture," and Scudder on "The Human Ecology of Big Projects: River Basin Development and Resettlement." Even though much of the research reviewed was collaborative, it was not clear how the role of the anthropologist would be defined vis-a-vis the other disciplines.

National Research Council. Committee on Germplasm Resources. CONSERVATION OF GERMPLASM RESOURCES: AN IMPERATIVE. Washington, D.C.: National Academy of Sciences, 1978. ix, 118 p. Paperbound. References.

With increasing population and industrial expansion, the world is losing many important natural habitat areas, and hence many species and variants essential to meet long-term human needs. The total array of living species, subspecies, genetically defined stocks, variants, and mutants making up the biological underpinning on which we live must be conserved in the natural habitat, and treated as an essential national resource. This committee report considers the problems involved and offers recommendations.

National Research Council. Committee on Resources and Man. RESOURCES AND MAN. San Francisco: W.H. Freeman and Co., 1969. xi, 259 p.

This book reports a study of national and world resources in the light of current and expected demands and makes recommendations concerning problems identified and topics needing further investigation. The resources considered include food and minerals from the sea and the land and energy.

National Research Council. Study Committee on Environmental Aspects of a National Materials Policy. MAN, MATERIALS, AND ENVIRONMENT. Cambridge: MIT Press, 1973. xviii, 236 p. Paperbound.

This study committee prepared this report for the National Commission on Materials Policy. The materials discussed include metallic and nonmetallic mineral resources, fuel materials, and forest products. The report emphasizes environmental effects but also considers economic and international implications for materials policy. The situation in Japan's natural resources is presented as a comparative case study.

NIPPON: A CHARTERED SURVEY OF JAPAN. Tokyo: Kokusei-Sha, 1957-59, 1961-- . Annual.

This is a compendium of statistical information about Japan: climate, population, labor, income, trade, agriculture, industry, energy resources, finance, communications, health, social security, and environmental pollution.

Turk, Jonathan; Wittes, Janet T.; Wittes, Robert; and Turk, Amos. ECOSYSTEMS, ENERGY, POPULATION. Philadelphia: W.B. Saunders Co., 1975. xi, 296 p. Paperbound. Bibliog.; Glossary.

This introductory text emphasizes the ecological and biological aspects of environmental science. The seven chapters are devoted to natural systems, natural populations, species diversity, extinction of species, the human population, resources, and agricultural systems. Each chapter contains problems for discussion.

Wagner, Richard H. ENVIRONMENT AND MAN. 3d ed. New York: W.W. Norton and Co., 1978. xiii, 591 p. Appendixes; References.

The text is presented in seven parts: (1) the physical and biotic environments; (2) how man reshapes the environment; (3) man's impact on the biota; (4) urbanization; (5) the capture and use of energy; (6) environmental contamination and pollution; and (7) the population problem and alternate solutions. Appendix 1 provides a selected list of professional and nontechnical publications; appendix 2, a list of environmental organizations.

A. AGRICULTURAL SYSTEMS

Biswas, Margaret R., and Biswas, Asit K., eds. FOOD, CLIMATE, AND MAN. New York: John Wiley and Sons, 1979. xvii, 285 p. Tables; Figures; References; Indexes.

Nine authors address the complex interrelations among food production, climate, and human uses of the environment and its resources: "Food, Climate and Man," F. K. Hare; "Natural Resources, Development Strategies and the World Food Problem," D. Norse; "Water and Food Production," G. Lindh; "Energy and Agriculture," D. Pimentel; "Energy and Food Production" and "Environment and Food Production," M.R. Biswas; "Soil Reclamation and Food Production," V.A. Kovda; "The Effects of Man's Activities on Climate," H.E. Landsberg; "Climate, Agriculture and Economic Development," A.K. Biswas; and "The Future of Man," A. Peccei.

Brown, Lester R. SEEDS OF CHANGE: THE GREEN REVOLUTION AND DEVELOPMENT IN THE 1970'S. New York: Praeger, 1970. xv, 205 p.

Brown views the Green Revolution as a response of agriculture to the problems of feeding the world's population. The high yields resulting from these new seeds produced a number of "second-generation problems" such as instability of production and overproduction. The consequences could be unemployment and increased urbanization. To counter these possibilities, Brown offers an agenda for the seventies which focuses on international trade relations, labor-intensive agriculture, and financing international development.

Cohen, Mark Nathan. THE FOOD CRISIS IN PREHISTORY: OVERPOPULATION AND THE ORIGINS OF AGRICULTURE. New Haven, Conn.: Yale University Press, 1977. x, 341 p. Bibliog.

Cohen asks two questions: Why did people adapted to a hunting and gathering life-style abandon it for farming? Why did the shift to agriculture take place at approximately the same time worldwide? An examination of the evidence suggests the hypothesis that it was increased pressure from population which caused the shift in subsistence from more palatable meat to less palatable but calorically rich cereals. Cohen then examines in considerable

detail evidence from archeology and ethnography in the Old World
and New World (North, Middle and South America) supporting or
refuting his hypothesis. He concludes that his hypothesis is tenable
and suggests avenues for further research.

Duckham, A.N.; Jones, John Gareth Watkins; and Roberts, E.H., eds. FOOD
PRODUCTION AND CONSUMPTION: THE EFFICIENCY OF HUMAN FOOD
CHAINS AND NUTRIENT CYCLES. Amsterdam: North Holland Publishing Co.;
New York: American Elsevier Publishing Co., 1976. xx, 541 p. Appendixes.

The editors and their colleagues make an objective and detailed
analysis of the human food chains, the flow of food from agricultural land to the individual consumer. The analysis is expressed
in terms of the efficiency of the energy use in the chains. The
material reviewed is presented in five parts. In the first, the
magnitude of the world's food problem is stated. The second focuses on flows of natural resources, flows and yields of agricultural
ecosystems, and environmental constraints acting on the food chains.
The third examines in detail the efficiencies of the biological components of the food chains, such as photosynthetic efficiency, efficiency of food production from animals, food preservation, use
of wastes, contaminants and health of organisms, and industrial
use of energy. In the fourth, the socioeconomic aspects of the
food chains are examined. The emphasis is on application of
systems research to planning and managing farming and marketing
systems. These details are brought together in the final part,
which deals with strategies for planning and administering human
food chains and nutrient cycles. There are four appendixes: de-
tailing symbols and abbreviations, providing conversion factors,
listing scientific and common names of plants, and defining economic classes and regions of the world.

FOOD, AGRICULTURE, AND THE ENVIRONMENT. Edited by John Lenihan
and William W. Fletcher. Environment and Man Series, vol. 2. New York:
Academic Press, 1976. xii, 130 p.

The cultivation of domesticated plants and animals intimately links
man to his environment. In this volume, the complex problems
arising from this vital linkage are examined: energy requirements,
the environmental impact of cultivation, optimal use of plants, and
agricultural chemicals. The final chapter focuses on the social,
political, and ethical issues arising from modern agricultural technology. The treatment of the various problems and issues is realistic and balanced.

Harlan, Jack R. CROPS AND MAN. Foundations for Modern Crop Science
Series. Madison, Wis.: American Society of Agronomy, Crop Science Society
of America, 1975. xi, 295 p.

This monograph is sponsored by the American Society of Agronomy
and Crop Science Society of America and written for upper-level

undergraduate students. The chief themes are evolution and domestication of crops important to man. Specific topics include
foods of hunters-gatherers; views and theories on agricultural origins;
descriptions of "a crop" and "a weed"; classification of cultivated
plants; dynamics of domestication; variation in crops in time and
space; centers of domestication in Near East, Africa, China, South-
east Asia and Oceania, and the Americas; the dispersal of selected
crops; and problems of modern agriculture such as management of
genetic resources and unconventional food sources.

Heiser, Charles B., Jr. SEED TO CIVILIZATION: THE STORY OF MAN'S
FOOD. San Francisco: W.H. Freeman and Co., 1973. xii, 243 p. Paperbound.

Heiser's monograph traces the role of domesticated plants in the
development of civilization, focusing particularly on cereal grasses,
legumes, roots, cocoa nuts, and plants used for beverages and
spices. The final chapter of the book deals with the problems of
environmental deterioration, growing population, and the need to
increase agricultural productivity. Solutions to the problems are
not offered, but the problems are tersely defined.

Hollingsworth, Dorothy, and Morse, Elizabeth, eds. PEOPLE AND FOOD
TOMORROW. London: Applied Science Publishers, 1976. xii, 173 p.

This volume comprises the proceedings of the British Nutrition
Foundation Conference held 1-4 April 1976 at Churchill College,
Cambridge. The papers deal not only with potential food production but also with constraints on adequate nourishment, such
as limited arable land and water, international relations, purchasing power, and sociopolitical forces. The fifteen papers are
arranged under topics: (1) food requirements, (2) nutritional requirements and national policies, (3) provision of food, and (4)
constraints on meeting needs and wants of people.

Hood, Lamartine F.; Wardrip, Edward K.; and Bollenback, G.N., eds. CAR-
BOHYDRATES AND HEALTH. Westport, Conn.: AVI Publishing Co., 1977.
ix, 147 p.

The papers in this volume were presented at a forum organized by the
Carbohydrate Division of the Institute of Food Technologists held in
Anaheim, Calif., 8 June 1976. The topics are world patterns of carbohydrate consumption; digestion, absorption, and metabolism of sugars,
polyols, and polysaccharides; fiber and health; carbohydrate-mineral
interactions; carbohydrates in diabetes mellitus and dental caries;
and carbohydrates as sweeteners.

Hutchinson, Joseph, ed. POPULATION AND FOOD SUPPLY: ESSAYS ON
HUMAN NEEDS AND AGRICULTURAL PROSPECTS. Cambridge: University
Press, 1969. vii, 144 p.

Hutchinson and his colleagues examine the diverse problems of maintaining a balance between agricultural production and demand for food. J.M. Thoday and A.S. Parkes address the question of expansion of the human population. R.T.F. King discusses the interrelations among population, food supplies, and economic growth. A.L. Banks examines the consequences of catastrophes and restraints. K.J. Carpenter summarizes man's dietary needs, and B.H. Farmer, available food supplies. W. Allan reviews land tenure and productivity, and J.B. Hutchinson, the resources of agriculture. The editor concludes that whereas agricultural productivity appears to be able to keep pace with demand for the short term, poverty makes it difficult for all people to satisfy their needs. Over the long run, productivity may not be able to keep pace. Thus, the growth of the population must be slowed.

Jackson, Ian Joseph. CLIMATE, WATER AND AGRICULTURE IN THE TROPICS. London: Longman Group, 1977. xii, 248 p. Tables; Figures; Bibliog.

Jackson discusses the influences of tropical rainfall and evaporation on man's activities. The principal topics reviewed are tropical climatology, the relation between water and plants, tropical agriculture, and man's impact on the hydrological cycle.

Lockeretz, William, ed. AGRICULTURE AND ENERGY. New York: Academic Press, 1977. xiii, 750 p.

At a conference sponsored by the National Science Foundation and convened at Washington University, St. Louis, Missouri, 17-19 June 1976, experts gathered to consider energy consumption and agriculture, particularly how production strategies might be adapted to available resources. Their discussions were organized around nine themes: energy use in agriculture: statewide and national analyses; crop production; irrigation; tillage; fertilizers and plant nutrients; livestock production; nondepletable energy resources; agriculture in developing countries; and implications of energy problems for U.S. agricultural policy.

McCarthy, F. Desmond. NUTRITION, FOOD AND PRICES IN PAKISTAN. INP Discussion Papers 75-4. International Nutrition Planning Program. Center for International Studies. Cambridge: MIT, 1975. viii, 74 p. Paperbound. Bibliog.

Drawing upon data collected in governmental household surveys, McCarthy presents an economic analysis of the relation between income among low-income classes and total food intake and intake of different types of food and then discusses policy options based on his findings.

National Research Council. Board on Agriculture and Renewable Resources. Study on World Food and Nutrition. WORLD FOOD AND NUTRITION STUDY:

ENHANCEMENT OF FOOD PRODUCTION FOR THE UNITED STATES. Washington, D.C.: National Academy of Sciences, 1975. xiii, 174 p. Paperbound. References.

> This report provides five groups of recommendations formulated in workshops attended by informed professionals. There are five groups of recommendations: (1) human nutrition; (2) natural resources base, input management, and the environment; (3) production of food and feed crops; (4) livestock, poultry, and fish production; and (5) food science and technology.

National Research Council. Committee on Agricultural Production Efficiency. AGRICULTURAL PRODUCTION EFFICIENCY. Washington, D.C.: National Academy of Sciences, 1975. ix, 199 p. Paperbound.

> This report evaluates the policies of the United States, and the country's knowledge and technology relative to research and education, particularly insofar as they apply to a sustained effort to provide food and other agricultural produce for the population of this and other countries. The members of the committee examined historical trends in agricultural production, various measures of change in production efficiency, the role of farmers, societal supports and constraints, energy, biological limitations on productivity, frontiers for scientific research, and projections on future productivity. A program of sustained agricultural productivity will require joint efforts of farmers, agribusinessmen, scientists, and educational institutions as well as enlightened governmental policies.

National Research Council. Committee on Climate and Weather Fluctuations and Agricultural Production. Board on Agriculture and Renewable Resources. Commission on Natural Resources. CLIMATE AND FOOD: CLIMATE FLUCTUATION AND U.S. AGRICULTURAL PRODUCTION. Washington, D.C.: National Academy of Sciences, 1976. ix, 212 p. Paperbound.

> Problems include climatic factors in agriculture, water and land resources, plant breeding, crop livestock and pest management, weather modification, strategies for developing countries, marine food production, and forest lands. The recommendations urge improved management and intensified research on weather-crop and animal relationships so that more reliable forecasts can be made of agricultural productivity during weather and climatic change.

Reed, Charles, ed. ORIGINS OF AGRICULTURE. World Anthropology. The Hague: Mouton Publishers, 1977. xvi, 1,013 p. References; Indexes.

> This volume contains papers contributed by botanists, zoologists, anthropologists, demographers, agricultural historians, and paleoenvironmentalists to discussions held at the ninth International Congress of Anthropological and Ethnological Sciences. The extensive material is arranged in six sections: (1) general principles,

(2) worldwide concepts, (3) beginnings of agriculture in the old world, (4) beginnings of agriculture in the new world, (5) general conclusions drawn by the editor, and (6) an appendix on a radio-carbon chronology related to origins of agriculture.

Renfrew, Jane M. PALAEOETHNOBOTANY: THE PREHISTORIC FOOD PLANTS OF THE NEAR EAST AND EUROPE. New York: Columbia University Press; London: Methuen and Co., 1973. xviii, 248 p. Bibliog.; Glossary; Plates.

Renfrew makes a detailed examination of the evidence regarding the origins and development of agriculture in the Near East and its spread to Europe in prehistoric times. Two chapters deal with the nature of the evidence and the problems of sampling and in-terpretation. There is an extended discussion of cereals (wheat, barley, rye, oats, and millets), pulses (horsebean, field peas, and lentils), legumes (bitter vetch, grass pea, and chickpea), flax, cultivated and wild fruits, nuts, drug plants, and edible wild plants. One chapter summarizes data on the food values of these plants.

Scrimshaw, Nevin S.; Austin, James E.; Harris, John R.; Rha, Chokyun; and Sinskey, Anthony J. HIGH PROTEIN PRODUCT DEVELOPMENT EFFORTS IN THAILAND: AN EVALUATION OF THE KASETART UNIVERSITY PROGRAM. MIT International Nutrition Planning Program, Technical Report Series, no. 1. Cambridge: MIT, 1973. xiii, 227 p. Paperbound. Tables; Figures; Appendixes.

The objectives of the evaluation were: identification of users of high protein products, appraisal of technical suitability of these products, economic feasibility of producing these products, and preparation of recommendations on product development strategies and manpower needed in program. Information was brought to-gether on community nutrition status, demographic data, dietary pattern, evaluation of high protein products, analysis of demand, supplies of raw materials, food processing industry, and nutrition policies; and recommendations were made.

Scrimshaw, Nevin S., and Behar, Moises, eds. NUTRITION AND AGRICUL-TURAL DEVELOPMENT: SIGNIFICANCE AND POTENTIAL FOR THE TROPICS. Basic Life Sciences, vol. 7. New York: Plenum Press, 1976. xxiv, 500 p.

Collected are papers and discussions from the Symposium on Nu-trition and Agricultural and Economic Development in the Tropics held in Guatemala City, 2-6 December 1974, to celebrate the twenty-fifth anniversary of the Institute of Nutrition of Central America and Panama. The principal topics are: (1) food and nutrition problems, particularly among children and members of the labor force; (2) technological and ecological problems limiting the production of food; (3) problems in the postharvest conserva-tion, processing, and distribution of food; (4) social and economic problems limiting food supplies and consumption; (5) alternate strategies to break the vicious cycle; and (6) application of science and technology to long-range solutions.

Takahashi, Koichiro, and Yoshino, Matatoshi M., eds. CLIMATIC CHANGE
AND FOOD PRODUCTION. Tokyo: University of Tokyo Press, 1978. xi,
433 p.

> This volume comprises the proceedings of an international sym-
> posium convened in Japan, 4-8 October 1976. The principal
> focus is the Far East. The general topics are: climatic change
> in monsoon Asia and the world; climatic change and crop pro-
> duction in South and Southeast Asia; climatic change and crop
> production in Japan; analysis of climatic change; and modelling,
> simulation and prediction of climatic change and crop production.

Ucko, Peter J., and Dimbleby, G.W., eds. THE DOMESTICATION AND
EXPLOITATION OF PLANTS AND ANIMALS. Chicago: Aldine-Atherton,
1969. xxvi, 581 p. Paperbound. Indexes.

> The papers were presented at a meeting of the Research Seminar
> in Archaeology and Related Subjects held 18-19 May 1968 at
> London University. In part 1, "Origins of Domestication," the
> authors consider environmental background and patterns of ex-
> ploitation. In part 2, the authors discuss how to undertake in-
> vestigations of exploitation and domestication. Part 3 focuses on
> regional and local evidence for domestication. The papers of
> part 4 emphasize studies of particular taxonomic groups of plants
> and animals. Early man's nutrition is the theme of part 5.

B. ENERGY

Battelle Memorial Institute. Columbus Laboratories. ENERGY INFORMATION
RESOURCES: AN INVENTORY OF ENERGY RESEARCH AND DEVELOPMENT
INFORMATION RESOURCES IN THE CONTINENTAL UNITED STATES, HAWAII
AND ALASKA. Compiled by Patricia L. Brown et al. Washington, D.C.:
American Society for Information Science, 1975. vi, 207 p. Paperbound.
Indexes.

> This publication, compiled under a grant from the National Science
> Foundation, is intended to provide those concerned with energy-
> related research and development with a list of potentially ap-
> plicable sources of information available to the user community.
> The two main sections list 193 information resources and 108 an-
> notated publications, with complete information about each entry.
> There are five indexes: (1) organization, (2) acronym, (3) geo-
> graphic location, (4) serial products, and (5) subject. The first
> three indexes relate only to the list of information resources, the
> last two to both main sections.

Brown, Norman L., ed. RENEWABLE ENERGY RESOURCES AND RURAL AP-
PLICATIONS IN THE DEVELOPING WORLD. American Association for the
Advancement of Science, Selected Symposium 6. Boulder, Colo.: Westview
Press, 1978. xviii, 168 p. Tables; Figures; Bibliog.

The special energy problems and needs of the less-developed countries are considered, especially in rural areas. Potential solutions are provided by small-scale, decentralized technologies for exploiting the sun's energy, received directly or as wind, flowing water, or biomass. The status of these technologies is discussed in eight papers, with special attention to problems in Brazil, India, and Ghana.

Burk, Creighton A., and Drake, Charles L., eds. THE IMPACT OF THE GEOSCIENCES ON CRITICAL ENERGY RESOURCES. American Association for the Advancement of Science, Selected Symposium 21. Boulder, Colo.: Westview Press, 1978. xvi, 114 p. Figures; Tables.

The seven papers presented at this symposium deal with federal objectives and organizations relative to the geosciences; the impact of university geoscience programs on critical energy resources; hydrocarbon resources and related problems; coal; geothermal resources; nuclear energy resources; and energy, environment, and the geosciences.

Darmstadter, Joel; Dunkerley, Joy; and Alterman, Jack. HOW INDUSTRIAL SOCIETIES USE ENERGY: A COMPARATIVE ANALYSIS. Baltimore: Johns Hopkins University Press, 1977. xvi, 282 p.

This research study, sponsored by the Center for Energy Policy Research of Resources for the Future, depicts comparative patterns of energy consumption for the United States, Canada, France, West Germany, Italy, Netherlands, United Kingdom, Sweden, and Japan. The study identifies those components of energy consumption that give rise to variations between countries in the relationship between energy use and national output. It also interprets the respective contributions of economic structure and of characteristics of energy use to the intercountry variations in energy use and output. Detailed statistical data are presented to support the final chapter on findings and interpretation.

Eddy, John A., ed. THE NEW SOLAR PHYSICS. American Association for the Advancement of Science, Selected Symposium 17. Boulder, Colo.: Westview Press, 1978. xxii, 214 p. References.

This volume presents recent developments in the study of the sun, written by scientists directly involved. Papers are: "Solar Physics in Broad Perspective," E. N. Parker; "Historical and Arboreal Evidence for a Changing Sun," John A. Eddy; "Neutrinos from the Sun," Raymond Davis, Jr. and John C. Evans, Jr.; "Streams, Sectors, and Solar Magnetism," Arthur J. Handhausen; and "Seismic Sounding of the Sun," Henry A. Hill.

ENERGY CRISIS IN AMERICA. Washington, D.C.: Congressional Quarterly, 1973. 93 p. Paperbound.

This is a compilation of articles which appeared between 1969 and 1973 in either the WEEKLY REPORT or EDITORIAL RESEARCH REPORTS, both published by Congressional Quarterly. Included are summaries of news, federal legislation, and court decisions on general energy problems, strip mining, natural-gas pipelines, energy ownership, nuclear power options, environmental problems, and pollution technology.

ENERGY RESOURCES AND THE ENVIRONMENT. Edited by John Lenihan and William W. Fletcher. Environment and Man Series, vol. 1. New York: Academic Press, 1976. xii, 194 p.

The authors examine the basic role of energy in modern society in a style understandable by scientist, engineer, and layman. The several contributions deal with man's energy needs, flow of energy through technological society, economical use of energy and materials, energy in the international scene, nuclear energy, and solar energy. The objectives are to demonstrate that conservation and minimal environmental disruption are feasible.

ENERGY SOURCE BOOK. Germantown, Md.: Aspen Systems Corp., 1977. ix, 724 p. Appendixes.

This book, compiled by the Center for Compliance Information, contains source material from government and private sources needed by U.S. business and industry to facilitate sound management and prudent corporate decisions in evaluating energy supplies, planning conservation measures, and dealing with energy regulation, from the present to 1990. The five chapters deal with (1) President Carter's energy proposals and congressional actions; (2) the national energy scene, with a forecast through 1990; (3) the sources of energy, with discussion of production and economics; (4) options for American industry; and (5) guidelines for industry. Appendixes list policy considerations for the states regarding energy conservation and energy issues facing the ninty-fifth Congress; also included is the full text of the Department of Energy Organization Act of 1977 (42 USC 7101).

Fisher, John C. ENERGY CRISES IN PERSPECTIVE. New York: John Wiley and Sons, 1974. ix, 196 p. Appendixes.

Fisher analyzes world energy activities: sources, consumption, availability of fuels, social and environmental factors, political factors, technology, and efficiency of utilization. The book is directed primarily to problems and opportunities in the use of inanimate energy (characteristic of the industrialized regions), with particular emphasis on electrical energy.

Ford Foundation. Energy Policy Project. A TIME TO CHOOSE; AMERICA'S ENERGY FUTURE. Cambridge, Mass.: Ballinger Publishing Co., 1974. xii, 511 p. Notes; Appendixes.

This is the final report of the project. It analyzes choices under three versions of possible U.S. energy futures in 1985 and 2000: a historical growth scenario, a technical fix scenario, and a zero energy growth scenario. Chapters deal with the American energy consumer; energy and the environment; government energy policy and regulation; research and development; conclusions and recommendations. Comments by individuals of the Energy Policy Project complete the text. Extensive appendixes.

Hammond, Allen L.; Metz, William D.; and Maugh, Thomas H. II. ENERGY AND THE FUTURE. Washington, D.C.: American Association for the Advancement of Science, 1973. xii, 184 p. Glossary; Bibliog.

This book consists of six sections, on energy from fossil fuels, nuclear energy, alternative energy sources, energy transmission, energy conservation, and energy policy. Its purpose is to discover and assess the technologies and research developments that will be the basis for future energy policies in the United States.

Hitch, Charles J., ed. ENERGY CONSERVATION AND ECONOMIC GROWTH. American Association for the Advancement of Science, Selected Symposium 22. Boulder, Colo.: Westview Press, 1978. xvi, 167 p. Figures; Tables; Charts; Bibliog.

This book consists of seven papers contributing to the debate on national energy policy. It considers a variety of responses to higher energy costs, especially the relative importance of conserving energy and of increasing energy supplies, with special focus on the impact of conservation on economic growth.

_____. RESOURCES FOR AN UNCERTAIN FUTURE. Baltimore: Johns Hopkins University Press, 1978. x, 105 p. Paperbound.

These seven papers, presented at a forum held by Resources for the Future in 1977, appraise the resource and environmental outlook for the United States during the next twenty-five years in the light of events of the recent past. Informed opinions are offered on selected issues, including resources in the past and the future; energy imperatives and the environment; three assessments (historical, scientific, economic) of coping with the future; and managing the relationship of the environment and the economy.

Hottel, Hoyt Clarke, and Howard, Jack Benny. NEW ENERGY TECHNOLOGY-- SOME FACTS AND ASSESSMENTS. Cambridge: MIT Press, 1971. xi, 364 p. Bibliog.

Chief source of information for this book was a six-month study done for the National Science Foundation by the Environmental Laboratory of Massachusetts Institute of Technology to identify specific research needs related to the overall problem of satisfying the energy requirements of the United States. Contents include a summary of energy supply and demand, past, present, and future

as projected; background for assessment of new energy technology;
and technical and economic data on various processes for fossil
fuel-to-fuel conversion, nuclear power, and central-station power
from fossil fuel. Also considered are utilization-related energy
problems and utilization of solar energy.

Illinois. Board of Higher Education. A WORK FORCE FOR ENVIRON-
MENT AND ENERGY: A MASTER PLAN FOR ENVIRONMENT/ENERGY
HIGHER EDUCATION IN ILLINOIS. [Springfield]: 1975. 418 p. Paper-
bound.

This study is a response to the emerging problems of energy resources. Its objective is to formulate a plan for training college
and university students and to retain adults for dealing with energy
problems. The volume contains detailed descriptions of curricula
and special facilities at community colleges, colleges, universities,
and other institutions of the state, as well as an inventory of research in progress which relates to energy use and conservation.

Inglis, David Rittenhouse. NUCLEAR ENERGY--ITS PHYSICS AND ITS SOCIAL
CHALLENGE. Reading, Mass.: Addison-Wesley Publishing Co., 1973. xiv,
395 p. Paperbound. Appendixes; Bibliog.; Index.

This college textbook is intended chiefly for the liberal arts student with little background in science, or for the general reader
interested in both the scientific and the humanistic aspects of
nuclear-energy problems, as a basis for present and future political
judgments. After five chapters on the basic physics and biology,
the remaining chapters deal with control of fissile materials; other
possible power sources and future needs; nuclear explosives; and
constraints on the arms race.

Inglis, K.A., ed. ENERGY: FROM SURPLUS TO SCARCITY? New York:
John Wiley and Sons, 1974. ix, 242 p.

The volume contains the proceedings of the summer meeting of the
Institute of Petroleum, held in Harrogate, London, 5-8 June 1973.
Fifteen papers deal with production and marketing of coal, oil,
natural gas, electricity, and nuclear energy; new and alternative
sources of energy; the Middle East countries and the international
oil industry; and future outlook in the United States and Europe.

Kwee, Swan Liat, and Mullender, J.S.R., eds. GROWING AGAINST OURSELVES:
THE ENERGY-ENVIRONMENT TANGLE; PROBLEMS, POLICIES, AND AP-
PROACHES. Leiden: A.W. Sijthoff; Lexington, Mass.: Lexington Books,
1972. xix, 252 p.

The volume includes papers presented at an international colloquium
on Electric Energy Needs and Environmental Problems held at The
Hague in June 1971 and sponsored by the John F. Kennedy Institute and the Future Shape of Technology Foundation. Its purpose

was to present a multidisciplinary approach to energy-environment problems as affecting public policy and future strategies. Part 1 deals in general and international terms with identifying the problems of electric energy and the environment. Part 2 concerns technical problems and national energy policies, specifically in the United States, the United Kingdom, France, and Poland. Part 3 considers future strategies and approaches.

Lewis, Richard S., and Spinrad, Bernard I., eds. THE ENERGY CRISIS. Chicago: Educational Foundation for Nuclear Science, 1972. 148 p.

Originally published in the BULLETIN OF ATOMIC SCIENTISTS in 1971, the articles in this volume comprise a science and public affairs book. Topics addressed are: (1) is there an energy crisis? (2) the radiation controversy; (3) economic aspects of energy; (4) technical alternatives; (5) an international survey of nuclear power development; and (6) patterns of protest.

National Research Council. Committee on Mineral Resources and the Environment. MINERAL RESOURCES AND THE ENVIRONMENT. Washington, D.C.: National Academy of Sciences, 1975. vi, 348 p. Paperbound. Bibliog.

This is the first report of a two-year study to provide a balanced, long-term review of problems affecting mineral resources and the environment within the four provinces of technology, supply, the environment, and demand. The supply panel considered two categories, the fossil fuels and copper; the environment panel studied only coal. The approach of the technology and demand panels was generalized. All four panels present policy recommendations, and a separate appendix volume for each is available, expanding and documenting certain aspects of the main report.

National Research Council. Geophysics Study Committee. ENERGY AND CLIMATE. Washington, D.C.: National Academy of Sciences, 1977. xiv, 158 p. Paperbound.

One of a series of studies on subjects related to geophysics, this report includes ten essays originally presented at a symposium of the American Geophysical Union held in December 1974 in San Francisco. All ten essays treat the question of possible constraints placed on energy use by the danger of climatic change. In addition to the overview and recommendations, the report contains three parts, covering the context of the problem; effluents of energy production; and monitoring and modelling.

Science and Public Policy Program, University of Oklahoma. ENERGY ALTERNATIVES: A COMPARATIVE ANALYSIS. Washington, D.C.: Government Printing Office, for the Council on Environmental Quality, 1975. xxxviii, 662 p. Paperbound. Glossary; Bibliog.; Tables; Figures.

This report is intended to help develop a methodology for identifying, assessing, and comparing energy alternatives in environmental

impact statements. Part 1 (thirteen chapters) gives descriptions
and data on the major energy resource systems of the United States
(coal, oil shale, crude oil, natural gas, tar sands, nuclear, geothermal, hydroelectric, organic wastes, solar energy, electric
generation), including for each the technologies, efficiencies,
environmental residuals, and economic costs. Part 2 (three chapters)
describes procedures for using part 1 data to compare and evaluate
a proposed energy action and its alternatives.

Stanford Research Institute. PATTERNS OF ENERGY CONSUMPTION IN THE
UNITED STATES. Washington, D.C.: Government Printing Office, 1972.
xi, 156 p. Paperbound. Appendixes.

This study, made for the Energy Policy Staff of the President's
Office of Science and Technology, presents statistics covering
1960 to 1968 on consumption of energy by the residential, commercial, industrial, and transportation sectors, based on the annual
data of the Bureau of Mines and other sources, some providing
estimates only. The purposes were to determine what significant
end uses fuels have served, what portion of energy requirements
were met by each fuel, what rate of growth of consumption each
fuel showed, and what technical efficiency can be expected when
each fuel is suitably used.

Steadman, Philip. ENERGY, ENVIRONMENT, AND BUILDING. Cambridge:
University Press, 1975. ix, 287 p. Bibliog.

Intended for architects, engineers, and builders, this is a compilation of information on energy conservation in building; solar
energy, especially solar space-heating; wind power; small-scale
water power; composting, waste treatment, and methane gas as a
fuel; and water conservation. An extensive bibliography on each
topic is included, together with lists of manufacturers of equipment
in these fields, and directories of existing buildings and projects
illustrating the techniques discussed. Drawings, schematic plans,
and design data are included in many cases.

Turvey, Ralph, and Anderson, Dennis. ELECTRICITY ECONOMICS: ESSAYS
AND CASE STUDIES. Baltimore and London: Johns Hopkins University Press,
1977. xvii, 364 p. Tables; Figures; Maps; Bibliog.

Studies prepared under the aegis of the World Bank, dealing with
the economic theory and practice of pricing and investment in
electricity supply. Part 1, on descriptive and case studies, includes specific information on Thailand, Tunisia, Sudan, and
Turkey. Part 2, on studies of principles and theory, deals with
tariffs and tariff structures, rate of return on projects, shadow
pricing, investment planning models, cost structure in hydro and
hydro-thermal systems, and optimal pricing.

United Nations. Economic Commission for Europe. Committee on Gas. THE GAS INDUSTRY AND THE ENVIRONMENT. Oxford, Engl.: Pergamon Press, 1978. xvi, 263 p.

Here are the proceedings of a symposium of the Committee on Gas held at Minsk, USSR, 20-27 June 1977, with 140 representatives of twenty-five countries participating. Of the twenty-seven papers included, twenty-five are in English and two in French. The problems of environmental protection considered arose from: (1) the use of natural gas in industry, agriculture, and energy production; (2) the use of gas in the commercial and domestic sectors; (3) exploration, preparation, transportation, storage, and distribution of natural gas; and (4) production, distribution, and use of manufactured gases.

U.S. Atomic Energy Commission. Office of Information Services. Technical Information Center. SOLAR ENERGY: A BIBLIOGRAPHY. (TID-3351). Washington, D.C.: 1974. iii, 218 p. Paperbound.

This is a comprehensive bibliography on solar energy research, arranged in broad subject categories, with three indexes: by personal author, detailed subject, and report number. The indexes total an additional 138 pages. Besides the items included in this publication, new references are being added on a continuing basis and are available on RECON, the on-line computer retrieval system developed under the Atomic Energy Commission and now supported by the Department of Energy.

U.S. Office of the President. Office of Science and Technology. Energy Policy Staff. ELECTRIC POWER AND THE ENVIRONMENT. Washington, D.C.: Office of Science and Technology, August 1970. xi, 71 p. Paperbound.

Assembled is information on institutional arrangements and standard setting, transmission lines and utility corridors, acquisition of plant sites, problems of power plant siting, and growth of electricity consumption. The staff and the agencies cooperating in the study present conclusions and recommendations on meeting national needs for electrical power and maintaining environmental quality.

C. WATER, WEATHER MODIFICATION, WEATHER CHANGE

Bryson, Reid A., and Murray, Thomas J. CLIMATES OF HUNGER: MANKIND AND THE WORLD'S CHANGING WEATHER. Madison: University of Wisconsin Press, 1977. xv, 171 p. Bibliog.

Bryson and Murray review the climatic record for the past several thousand years. They demonstrate that the climate has been variable, more often than not unfavorable for sustained agricultural production. They examine in some detail several periods when mankind suffered particularly from these fluctuations: a drought in Greece in 1200 B.C., an American drought of 1200 A.D., the "little ice age" of 1550-1850, and the recent drought in the Sahel. Because the climate again seems to be deteriorating, special attention should be given to measuring and evaluating trends and anticipating consequences.

Changnon, Stanley A., Jr., et al. HAIL SUPPRESSION: IMPACTS AND ISSUES. Urbana: Illinois State Water Survey, 1977. xv, 432 p. Paperbound. Tables; Figures; References.

This volume is the final report of a Technology Assessment of the Suppression of Hail supported by the National Science Foundation. The authors discuss the hail problem and the technology of its suppression, the individuals and organizations having a stake in the problem, and societal influences of weather modification and hail suppression. They consider the future of hail suppression, its costs and benefits, the social constraints, and various models for anticipating the outcomes of suppression activities. Finally, they examine public policy options for continuing, supporting, regulating, and evaluating this form of weather modification technology.

Chroley, Richard J., ed. WATER, EARTH, AND MAN: A SYNTHESIS OF HYDROLOGY, GEOMORPHOLOGY, AND SOCIO-ECONOMIC GEOGRAPHY. London: Methuen and Co., 1969. xix, 588 p. Bibliog.

British, American, and Australian scientists in many fields and from many universities have contributed to this compilation, which is organized under twelve topics: the world; the basin; precipitation; evapotranspiration; surface runoff; ground water; channel flow; snow and ice; short-term runoff patterns; annual runoff characteristics; long-term trends; and choice in water use.

Coker, Robert E. STREAMS, LAKES, PONDS. Chapel Hill: University of North Carolina Press, 1954. Reprint. New York: Harper and Row, 1968. xvi, 327 p. Paperbound. Bibliog.

This is a semitechnical introductory treatment of inland surface waters. It includes sections on water and its content, running waters, and still waters (lakes and ponds) with their plants and animals. One chapter is devoted to stream pollution.

Davis, Ray Jay, and Grant, Lewis O., eds. WEATHER MODIFICATION: TECHNOLOGY AND LAW. American Association for the Advancement of Science, Selected Symposium 20. Boulder, Colo.: Westview Press, 1978. xviii, 124 p.

The four principal topics are: (1) weather modification technology, (2) options for legal regulation, (3) societal and scientific criteria for development, and (4) interactions of scientists and lawyers.

Giefer, Gerald J. SOURCES OF INFORMATION IN WATER RESOURCES;

AN ANNOTATED GUIDE TO PRINTED MATERIALS. Port Washington, N.Y.: Water Information Center, 1976. xvii, 290 p. Index.

This guide cites and annotates over eleven-hundred titles useful for reference purposes in the water resources field, including many secondary sources from allied fields such as environmental sciences. Emphasis is on the literature of the United States; some state publications are included. The period covered is 1960 to 1975, although some earlier works are listed if noteworthy. Following the section on general works, the subject sections cover the nature of water; the water cycle; water supply; water quality: management and protection; water resources planning; and engineering works.

Halacy, Daniel S., Jr. THE WEATHER CHANGERS. New York: Harper and Row, 1968. viii, 246 p.

This discussion of weather forecasting and attempts at modification covers the history of rainmaking; lightning suppression; weather as a weapon; changing the climate; modification by accident; the dangers of tampering; weather modification and the law; weather-changing around the world; and outlook for the future.

Hamilton, C.E., ed. MANUAL ON WATER. 4th ed. ASTM Special Publication 442 A. Philadelphia: American Society of Testing and Materials, 1978. [vii], 472 p. Paperbound. Tables; Charts; References.

The manual provides information on water. The principal topics addressed are sources and supply; industrial uses; natural and technical means of purification; thermal loading; monitoring flow and quality; analysis of water, waste water and deposits; and radioactive nuclides in water and their measurement.

Leopold, Luna Bergere. WATER: A PRIMER. San Francisco: W.H. Freeman and Co., 1974. xvi, 172 p. Figures; Tables; Glossary; Index.

This book is designed to cover the general principles of hydrology and the facts about water use which must precede study of its impact on the environment. The book may be used either by the nonspecialist reader or as a textbook for undergraduates.

Murray, C. Richard, and Reeves, E. Bodette. ESTIMATED USE OF WATER IN THE UNITED STATES IN 1975. Geological Survey Circular 765. Arlington, Va.: U.S. Geological Survey, 1977. vi, 39 p. Paperbound. Illus.; Tables; Bibliog.

Based on statistics collected by the district offices of the Geological Survey, this report presents data on water withdrawn and consumed, by states and regions, for five categories of use: public supply, rural, irrigation, self-supplied industrial, and hydroelectric power. A tabulation shows trends in water use by five-year periods from 1950 to 1975.

National Research Council. Committee on Atmospheric Sciences. THE AT-
MOSPHERIC SCIENCES: PROBLEMS AND APPLICATIONS. Washington, D.C.:
National Academy of Sciences, 1977. xiii, 124 p. Paperbound.

> Members of the committee examined the scope and recent progress
> in the atmospheric sciences and summarized the nature of problems
> now under study. The first chapter treats atmospheric science and
> society. The second, "Impacts of Weather and Climate," discusses
> water, food, energy, and violent storms. The third, "Need for
> Skillful Predictions of Weather and Climate," reports that some
> progress has been made in short-term but not long-term forecasts.
> The fourth, "Environmental Preservation and Management," dis-
> cusses air quality, weather modification, and the upper atmosphere.
> Understanding man's impact on weather systems is considered most
> urgent. The fifth chapter emphasizes the need for new institu-
> tional arrangements in government for better planning and manage-
> ment of atmospheric research. The style of the presentation is
> nontechnical.

_____. THE ATMOSPHERIC SCIENCES AND MAN'S NEEDS: PRIORITIES
FOR THE FUTURE. Washington, D.C.: National Academy of Sciences, 1971.
viii, 88 p. Paperbound. Bibliog.

> This study, involving fifty-five participants, had eleven subject-
> matter panels covering the scientific and technical disciplines to
> review problems, constraints, recent achievements, and existing
> research plans, and to discuss the contribution of each subject
> area to the fulfillment of specific human needs. For each of the
> areas of major application--prediction, atmospheric quality, modi-
> fication, and information services--relevant material from the
> panels was summarized and interpreted. Resources required through
> the 1970s were estimated; and objectives and recommended actions
> for the nation were listed.

_____. WEATHER AND CLIMATE MODIFICATION: PROBLEMS AND PROG-
RESS. Washington, D.C.: National Academy of Sciences, 1973. xxi, 258 p.
Paperbound. Bibliog.

> This report of the Committee's Panel on Weather and Climate
> Modification is concerned with work in the field between 1966
> and 1973. It describes technical and scientific advances in weather
> modification; summarizes twelve programs for modifying precipi-
> tation (chiefly in the United States, but also in Mexico and Israel);
> reviews the modification, both intentional and inadvertent, of
> hazards such as fog, hail, hurricanes, and tornadoes; and analyzes
> the role of statistics in weather modification. The summary offers
> recommendations for research, national goals, and public-policy
> issues.

National Research Council. Committee on Atmospheric Sciences. Panel on
Short-Range Prediction and Panel on Severe Storms. SEVERE STORMS: PRE-

DICTION, DETECTION, AND WARNING. Washington, D.C.: National
Academy of Sciences, 1977. ix, 78 p. Paperbound. References.

> This pamphlet contains the reports of the two panels established
> in 1973 to look into the problems of the short-range prediction
> of general weather and violent storms. Their work concentrated
> on techniques for improved capability to predict important weather
> variables up to twelve hours in advance, especially by the use of
> modern computer techniques; and on the observational problems of
> detecting and tracking violent storms, as well as the communica-
> tion problems of providing adequate warnings. Each report con-
> tains a summary and recommendations.

National Research Council. Committee on Atmospheric Sciences. Panel on
Weather and Climate Modification. WEATHER AND CLIMATE MODIFICATION:
PROBLEMS AND PROSPECTS. Vol. 1, SUMMARY AND RECOMMENDATIONS.
National Academy of Sciences-National Research Council Publication, no. 1350.
Washington, D.C.: National Academy of Sciences, 1966. xi, 28 p. Paper-
bound.

> Appointed in 1963, the Panel on Weather and Climate Modifica-
> tion was instructed "to undertake a deliberate and thoughtful re-
> view of the present status and activities in this field, and of its
> potential and limitations for the future." This final report, in
> two volumes, completely supersedes a preliminary report dated
> October 1964. Volume 1 contains a summary of the status of the
> problem, suggestions for essential research, and recommendations
> for mandatory actions to ensure orderly and rapid progress.

_____. WEATHER AND CLIMATE MODIFICATION: PROBLEMS AND PROS-
PECTS. Vol. 2, RESEARCH AND DEVELOPMENT. National Academy of
Sciences-National Research Council Publication, no. 1350. Washington, D.C.:
National Academy of Sciences, 1966. xii, 198 p. Paperbound. Appendixes;
References.

> Volume 2 presents a general assessment covering these topics:
> modifying clouds and storm systems; modifying the weather and
> climate of large areas; modifying local and regional climates;
> inadvertent modification of atmospheric properties and processes;
> special problem areas in weather modification.

National Research Council. Geophysics Study Committee. CLIMATE, CLIMATIC
CHANGE, AND WATER SUPPLY. Studies in Geophysics. Washington, D.C.:
National Academy of Sciences, 1977. ix, 132 p. Paperbound.

> The essays were presented at a meeting of the American Geo-
> physical Union in April 1976. They deal with climate, climatic
> change, water, water-resources planning, water law, and the so-
> cioeconomic impacts of water shortages. The committee drew con-
> clusions and recommendations framed to aid policymakers in social
> decisions that involve geophysics. It was evident that not much

was known about socioeconomics impacts of drought and that the
ability to forecast climatic change, water shortage, and crop
yield was presently underdeveloped and inaccurate.

National Science Foundation. HUMAN DIMENSIONS OF THE ATMOSPHERE.
Washington, D.C.: Government Printing Office, 1968. vi, 174 p. Paperbound. Bibliog.

In 1966 a task group on human dimensions of the atmosphere was formed
with representatives from the fields of economics, geography, sociology,
political science, law, ecology, and meteorology. Its objective
was to identify areas of research in human uses of the atmosphere
and to foster interest in these problems among physical and social
scientists. After four sessions, with advice from other specialists
and from representatives of industry and government, twelve papers
were prepared on the various areas discussed. Included is a report from the task group chairman, W.R. Derrick Sewell, featuring
conclusions and recommendations.

National Science Foundation. Special Commission on Weather Modification.
WEATHER AND CLIMATE MODIFICATION. Washington, D.C.: 1965. vi,
149 p. Paperbound. Bibliog.

Under the chairmanship of A.R. Chamberlain, vice-president of
Colorado State University, the special commission examined the
physical, biological, legal, social, and political aspects of the
field and made recommendations on future policies and programs.
Its work is summarized in this report, which considers also the
statistical aspects of weather modification, its human effects, and
its impact on international relations.

Oglesby, Ray T.; Carlson, Clarence A.; and McCann, James A., eds. RIVER
ECOLOGY AND MAN. New York: Academic Press, 1972. xvii, 465 p.
References.

The papers of twenty-four contributors comprise these proceedings
of the International Symposium on River Ecology and the Impact of
Man held in Amherst, Massachusetts, 20-23 June 1971. Four
general topics were considered: what is a river?; uses of a river--
past and present; effects of river uses; rationalization of multiple
use. Case histories are given of the following rivers: Columbia,
Delaware, Illinois, Nile, Danube, and Thames.

Rosenberg, Norman J., ed. NORTH AMERICAN DROUGHTS. American Association for the Advancement of Science, Selected Symposium 15. Boulder,
Colo.: Westview Press, 1978. xx, 177 p. Tables; Figures.

This volume consists primarily of papers presented at a symposium
of the American Association for the Advancement of Science held
in Denver, 21 February 1977. The nine authors seek to organize
available evidence of both prehistoric and modern drought events;

to provide information on the impacts of droughts on social, political, and economic life in North America; to describe technological defenses against drought; and to examine the possibility of
forecasting future droughts.

Sewell, W.R. Derrick, ed. HUMAN DIMENSIONS OF WEATHER MODIFI-
CATION. University of Chicago, Department of Geography, Research Paper,
no. 105. Chicago: University of Chicago Press, 1966. xii, 423 p. Paperbound. Tables; Illus.; Bibliog.

This volume consists of twenty-seven papers presented at a Symposium on the Economic and Social Aspects of Weather Modification held 1-3 July 1965 in Boulder, Colorado. Topics were
physical capacity to modify the weather; economic evaluation of
weather modification; impacts on agriculture, forestry, outdoor
recreation, airlines, public utilities, and the insurance industry;
impacts on urban regions; legal and governmental aspects; perceptions of weather effects and attitudes toward weather; research
effort in this field; and behavioral and social implications of weather
modification.

Taubenfeld, Howard J., ed. WEATHER MODIFICATION AND THE LAW. Dobbs
Ferry, N.Y.: Oceana Publications, 1968. xii, 228 p.

This volume contains papers presented at a lecture-workshop program held 7-8 December 1967 at the Law School of Southern
Methodist University, under a grant from the National Science
Foundation. Group discussions following the presentation of papers
are also reported in summary form, with emphasis on the implications for society in the United States of the interplay of science,
technology, and law. Conferees representing both government
and private industry were present, as well as lawyers and scientists, both physical and social.

Thomas, William A., ed. LEGAL AND SCIENTIFIC UNCERTAINTIES OF WEATHER
MODIFICATION. Durham, N.C.: Duke University Press, 1977. viii, 155 p.

This volume comprises the proceedings of a symposium held at Duke
University 11-12 March 1976 under the sponsorship of the National
Conference of Lawyers and Scientists. The objective of the symposium was to make available scientifically valid and legally acceptable advice on weather modification so as to promote sound
decision making. There were papers of various aspects of weather
modification technology and their legal implications, a report on
the Yuba City episode, and panel discussions on social implications of weather modification, institutional arrangements and dissemination of information, and risk-benefit analysis. Scientific
and legal documentation was included.

U.S. Bureau of Reclamation. PARK RANGE ATMOSPHERIC WATER RESOURCES

PROGRAM, PHASE 1. Water Resources Technical Publication Research Report, no. 5. Washington, D.C.: Government Printing Office, 1967. x, 111 p. Paperbound. Tables; Figures; Graps; Maps; Photos.

The purpose of the Park Range Atmospheric Water Resources Program, operated by E. Bollay Associates for the Bureau of Reclamation, was to determine to what extent the precipitation in a mountainous region can be augmented by artificial nucleation. Phase 1 covers operations of the program from 1 November 1964 through 1 July 1965 and data collected through 1 May 1965. Operations were centered at Steamboat Springs, Colorado, in the Park Range of the Rocky Mountains.

U.S. Water Resources Council. WATER FOR ENERGY SELF-SUFFICIENCY. Washington, D.C.: Government Printing Office, 1974. ix, 184 p. Paperbound. Tables.

The Water Resources Council, an independent executive agency of the federal government, directed a task force representing thirteen organizations to analyze the energy-related water needs of the nation and to offer recommendations for meeting problems in this field. The task force membership included federal agencies, river basin commissions and other regional bodies, and states. This resulting report contains five chapters, on the topics of background information; regional analyses; state aspects; problems and constraints; and conclusions and recommendations.

Van der Leeden, Frits, comp. and ed. GROUND WATER: A SELECTED BIBLIOGRAPHY. 2d ed. Port Washington, N.Y.: Water Information Center, 1974. viii, 146 p.

This bibliography of important books and journal articles in the field includes 1,750 references listed under thirty-two topics, each dealing with a particular aspect of ground-water hydrology. Each item is listed only once, alphabetically by author; there are no annotations and no indexes.

WATER FROM A THIRSTY LAND; SONORAN DESERT AND MOUNTAIN RIVER HISTORY. Prescott, Ariz.: Pinon Press, 1978. 90 p.

The five chapters in this volume were reprinted from JOURNAL OF ARIZONA HISTORY (19, no. 1, Spring 1978). Each depicts the history of man's struggles since the eighteenth century to obtain and conserve water for agricultural, industrial, and domestic needs in the Sonoran Desert and from major rivers of Arizona.

World Meteorological Organization. METEOROLOGY AND THE HUMAN ENVIRONMENT. WMO no. 313. Geneva: 1971. 40 p. Paperbound.

This booklet describes the steps taken to identify the role of meteorology in human environment affairs, and to explain the programs of the World Meteorological Organization in this field to serve its member countries as well as the United Nations and specialized agencies in both meteorology and operational hydrology. The four chapters cover efficient use of natural resources; air pollution; water pollution; and modification of weather and climate. There are brief descriptions of the World Weather Watch and the Global Atmospheric Research Programme.

Zikeev, Nikolay, and Doumani, George A. WEATHER MODIFICATION IN THE SOVIET UNION, 1946-1966: A SELECTED ANNOTATED BIBLIOGRAPHY. Washington, D.C.: Library of Congress, 1967. x, 78 p. Paperbound. Appendixes.

This bibliography lists 503 items received in the Library of Congress before 1 November 1966. The entries are arranged into seven subject categories: physics of clouds and fog; seeding of clouds and fog; atmospheric electricity; hail suppression; radar applications; reagents: dispersion properties, equipment, and methods; and climate modification. Appendix 1 contains the titles and Library of Congress call numbers of the fifty-four Russian scientific serials represented in the bibliography. Appendix 2 lists Soviet specialists active in research in this field, with the affiliation and research subject of each. Appendix 3 contains addresses and phone numbers, if available, of the Soviet institutions active in operations of weather and climate modification.

D. LAND (CITIES, FARMS, MINING, RECREATION, WILDERNESS)

Abler, Ronald, and Adams, J.S., eds. A COMPARATIVE ATLAS OF AMERICA'S GREAT CITIES; TWENTY METROPOLITAN REGIONS. Association of American Geographers. Comparative Metropolitan Analysis Project, vol. 3. Minneapolis: University of Minnesota Press, 1976. xxii, 503 p.

The atlas comprises tabular and cartographic data for twenty metropolitan regions: Boston, New York and northern New Jersey, Philadelphia, Hartford and Connecticut Valley, Baltimore, New Orleans, San Francisco and Oakland, Pittsburgh, St. Louis, Cleveland, Chicago, Detroit, Minneapolis and St. Paul, Seattle, Dallas and Fort Worth, Houston, Los Angeles, Miami, Atlanta, and Washington, D.C. The methodologies for constructing the atlas are discussed in part 1. The geographic and demographic patterns of these cities are described in part 2. Part 3 focuses on such metropolitan problems as water supply, sewage disposal, housing, transportation and communication, growth, education, employment and poverty, and urban development. Part 4 deals with matters of policy.

Adams, John S., ed. CONTEMPORARY METROPOLITAN AMERICA. Vol. 1: TWENTY GEOGRAPHICAL VIGNETTES. Part 1: CITIES OF THE NATION'S

HISTORIC METROPOLITAN CORE; Part 2: NINETEENTH CENTURY PORTS; Part 3: NINETEENTH CENTURY INLAND CENTERS AND PORTS; Part 4: TWENTIETH CENTURY CITIES. Cambridge, Mass.: Ballinger Publishing Co., 1976. xvi, 354 p.; xiii, 314 p.; xix, 507 p.; xvi, 350 p. Maps; Photos.; Diagrams.

This first volume (comprising a four-book series) of the Comparative Analysis Project of the Association of American Geographers provides detailed analysis of twenty metropolitan centers of the United States. The first part focuses on the urban development in the historic cities of Boston, New York-New Jersey metropolitan region, Philadelphia, and central Connecticut. The second part is devoted to discussions of the urban growth in Baltimore, New Orleans, and the cities of San Francisco Bay during the nineteenth and twentieth centuries. In the third part, there are discussions of the urban growth in Pittsburgh, St. Louis, northeastern Ohio (Cleveland and Akron), Chicago, Detroit, St. Paul and Minneapolis, and Seattle during the nineteenth and twentieth centuries. The fourth part deals with the urban growth in the Dallas-Fort Worth region, Miami, Houston, Atlanta, Los Angles, and Washington during the nineteenth and twentieth centuries. In each discussion, attention is given to the issues and problems which growth has precipitated, such as land use, transportation, housing, communication, and pollution.

Berry, Brian Joe Lobley, and Kasarda, John D. CONTEMPORARY URBAN ECOLOGY. New York: Macmillan Publishing Co.; London: Collier Macmillan Publishers, 1977. xiii, 497 p. Bibliog.; Indexes.

Aimed at advanced undergraduate and graduate students of urban ecology, the authors first discuss recent trends in the conceptualization of social and spatial organization. The main body of the text is organized hierarchically into five parts: (1) local communities; (2) intraurban groups; (3) metropolitan organization; (4) urban systems; and (5) comparative urban structure and planned change. In the final section, the authors look at the future of ecology.

Chapman, G.P. HUMAN AND ENVIRONMENTAL SYSTEMS; A GEOGRAPHER'S APPRAISAL. London: Academic Press, 1977. xiv, 421 p.

Chapman critically summarizes the theoretical and practical applications of the concept of systems to geographical study. The first part deals with wholes and how they are treated hierarchically and in space and time. In the second part, Chapman discusses how interdependent parts are brought together as systems. Part 3 is devoted to information theory, and part 4 to energetics. In the fifth part, Chapman considers some empirical examples from geographical studies of land use. He concludes that it will be some years before systems theory has any operational consequences for geography, that the systems of specific disciplines really have

much in common, and that the manner of data collection is crucial
for their usefulness in developing and testing systems.

Collier, George Allen. FIELDS OF THE TZOTZIL: THE ECOLOGICAL BASES
OF TRADITION IN HIGHLAND CHIAPAS. Austin: University of Texas Press,
1975, xv, 255 p. Appendix; Bibliog.

Collier discusses the cultural traditions regarding land use among
the Tzotzil Indians of southeastern Mexico. He considers the
forms of land use, the inheritance of land, the Indians' impact
on the land, its marginal nature, the role of ethnicity, and the
refuge-region hypothesis as well as the interaction between these
Indians and the state and the nation. He concludes that the ecological nature of the cultural traditions cannot be understood un-
less studies in relation to the local habitat and the constraints
imposed by state and nation.

Cox, Kevin R. MAN, LOCATION, AND BEHAVIOR: AN INTRODUCTION
TO HUMAN GEOGRAPHY. New York: John Wiley and Sons, 1972. xi,
399 p. Bibliog.

Intended as a textbook for beginning undergraduate students in
geography, this book simplifies the essential ingredients of scientific human geography, reflecting the conceptual rather than the
technical advances in the field in the past fifteen years. The
book stresses the general concept of spatial pattern or locational
predictability; also it draws upon work in so-called behavioral
geography, which emphasizes the role of human behavior and the
spatial interpretation of real-world human problems. There are
six sections, the first dealing with the topic of movement, the
second with migration and the decisions underlying it. The next
three sections deal with the patterns created by lines (e.g., communication channels), points, and areas. The last section considers the application of knowledge to three pressing problems of
society: the urban crisis, environmental quality, and economic
development.

Detwyler, Thomas R., and Marcus, Melvin G., eds. URBANIZATION AND EN-
VIRONMENT: THE PHYSICAL GEOGRAPHY OF THE CITY. Belmont, Calif.:
Duxbury Press, 1972. viii, 287 p. Paperbound. References.

The volume answers three questions: (1) How has urbanization
changed the natural environment? (2) How do physical features
and processes influence growth and functions of cities? (3) What
are some of the feedbacks between man's actions and environmental processes? The specific topics addressed include topo-
graphic setting, climate, air pollution, water, soil, natural risks,
noise, vegetation, and habitat for wildlife and man.

Doxiadis, Constantinos A. EKISTICS: AN INTRODUCTION TO THE SCIENCE OF HUMAN SETTLEMENTS. New York: Oxford University Press, 1968. xxix, 527 p. Appendixes; Notes; Glossary; Bibliog.; Illus.

Doxiadis sets out his personal experiences and traces the development of ekistics in four parts. The first describes human settlements and their study. The second deals with ekistic analysis, evolution, pathology, and diagnosis. In the third, he develops an ekistic theory. Action is the subject of the fourth.

Dregne, Harold E., ed. ARID LANDS IN TRANSITION. AAAS Publication, no. 90. Washington, D.C.: American Association for the Advancement of Science, 1970. xiii, 524 p. Appendix.

This volume comprises the proceedings of an international conference held in June 1969 and cosponsored by AAAS and UNESCO. Three groups of papers are devoted to present knowledge, problems, and potentials. The first two emphasize alternate uses and constraints resulting from availability of water and finance, politics, and education. In the third, the papers deal with such arid regions as Africa south of the Sahara, North Africa, Asia, Australia, Mexico, and South America. Another group of papers focuses on mechanisms and institutions for problem-solving. The final two papers evaluate arid lands as neglected resources and unresolved issues.

Eames, Edwin, and Goode, Judith Granich. ANTHROPOLOGY OF THE CITY: AN INTRODUCTION TO URBAN ANTHROPOLOGY. Englewood Cliffs, N.J.: Prentice-Hall, 1977. viii, 344 p. Footnotes; Bibliog.; Indexes.

Eames and Goode consider the history of urban anthropology and the meaning of such studies; the role of cities; urban ethnography; methods, techniques, and ethics; and the culture of poverty.

Haggett, Peter; Cliff, Andrew David; and Frey, Allan E. LOCATIONAL ANALYSIS IN HUMAN GEOGRAPHY. 2d ed. New York: John Wiley and Sons; Halsted Press, 1977. xiv, 605 p. Glossary; Tables; Bibliog.

Considerably revised from the first edition of 1965, this edition has three objectives: (1) to describe the patterns of human geographical aggregation in space, (2) to discuss methods of detecting these patterns, and (3) to suggest how such information may be used in regional analysis. The text has three parts. In the first, models of locational structure are discussed. In the second, the authors consider methods of locational analysis. In the third, regional applications in building, allocating, and forecasting are reviewed.

Hyams, Edward. SOIL AND CIVILIZATION. London: Thomas and Hudson, 1952. Reprint. Harper Colophon Books CN 458. New York: Harper and Row Publishers, 1976. vii, 312 p. Paperbound.

Hyams examines man's relation to and use of the soil, with both destructive and nondestructive results. His thesis is illustrated with case studies from both ancient and contemporaneous societies.

International Institute for Environment and Development. HUMAN SETTLE-MENTS; AN ANNOTATED BIBLIOGRAPHY. Elmsford, N.Y.: Pergamon Press, 1976. viii, 220 p.

This document was prepared for Habitat: United Nations Con-ference on Human Settlements, Vancouver, 31 May-11 June 1976. Included are bibliography of books, journals, articles, reports, and documents; a bibliography of bibliographies; national reports; and conferences documents. More than seventeen-hundred citations are annotated in English.

Knight, C. Gregory. ECOLOGY AND CHANGE: RURAL MODERNIZATION IN AN AFRICAN COMMUNITY. New York: Academic Press, 1974. xx, 300 p. Appendixes; References; Glossary.

Knight discusses a geographical study of the Nhiha of the Mbozi area of East Africa. His presentation blends the viewpoints of ecology, ethnogeography, and spatial organization of society and landscape and his focus is the implications of modernization for this rural community. He considers the people, their resources and their agricultural systems and patterns. He examines the sources of change, various models of change, and the implications of change. There are three appendixes: (1) "Vegetation of Unyiha," (2) "The Mbozi Economic Survey," and (3) "Key to Alienations."

Laconte, Pierre, ed. THE ENVIRONMENT OF HUMAN SETTLEMENT: HUMAN WELL-BEING IN CITIES. 2 vols. Oxford, Engl.: Pergamon Press, 1976. liv, 373 p.; x, 311 p.

These two volumes comprise the proceedings of the Conference on Human Well-Being in Cities held in Brussels, April 1976. Com-missioned by the World Environment and Resources Council, these volumes provided input to the United Nations Conference on Hu-man Settlement. The papers are grouped under the themes: modern technology of cities, decision making for human well-being in cities, urban and land use planning, and design as an aid to solving problems. Volume 2 includes addresses and reports of dis-cussion from the floor as well as a "Declaration of Brussels on Human Well-Being in Cities" adopted by the participants.

National Research Council. Division of Biology and Agriculture. Committee on Agricultural Land Use and Wildlife Resources. AGRICULTURAL LAND USE AND WILDLIFE RESOURCES. Washington, D.C.: National Academy of Sciences, 1970. vii, 262 p. Paperbound.

The committee evaluated the interrelations between the use of land for agriculture and protection and production of wildlife and other resources. It examined areas of conflict between agriculture and wildlife management. Wildlife was viewed broadly as including vertebrate animals, particularly mammals, birds, and fish, which were of social and economic interest. The report covers such topics as history, wildlife values, new patterns of use of land and water, influence of land management on wildlife, special problems of waters and watersheds, pesticides, wildlife damage and control, and legislation and administration. The recommendations include policy proposals for control of birds and mammals, protection of waters and watersheds, and management of river basin and open lands.

Perloff, Harvey S., ed. THE QUALITY OF THE URBAN ENVIRONMENT: ESSAYS ON "NEW RESOURCES" IN AN URBAN AGE. Washington, D.C.: Resources for the Future, 1969. xii, 332 p. Paperbound.

The nine papers were prepared for a conference on the urban environment sponsored by Resources for the Future and held in Washington, D.C., in November 1967. The conference was organized to evaluate the current state of the art and to stimulate research in the field. The choice of subjects and authors was highly selective, to provide a sampling of current work dealing with issues and methods relevant to public policymaking. Five papers are concerned with urban space, its uses, values, and amenity features. Two papers suggest broad settings within which the problems of the urban environment might be fruitfully viewed. Other papers deal with environmental quality and with transport. A unifying element in all papers is the search for better informational and measurement tools ultimately useful for decision making.

Popcock, Douglas, and Hudson, Ray. IMAGES OF THE URBAN ENVIRONMENT. Focal Problems in Geography Series. London: Macmillan Press, 1978. x, 181 p. Bibliog.; Indexes.

Introductory text in which Popcock and Hudson explore aspects of man's perception of his surroundings, particularly those comprising the urban environment. They write of the nature of environmental images, how these images are described and evaluated, the role of learning, and the implications of environmental images for planning and policy.

RECLAMATION. Edited by John Lenihan and William W. Fletcher. Environment and Man Series, vol. 4. New York: Academic Press, 1976. xii, 172 p.

Both the storms of nature and the exploitive behavior of man ravage the landscape. This volume provides five case histories demonstrating principles and works which can restore the landscape. The first case relates how the estate of Culbin in England devastated by a storm was restored. In the second, the subject is reclamation of spoil heaps of coal mine wastes. The third deals with procedures to restore the productivity of land subjected to

surface (strip) mining. In the fourth, the topic is the improvement of marginal land (for example, hills and uplands of Scotland)
so that it will produce food. Urban renewal is the topic of the
final case and the subject is the Gorbals district of Glasgow.

Rodefeld, Richard D.; Flora, Jan; Voth, Donald; Fujimoto, Isao; and Converse,
Jim, eds. CHANGE IN RURAL AMERICA: CAUSES, CONSEQUENCES, AND
ALTERNATIVES. St. Louis: C.V. Mosby Co., 1978. xvii, 511 p. Paper-
bound.

The readings are arranged in five sections: (1) nature of changes
in agricultural technology; (2) nature of changes in farm organizational, occupational, and class structure; (3) causes of changes
in farm technology, size, and organizational structure; (4) historical overview of U.S. rural communities; and (5) alternative
responses to change. Each section is introduced by an essay
written by one or more of the editors.

Shepard, Paul. MAN IN THE LANDSCAPE; A HISTORIC VIEW OF THE ES-
THETICS OF NATURE. New York: A.A. Knopf, 1967. xxv, 290 p.

The author examines the conflicting feelings that have developed
when man views the man-made landscape against the natural landscape: despair, hatred, love, sentimentality, conservationism, and
alienation. He concludes that social experiences are natural and
that the natural history of man should not be limited to nature
alone.

Smith, David M. PATTERNS IN HUMAN GEOGRAPHY: AN INTRODUCTION
TO NUMERICAL METHODS. Newton Abbot Devon, Engl.: David and Charles;
New York: Crane Russak and Co., 1975. 373 p. Bibliog.

In view of the recent "quantitative revolution" in human geography,
through which conventional statistical methods have been applied,
modified, and extended in geographical research, the author attempts a wide range of commonly used numerical techniques, applied in a descriptive context in human geography. The expo-
sition is informal, with illustrations (worked applications using
simple imaginary data) and examples (actual research applications
using data from real-world situations). Topics covered include the
following: type of data used by the geographer; the map as a
descriptive device; simple descriptive statistics; means of comparing sets of numerical observations; scale transformation and the
combination of data; measures of areal distribution patterns; geographical surfaces; the measurement of association; networks and
patterns of movement; areal classification and regions.

Smole, William J. THE YANOAMA INDIANS: A CULTURAL GEOGRAPHY.
Austin: University of Texas Press, 1976. xiv, 272 p. Appendix; Notes;
Glossary; Bibliog.

Smole writes about the Barafiri who live in the Parima highlands. He examines their subsistance and social activities in an ecological context. His principal topics include the people and their habitat; settlement patterns; livelihood; collecting, hunting, and horticulture; food allocation and consumption; and modification of landscape.

Trewartha, Glenn T., ed. THE MORE DEVELOPED REALM; A GEOGRAPHY OF ITS POPULATION. Oxford, Engl.: Pergamon Press, 1978. viii, 275 p.

This book focuses on the population geography of the developed regions: Europe, the Soviet Union, the United States and Canada, Japan and Australia and New Zealand. The book is intended for nonprofessional readers.

Whyte, William H. THE LAST LANDSCAPE. Garden City, N.Y.: Doubleday and Co., 1968. vi, 376 p.

Whyte examines land-use planning for metropolitan areas. The topics include devices to obtain land, planning for the future, examples of development projects such as "new towns," strategies for maintaining open space, and design and density. The author emphasizes the importance of open spaces.

Section V

ENVIRONMENTAL QUALITY

There has been much recent attention given to the fact that man's
behavior and his behavioral products have given rise to a deterioration in the quality of the environment. As a consequence
man's perception of the resources of his environment has begun to
change. He is coming to realize that he faces a crisis of unprecedented dimensions, unprecedented for that crisis threatens the
very survival of the human species. In view of this greater ecological sensitivity, Theobold emphasizes, 'It is no longer sufficient
to argue that a person 'meant well' when his intervention in a
personal or social or ecological situation worsened rather than improved the situation. Today it is necessary to possess information,
knowledge and wisdom before acquiring the right to interfere.'[1]

INADVERTENT DETERIORATION

That the quality of the environment is deteriorating, few would
dispute. This environmental condition has been created by man.
He brought it about before he fully realized the implications of
his impact. Those changes--he called them inadvertent--seem to
have been motivated by a religious viewpoint which held that the
bountifulness of the environment was for him to draw upon and to
utilize in any way he desired.[2] That the bountifulness of the environment was exhaustible or that biological productivity might be
disrupted does not seem to have been a serious consideration.
Rather suddenly it became evident to him that his actions were
deleterious. He discovered, for example, that there was insufficient
water to fulfill the diverse and heavy demands placed upon it by
industrial processes, power generating facilities, sanitary systems,
irrigation, and human requirements. Chemical pollution, thermal

---

1. R. Theobold, "Compassion or Destruction: Our Immediate Choice," in
HUMAN VALUES AND ADVANCING TECHNOLOGY, compiled by C.P. Hall
(New York: Friendship Press, 1967).

2. L. White Jr., "The Historical Roots of Ecological Crisis," SCIENCE 155
(1967): 1,203-07.

pollution, and eutrophication suddenly loomed as problems of stag-
gering proportions. The alternative use of the atmosphere for
waste disposal led to air pollution and showed him that vast as
the earth's air resources were they were limited and subject to
measurable alterations. Because biological productivity could be
enhanced in managed ecosystems by fertilizers and biocides, their
application was expanded. Then it became clear that excessive
use of fertilizers contributed to eutrophication, and that biocides
had effects on the biosphere far beyond their point of application.

These uses of the resources of the environment had not been planned
as part of a soundly based program of resource management. They
were undertaken by particular groups whose concerns and goals
were immediate and parochial. When it became clear that such
schemes were leading to a depletion of resources and a deterioration of the environment, there arose the need for a strategy to
conserve resources and restore the quality of environment.[3]

A. GENERAL DETERIORATION OF THE ENVIRONMENT

American Medical Association. Congress on Environmental Health. ENERGY,
ENVIRONMENT, AND HUMAN HEALTH. Edited by Asher J. Finkel. Acton,
Mass.: Publishing Sciences Group, 1974. xxiv, 288 p.

The volume contains proceedings (twenty-two papers) of the 1973
Congress on Environmental Health, held in Chicago, dealing
with the topics of energy requirements, both world and United
States; energy sources; environmental impacts; energy production
and human health; socioeconomic considerations; and energy-
use policies, present-day and long-term.

Brierley, John K. BIOLOGY AND THE SOCIAL CRISIS: A SOCIAL BIOLOGY
FOR EVERYMAN. First American ed. Rutherford, N.J.: Fairleigh Dickinson
University Press, 1970. xix, 260 p. Bibliog.

The author identifies seven major social problems: (1) numbers of
people, (2) food production and distribution, (3) uniqueness of
individuals, (4) aggression between men, (5) automobile traffic,
(6) diversity of resources in man's habitat, and (7) the aging
population. Brierley discusses these problems in terms of human
heredity, race, health and food, the crisis of numbers, youth
and age, and brain and behavior.

Commoner, Barry. SCIENCE AND SURVIVAL. New York: Viking Press,
1967. 150 p. Paperbound.

---

3. Frederick Sargent II, "Informed Forces for Environmental Quality," JOURNAL
OF ENVIRONMENTAL EDUCATION 1, no. 2 (1969): 50-53.

Commoner offers his view of the implications of man's technological exploitation of his environment.

Dansereau, Pierre, ed. CHALLENGE FOR SURVIVAL: LAND, AIR, AND WATER FOR MAN IN MEGALOPOLIS. New York: Columbia University Press, 1970. xii, 235 p.

The volume contains papers and commentaries presented at a symposium on land, air, and water for man in megalopolis held in 1968. The principal themes are land use in urban and rural areas, atmospheric pollution, and the management of water and wetlands in metropolitan regions.

Detwyler, Thomas R., ed. MAN'S IMPACT ON ENVIRONMENT. New York: McGraw-Hill Book Co., 1971. xiii, 731 p. Paperbound. Glossary.

Detwyler drew together fifty-two selections from recent literature which should as a whole demonstrate to the college-level student the problems created by man's use of the environment. The selections, each introduced by an editorial comment, deal with a variety of different impacts: air pollution, water pollution, soil erosion and subsidence, invasions of plant and animals, destruction of vegetation and animals, and domestication and genetic variation. Other selections examine the basic reasons for man's use and abuse of the environment and the outlook for the future. Detwyler sees a change in social values as crucial in environmental management.

De Vos, Antoon. AFRICA, THE DEVASTATED CONTINENT? The Hague: Dr. W. Junk, Publishers, 1975. 236 p.

De Vos describes man's impact on the African continent and examines some of the immediate and ultimate consequences of these actions. In the six parts, he discusses the African environment; ecological zones; man as an environmental agent; specific environmental problems, such as nomadism, desertification, endangered species, and parks; problems, needs, and potentials in land use, such as agriculture, land management, and soil and water conservation; and planning for the future.

Ehrlich, Paul R., and Ehrlich, Anne H. POPULATION, RESOURCES, ENVIRONMENT: ISSUES IN HUMAN ECOLOGY. San Francisco: W.H. Freeman and Co., 1970. 383 p. Appendixes; Bibliog.

The Ehrlichs write of the crises with which man must deal: people and the carrying capacity of the earth, pollution of air, water, and land, exhaustion of resources, family planning, and social, political, and economic change. They recommend a program of actions to ameliorate these crises. There are several appendixes: demographic data and population projections, essential nutrients, ecological case study of fire ant program, properties of important pesticides, and reproductive anatomy and physiology.

Ehrlich, Paul R.; Ehrlich, Anne H.; and Holdren, John P. ECOSCIENCE: POPULATION, RESOURCES, ENVIRONMENT. 3d ed. San Francisco: W.H. Freeman and Co., 1977. xv, 1,051 p. References; Indexes; Appendixes.

Originally published in 1970 and 1972 as POPULATION, RE-SOURCES, ENVIRONMENT, this third edition has an amended title. The authors examine man's predicament in considerable detail: natural resources and human well-being, population and renewable resources, energy and materials, environmental disruption, and alternate solutions to problems. There are four appendixes: (1) world demography, (2) food and nutrition (production, consumption, and nutrient requirements), (3) pesticides (properties and toxicity), and (4) reproduction and birth control (physiology and programs).

Eisenbud, Merril. ENVIRONMENT, TECHNOLOGY, AND HEALTH: HUMAN ECOLOGY IN HISTORICAL PERSPECTIVE. New York: New York University Press, 1978. x, 384 p.

Eisenbud makes an appraisal of the contemporary environmental movement with particular reference to issues of public health. There are four parts. In the first, man's impact on the environment is reviewed in historical perspective. In the second, the question of maintaining a balance among people, energy, and resources is discussed. In the third, the health implications of environmental contamination are considered. Eisenbud concludes, in the fourth, that the environmental movement distorted priorities, misinterpreted key health issues, and caused confusion in the public through politicization and polarization of environmental issues.

Elder, Frederick. CRISIS IN EDEN; A RELIGIOUS STUDY OF MAN AND ENVIRONMENT. Nashville, Tenn.: Abington Press, 1970. 172 p.

The author examines the implications of the two conflicting views of man and nature: the one being that man must live in harmony with nature, the other that man should dominate and exploit nature. He argues that to live in harmony with nature, man must adopt a new set of values, an environmental theology, and an environmental ethic.

Farvar, M. Taghi, and Milton, John P., eds. THE CARELESS TECHNOLOGY: ECOLOGY AND INTERNATIONAL DEVELOPMENT. Garden City, N.Y.: Natural History Press, 1972. xxix, 1,030 p.

This volume contains a report of a Conference on the Ecological Aspects of International Development convened by the Conservation Foundation and the Center for the Biology of Natural Systems, Washington University, 8-11 December 1968, Airlie House, Arlington, Virginia. The objective of the discussions was to assess the ecological impacts of technology in the developing countries. Five major impacts were considered: (1) health and nutritional

consequences of selected development programs, (2) irrigation and
water development, (3) intensification of plant productivity, (4)
intensification of animal production, and (5) special problems of
environmental degradation. Because serious environmental deterioration has been brought about by technology, it was concluded
that great care must be exercised in planning and implementing
economic development.

Hall, Cameron P., comp. HUMAN VALUES AND ADVANCING TECHNOLOGY:
A NEW AGENDA FOR THE CHURCH IN MISSION. New York: Friendship
Press, 1967. 175 p. Paperbound.

This is a compilation of major addresses and reports of a working
group presented at Consultation in Technology and Human Values,
Chicago, 2-4 May 1967. The addresses deal with "Technology and
Human Values: This American Moment"; "Compassion or Destruction:
Our Immediate Choice"; "Human Values in an Evolving World"; "Brain
Technology and Psychocivilization"; and "Twenty-First Century Institutions: Prerequisites for a Creative and Responsible Society." The reports examine technology and (1) world population-hunger problems,
(2) work-income issue, (3) youth, (4) urban issues, (5) man's nature, and (6) man's relation to nature. The thesis of the book is
that decisions for environmental exploitation and social change
must be based on prior information, knowledge, and wisdom about
the implications and consequences of the change both for man and
his environment.

Harte, John, and Socolow, Robert H. PATIENT EARTH. New York: Holt,
Rinehart and Winston, 1971. xv, 364 p. Appendixes; References.

Harte and Socolow and other authors treat the earth as a patient,
ill with a cruel and debilitating disease but probably not incurable.
As geophysicians, they examine the illness and consider the treatment in not only scientific terms but also moral and social ones.
The first part deals with lessons from the past. In the second
part are ten case studies devoted to the quest for environmental quality by man alone, governmental agencies, the military,
and environmentalists. The chapters of the third part are devoted
to steady states in society. In the fourth part, there are chapters
on water, energy, and radiation which provide a scientific background for the case studies. The four appendixes provide information about the mathematics of demography, conversions of physical
units, and facts about the earth.

"The Hostile Environment of Man." JOURNAL OF THE ROYAL COLLEGE OF
GENERAL PRACTITIONERS 24, Supplement 1 (September 1974): 1-46. Paperbound.

Papers and discussion are included in this report of a symposium
held 1 May 1974: Papers are: "Man as a Competitive Animal,"
by C.L. Oaklay; "The Unloving Family," J.G. Howells; "The

Harm We Doctors Do--Iatrogenic Disease," K. Hodgkin; "The
Nutritional Problems of the Affluent Society," M. Crawford;
"Death in the Air We Breathe," L.M. Swinburne; "Hazards of
Soil and Water," R.J.F.H. Pinsent; and "The World We Want
Our Children to Live in," R.W. Smithells.

Institute of Ecology. MAN IN THE LIVING ENVIRONMENT. N.p.: n.p.,
[1971]. 267 p. Paperbound. Available from the Institute of Ecology, P.O.
Box A, University Hill, Logan, Utah 84321.

This is a report of a Workshop on Global Ecological Problems held
in June 1971 at the University of Wisconsin. The objective was
to formulate ecologists' views on problems of environmental quality
to transmit to the forthcoming (1972) UN Conference on the Human
Environment. Position papers from four task groups were presented
and discussed: (1) biogeochemical cycles of elements essential to
protein production; (2) ecological constraints on man's use of land,
particularly as a result of vegetation-soil interactions; (3) terrestrial
food webs, diversity, and stability; and (4) man's impact on aquatic
systems, particularly the coastal zone.

Johnson, Huey D., ed. NO DEPOSIT--NO RETURN. MAN AND HIS EN-
VIRONMENT: A VIEW TOWARD SURVIVAL. Reading, Mass.: Addison-
Wesley Publishing Co., 1970. xvi, 351 p. Paperbound.

The book is an anthology of papers presented at the thirteenth
National Conference of the U.S. National Commission for UNESCO
held in November 1969. There are five parts: (1) introduction;
(2) facts about man-environment interactions, resources and their
management, and institutional arrangements in environmental management; (3) the viewpoint of youth; (4) viewpoints on individuals
and activism; and (5) suggestions for action. The thrust of the
conference was achieving a balance between man and nature through
effective social policy.

Johnson, Warren A., and Hardesty, John, eds. ECONOMIC GROWTH VS.
THE ENVIRONMENT. Belmont, Calif.: Wadsworth Publishing Co., 1971. v,
201 p.

This is an anthology of publications dealing with the economic
aspects of environmental problems. Economic thinking is the principal focus and ecological thinking is secondary. There are four
divisions: the ecologist's perspective, arguments against economic
growth, the traditional wisdom of economic growth, and precedents
and prospects. The theme is "sustainable balance with the environment." The editors provide continuity to their selections with
a general introduction and an introductory commentary for each
section.

Kaplan, Sylvan J., and Kivy-Rosenberg, Evelyn, eds. ECOLOGY AND THE
QUALITY OF LIFE. Springfield, Ill.: Charles C Thomas, 1973.

Most of the papers brought together here were presented at either a meeting of human ecologists at Jersey State College, Jersey City, 23 April 1971 or the meeting of the World Future Society, Washington, D.C., 14 May 1971. The twenty-six papers are arranged in four groups. Those of the first group focus on problems, issues, and questions. In the second part, the emphases are population, food, and resources. Papers on attitudes toward work, religion, resources, and planning comprise the third group. Some answers are provided in the fourth group, the principal one being that the time is short for mankind to adjust its attitudes about resources and quality of life.

Matthews, William Henry; Smith, Frederick G.; and Goldberg, Edward D., eds. MAN'S IMPACT ON TERRESTRIAL AND OCEANIC ECOSYSTEMS. Cambridge: MIT Press, 1971. xiv, 540 p.

Brought together here are background papers and other documents prepared for the Study of Critical Environmental Problems (SCEP) conducted in 1970. The topics are general ecological effects of man's activities, pollution and terrestrial ecosystems, climatic change and terrestrial ecosystems, pollution and oceanic ecosystems, measurements and monitoring, modelling: a tool for understanding and management, and implications of change.

Murdock, William W., ed. ENVIRONMENT RESOURCES, POLLUTION AND SOCIETY. Stamford, Conn.: Sinauver Associates, 1971. vi, 440 p. Paperbound.

This book, written by twenty-one different authorities on various aspects of the environmental problems now facing man, was designed primarily for undergraduate interdisciplinary courses. The objective of the book is to assist readers in thinking ecologically. The text is divided into three main sections: (1) population and resources, (2) environmental degradation, and (3) environment and society. The editor sets the stage in an opening chapter devoted to ecological systems and a concluding chapter on environment and the equilibrium population. Although some of the implications of a society in equilibrium are dealt with, for example, social inequity and power structure, making a systematic synthesis of the many issues and problems is left to the reader.

Novick, Sheldon, and Cottrell, Dorothy, eds. OUR WORLD IN PERIL: AN ENVIRONMENTAL REVIEW. Greenwich, Conn.: Fawcett Publications, 1971. xi, 498 p. Paperbound.

The chapters comprise articles originally published in the magazine ENVIRONMENT between 1967 and 1971. The material is organized in six sections: (1) global problems, (2) government, (3) industry, (4) agriculture, (5) the city, and (6) the search for alternatives.

Odum, Howard T. ENVIRONMENT, POWER, AND SOCIETY. New York: Wiley Interscience, 1971. ix, 331 p. Appendix.

Odum discusses the application of general systems theory to ecological systems and to problems of power, pollution, population, food, and war. He limits his discussion to the flow of energy (power). The presentation is designed for the general reader and for undergraduates in courses on human ecology.

Owen, Dennis Frank. MAN IN TROPICAL AFRICA: THE ENVIRONMENTAL PREDICAMENT. New York: Oxford University Press, 1973. ix, 214 p. Tables; Bibliog.

Intended as an introduction to the ecology of man in tropical Africa, this book covers: the environment; the population; vital statistics for rural and urban areas; the ecology of cultivation; weeds, pests, and diseases of cultivation; wild and domestic animals; food and nutrition; human diseases; natural selection and genetics; and the ecology of development.

Passmore, John. MAN'S RESPONSIBILITY FOR NATURE: ECOLOGICAL PROBLEMS AND WESTERN TRADITIONS. London: Gerald Duckworth and Co., 1974. x, 213 p.

Passmore sets the current ecological problems in the context of Western traditions. He first examines the history of the ideas that man is a despot and that he exercises stewardship and cooperation with nature. Then he discusses the four major ecological problems-- pollution, conservation, preservation, and multiplication. When he brings the problems and the traditions into confrontation with one another, he concludes that for the problems to be solved, there must be a moral revolution.

Ramparts, editorial staff. ECO-CATASTROPHE. San Francisco: Canfield Press, 1970. xiii, 158 p. Paperbound.

This is a collection of essays previously published in RAMPARTS which portray one view of the "ecological crises" of the early 70s, namely, that the many problems are expressions of a malfunctioning social order. Their solution is: a reconstruction of the social order. Included are "Eco-Catastrophe," P. Ehrlich; "The Eco-Establishment," K. Barkley and S. Weissman; "Why the Population Bomb is a Rockefeller Baby," S. Weissman; "Toward an Ecological Solution," M. Bookchin; "Catch 24,400 (or, Plutonium is My Favorite Element)," R. Rapoport; "Science and the Gross National Pollution," G.M. Woodwell; "The Making of a Pollution-Industrial Complex," M. Gellen; "Santa Barbara: Oil in the Velvet Playground," H. Molotch; "The Ecology of Oil; Raping Alaska," B. Weisberg; "California Water Plan: The Most Expensive Faucet in the World," G. Marine; and "Rural Renewal; Trouble in Paradise," S. Stern.

Revelle, Roger; Khosla, Ashok; and Vinovskis, Maris, eds. THE SURVIVAL EQUATION: MAN, RESOURCES, AND HIS ENVIRONMENT. Boston: Houghton Mifflin Co., 1971. xiii, 508 p.

> The editors have brought together articles which examine man's relationship to and use of the whole environmental system. The papers have been arranged under the following topics: populations-- humanity's problem, including future human numbers, determinants and consequences of population growth, controlling human fertility, and population policy; resources, food, and environment, including minerals and energy, world food problem, enough food for all, and closing the economic gap; and the environmental crisis, in- cluding decay of the environment and environmental improvement.

Revelle, Roger, and Landsberg, Hans H., eds. AMERICA'S CHANGING EN- VIRONMENT. Boston: Houghton Mifflin Co., 1970. xxxvii, 314 p.

> The principal theme is decision making in planning and imple- menting strategies for improving environmental quality. The editors suggest that action should be taken in four areas: elimination of pollution, adoption of an ethic about land, reconstruction of urban regions, and development of a balance between population and resources. The several essays deal with such topics as ecology as an ethical science; water, air, and land; economics and politics; the humane city; playgrounds for people; and the roles of education. The essays suggest that there is considerable ignorance about physical processes in the environment, little knowledge about what quality of environment people really want, and "a lack of new managerial principles, institutions, new attitudes, new administrative devices-- or old ones shaped to new purposes."

SCIENCE FOR BETTER ENVIRONMENT. Proceedings of the International Congress on the Human Environment (HESC), Kyoto, 1975. Oxford, Engl.: Pergamon Press, 1977. xiv, 992 p.

> The participants at this congress addressed themselves to a detailed study of environmental problems with a view to formulating plans for further research and action in the sphere of social policy. In- cluded in the proceedings are proposals for action; lectures on man's place in and impact on ecosystems, environment and tech- nology, and role of scientists in environmental improvements; re- ports on current environmental problems in Japan; and papers on analytical tools and policy instruments for conserving and improving the environment. Included also are four groups of discussion papers: (1) man's impact on terrestrial ecosystems (e.g., agro- and urban ecosystems and regions); (2) problems within purview of natural sciences (e.g., pollution, toxicology and monitoring, as- sessment, and alternate technologies); (3) problems within purview of social sciences (e.g., rights, legislation, economics, and de- velopment), and (4) problems in the field of cultural studies (e.g., aesthetics, information, and education).

Shepard, Paul, and Mckinley, Daniel, eds. ENVIRON/MENTAL: ESSAYS ON THE PLANET AS A HOME. Boston: Houghton Mifflin Co., 1971. xii, 308 p. References.

The editors focus on environmental and social problems man has created for himself. The material is organized under four section headings: (1) "Genesis and Perception" (enlightenment about ecological problems), (2) "Society and Its Creations" (population and urbanization), (3) "Positions" (different ecological viewpoints), and (4) "The Crunch" (food production and population).

Skipp, Victor. CRISIS AND DEVELOPMENT: AN ECOLOGICAL CASE STUDY OF THE FOREST OF ARDEN 1570-1674. Cambridge: University Press, 1978. xii, 132 p. Notes.

Based on extensive research under the auspices of the University of Birmingham, Skipp considers, from an ecological point of view, the historical development of a block of five parishes situated on what was once the northern fringe of the Forest of Arden in Warwickshire, now the eastern periphery of the city of Birmingham. Since the population of the area doubled in size in the century 1570-1670, the responses to this demographic crisis--agrarian, economic, social, and ecological--were significant, and are considered in detail. Appended are notes on the practice of birth control, estimates of population size, and chapter notes with references.

Southwick, Charles H. ECOLOGY AND THE QUALITY OF OUR ENVIRONMENT. 2d ed. New York: Van Nostrand Reinhold Co., 1976. xxi, 426 p. Paperbound. References; Glossary; Bibliog.

This book, first published in 1972, was written to demonstrate to the student of business, law, education, liberal arts, engineering, agriculture, health sciences, social services, and other nonbiological fields the relevance of ecology to the analysis and solution of the problems arising from man's use and abuse of the environment. The second edition, updated and expanded, included a greater emphasis on interrelations among ecology, economics, and sociology. There are six parts. The first deals with environmental deterioration and population dynamics in ecological perspective. The second part discusses the rise of agriculture, man's attitudes toward environment, and historical roots of ecology. In the third, the principles of ecology are described. The fourth part is devoted to population ecology and the fifth looks at community ecology. The sixth part examines man's future prospects.

Study of Critical Environmental Problems. MAN'S IMPACT ON THE GLOBAL ENVIRONMENT: ASSESSMENT AND RECOMMENDATIONS FOR ACTION; A REPORT. Cambridge: MIT Press, 1970. xxii, 319 p. Paperbound.

This is a report of the Study of Critical Environmental Problems

(SCEP) prepared from a conference in 1970. The report includes general assessments of major global problems--climatic and ecological effects of man's activities and implications of change and remedial action--and detailed analyses by various working groups: climatic effects, ecological effects, monitoring, implications of change, industrial products and pollutants, domestic and agricultural wastes, and energy products. The SCEP report was viewed as a useful input for the forthcoming (1972) UN Conference on the Human Environment.

Thomas, William L., Jr., ed. MAN'S ROLE IN CHANGING THE FACE OF THE EARTH. Chicago: University of Chicago Press, 1956. xxxviii, 1,193 p.

This book reports a International Symposium on Man's Role in Changing the Face of the Earth sponsored by Wenner-Gren Foundation for Anthropological Research and the National Science Foundation held at Princeton, New Jersey, 16-22 June 1955. The scholars discussed the transformations that man had made on the earth and in the air and examined the implications of these transformations. The papers of the first part look into man's past and examine cultural views, subsistence economies, commercial economies, and the industrial and urban revolutions. The papers of the second part focus on the processes characterizing the transformations of the waters, the land, the atmosphere, the soil, biotic communities, wastes, and urban-industrial demands on the land. In the third part, man's future, constrained by limited resources, is considered. In the fourth part, there are summaries of the earlier sections. The overall conclusion of the participants is that man-in-nature is in an unstable equilibrium. A policy of sustained yield rather than continued exploitation of resources might provide a solution for some of man's problems.

Watt, Kenneth E.F.; Molloy, Leslie F.; Varshney, C.K.; Weeks, Dudley; and Wirosardjono, Soetjipo. THE UNSTEADY STATE: ENVIRONMENTAL PROBLEMS, GROWTH, AND CULTURE. An East-West Center Book. Honolulu: University Press of Hawaii, 1977. xi, 287 p.

This book is an outgrowth of an Open Grants project, "Cultural Dimensions of Environmental Problems," sponsored in the spring of 1975 by the East-West Center. The chapters treat: (1) environmental problems and quality of life; (2) cultural dimensions of environmental problems; (3) ecosystem and economic system balance; (4) basic human needs--problems of poverty, affluence, and inequity; (5) interrelations of technology, culture, and environment; (6) control of information about environment; and (7) an option for a new environmental order. The thesis of the book emphasizes two points. First, to solve environmental problems, beliefs and economic systems causing the problems must be studied carefully. Second, rapid economic and technological growth is at the root of the problems disrupting the natural and social environment.

B. ENVIRONMENTAL POLLUTION

Berkowitz, David A., and Squires, Arthur M., eds. POWER GENERATION
AND ENVIRONMENTAL CHANGE. Cambridge: MIT Press, 1971. xxiii,
440 p. References; Index; Glossary.

> This book comprises the proceedings of the Symposium of the Com-
> mittee on Environmental Alteration, American Association for the
> Advancement of Science, held 28 December 1969, with additional
> invited contributions. The main subject areas are nuclear power,
> hydroelectric power, and fossil-fuel power, with discussions of
> waste heat; health and safety aspects of nuclear radiation; sulfur
> in residual fuel oil; and atmospheric chemistry. The time frame
> for most papers is the next twenty to thirty years, or up to the
> year 2000.

Boulding, Kenneth E.; Stahr, Elvis J.; Fabricant, Solomon; and Gainsbrugh,
Martin R. ECONOMICS OF POLLUTION. New York: New York University
Press, 1971. 158 p.

> At the 1971 Charles C. Moskowitz Lectures, Boulding spoke on
> "What Do Economic Indicators Indicate?: Quality and Quantity
> of GNP"; Stahr, on "Antipollution Policies, Their Nature and
> Their Impact on Corporate Profits"; Fabricant, on "Economic Growth
> and the Problem of Environmental Pollution"; and Gainsbrugh, on
> "The Economic Growth: Its Costs and Profits."

Butler, Gordon Cecil, ed. PRINCIPLES OF ECOTOXICOLOGY. SCOPE Report 12. Chicester, Engl. and New York: John Wiley and Sons, 1978. xxii,
350 p. Paperbound.

> Prepared under the auspices of the Scientific Committee on Prob-
> lems of the Environment (SCOPE), International Council of Scien-
> tific Unions, Butler and eighteen colleagues discuss the impact of
> pollutants on ecosystems. The first section deals with the environ-
> mental behavior of pollutants, such as abiotic and biotic processes,
> transport models, and estimation of doses. In the second section,
> the statistical analysis of dose-effect relationships is discussed.
> The third section is devoted to discussions of ecotoxicology, for
> example, terrestrial and aquatic animals, terrestrial and aquatic
> plant communities, microbial toxicology, and indirect biological
> effects of environmental pollutants. The response of the ecosystem
> is discussed in the fourth part, and in the fifth, the editor draws
> some general conclusions.

Calabrese, Edward J. POLLUTANTS AND HIGH-RISK GROUPS: THE BIO-
LOGICAL BASIS OF INCREASED HUMAN SUSCEPTIBILITY TO ENVIRON-
MENTAL AND OCCUPATIONAL POLLUTANTS. New York: John Wiley and
Sons, 1978. xviii, 266 p. Glossary; Bibliog.

This book represents the first comprehensive synthesis of the bio-medical literature in which the various hypersusceptible segments of the population with respect to pollutant toxicity have been identified and quantified. This information, useful in setting standards and making policy in environmental and occupational health, includes biological factors, genetic disorders, nutritional deficiencies, disease processes, and behavioral factors which pre-dispose individuals to the toxic effects of pollutants. A discussion follows of the role of high-risk groups in the development of health policy with regard to standard setting; economic health cost as-sessment; environmental impact statements; and the new toxic sub-stances control act.

THE CHEMICAL ENVIRONMENT. Edited by John Lenihan and William W. Fletcher. Environment and Man Series, vol. 6. New York: Academic Press, 1977. x, 163 p. References.

The authors review the hazards created by the man-made chemicals in the environment, emphasizing harmful effects, control measures, and prospects for the future. There are six chapters: (1) "Natural Cycles of the Elements and Their Perturbations by Man," Humphry J.M. Bowen; (2) "Mercury," Leonard A. Goldwater and Woodhall Stopford; (3) "Lead," Michael R. Moore, Brian C. Campbell, and Abraham Goldberg; (4) "Arsenic," M.D. Kipling; (5) "Aflatoxins," C. Allen Linsell; and (6) "Asbestos," Muriell Newhouse.

Commission of the European Communities. PROCEEDINGS, INTERNATIONAL SYMPOSIUM--RECENT ADVANCES IN THE ASSESSMENT OF THE HEALTH EFFECTS OF ENVIRONMENTAL POLLUTION, PARIS, 24-28 JUNE 1974. 4 vols. Luxembourg: 1975. xix, 2,522 p., cxiii-cxxii. Paperbound.

These volumes contain the full proceedings of the symposium, which was organized jointly by the Commission of the European Com-munities, the U.S. Environmental Protection Agency, and the World Health Organization. Volumes 1 and 4 include the broad-coverage papers presented at plenary sessions, all panel discussions, and the opening and closing sessions. Volumes 2 and 3 contain all papers presented at specialized sessions plus the supplementary reports. The original language of each report is used (Dutch, English, French, German, or Italian), with English translations of the abstracts. The opening and closing sessions were published in the original language and English. The topics covered in volume 1 include population studies, human effects studies, toxicological studies, and exposure monitoring; volume 2, human effects studies, animal studies, metabolism, interactions, and indicators of ex-posure; volume 3, tissue measurements, monitoring needs, envi-ronmental measurements, exposure monitoring, and models; and volume 4, scientific data base required for decisions to protect human health, experimental investigations, monitoring needs, tissue measurements, and health effects studies.

Council on Environmental Quality. ENVIRONMENTAL QUALITY; SECOND ANNUAL REPORT OF THE COUNCIL ON ENVIRONMENTAL QUALITY. Washington, D.C.: Government Printing Office, 1971. xxiv, 360 p. Paperbound.

The report to Congress reviews (1) federal and international activity; (2) state and local activities; (3) private activity; (4) economy and the environment; (5) law and the environment; (6) inner city environment; (7) status and trends of environmental quality; and (8) the year in perspective.

_____. ENVIRONMENTAL QUALITY; THE FIRST ANNUAL REPORT OF THE COUNCIL ON ENVIRONMENTAL QUALITY. Washington, D.C.: Government Printing Office, 1970. xxv, 326 p. Paperbound.

Topics are: (1) understanding environmental problems; (2) federal organization for environmental quality; (3) water pollution; (4) air pollution; (5) weather and climate modification; (6) solid wastes; (7) noise, pesticides, and radiation; (8) population growth and resources; (9) land use; (10) international cooperation; (11) citizen participation; (12) environmental education; and (13) present and future environmental needs.

Ducsik, Dennis W., ed. POWER, POLLUTION, AND PUBLIC POLICY: ISSUES IN ELECTRIC POWER PRODUCTION, SHORELINE RECREATION, AND AIR AND WATER POLLUTION FACING NEW ENGLAND AND THE NATION. MIT Report, no. 24. Cambridge: MIT Press, 1971. xiii, 322 p. Paperbound.

This book developed from a design project conducted under the Sea Grant Program by a group of MIT students. Chapters cover offshore siting of electric power plants; the crisis in shoreline recreation; controlling sulfur oxide emissions; water quality improvement in Boston Harbor; and regional government in New England--a prototype.

Hemphill, Delbert D., ed. TRACE SUBSTANCES IN ENVIRONMENTAL HEALTH-- IX. Columbia: University of Missouri, 1975. xvii, 495 p. Paperbound.

The volume comprises the proceedings of the Ninth Annual Conference on Trace Substances in Environmental Health sponsored by the Environmental Trace Substances Research Center, University of Missouri, June 10-12, 1975. The participants addressed the biological, ecological, and health significance of inorganic and organic substances present in trace amounts in air, food, and water. Fifty-four papers were assembled in five groups: epidemiology, environmental geochemistry and health, environmental pollution, analytical methodology, and health effects of trace substances.

Japan. Environmental Agency. QUALITY OF THE ENVIRONMENT IN JAPAN 1977. Tokyo: Ministry of Finance, 1977. Printing Bureau, 1977. v, 274 p. Paperbound. Tables; Figures.

This volume is a condensed version of the "White Paper on the Environment" submitted to the eightieth session of the Diet in 1977. Part 1 deals generally with the current state of the environment and pollution control expenditures and technology. Part 2 is devoted to details of present state of pollution and countermeasures initiated with regard to air pollution, water pollution, other pollution problems, health damage, environmental conservation, environmental research, international cooperation, and environmental administration. Appended are tables of standards for air quality, emissions, water quality, effluents, aircraft and railway noise. The main text contains fifty-three tables and sixty-five figures.

Kates, Robert William. RISK ASSESSMENT OF ENVIRONMENTAL HAZARD. SCOPE Report 8. Chicester, Engl. and New York: John Wiley and Sons, 1978. xvii, 112 p. Paperbound.

In this monograph sponsored by the Scientific Committee on Problems of the Environment (SCOPE) of the International Council of Scientific Unions, Kates discusses the complex problems of evaluating the hazardness of environment for the health and well-being of living organisms. The first chapter is devoted to ways society copes with environmental hazards. In the second chapter, devoted to methodology, he reviews means of identifying hazards, and estimating risks, and the ways society evaluates information. In the third chapter, his focus is on organized modes of assessment and decision making. The fourth chapter considers recent trends and attitudes in the assessment of environmental threats. Case studies are included.

Lee, Douglass H.K., ed. METALLIC CONTAMINANTS AND HUMAN HEALTH. Fogarty International Center Proceedings, no. 9. New York: Academic Press, 1972. xvii, 241 p.

Topics include concepts of environmental toxicology, major environmental contaminants (mercury, lead, cadmium), other contaminants (beryllium, chromium, manganese, nickel, vanadium, arsenic, fluorides), nutritional aspects of metals problems with case finding, and analytical techniques.

Lippmann, Morton, and Schlesinger, Richard B. CHEMICAL CONTAMINATION OF THE HUMAN ENVIRONMENT. New York: Oxford University Press, 1979. ix, 456 p. Figures; Tables; Bibliog.

In this graduate-level monograph, Lippmann and Schlesinger provide a current overview of chemical contamination of man's environment. The emphasis is on those substances which directly influence man's health and welfare. Topics are environmental characteristics and processes; sources, distribution, and fate of contaminants; effect of contaminants on environmental quality and human health; criteria for judging environmental quality; and sampling, measurement, and control of contaminants.

Lowrance, William W. OF ACCEPTABLE RISK: SCIENCE AND THE DETER-
MINATION OF SAFETY. Los Altos, Calif.: William Kaufman, 1976. x,
180 p. References.

> Lowrance explores the difficult problem of assuring some degree of
> safety for man among the hazards of nature and those man himself
> has created. Topics are measuring risk; judging safety, that is,
> acceptable risk; safety issues as public problems; and how things
> and places are made safe. He reviews the history of DDT as an
> archetypal modern problem.

McIntyre, A.D., and Mills, C.F., eds. ECOLOGICAL TOXICOLOGY RE-
SEARCH: EFFECTS OF HEAVY METAL AND ORGANOHALOGEN COMPOUNDS.
Environmental Science Research, vol. 7. New York: Plenum Press, 1975.
xi, 323 p.

> This volume contains the proceedings of a conference on ecotoxi-
> cology organized by the Science Committee of the North Atlantic
> Treaty Organization, Mont Gabriel, Quebec, 6-10 May 1974.
> Its task was to identify those areas of the subject in which inade-
> quate knowledge of the processes influencing entry, metabolism,
> and toxic action of the pollutants considered was hindering assess-
> ment of the significance of the hazards they create within eco-
> systems. Eight lectures presented by participants from several
> disciplines form the plenary papers found in part 1 of the pro-
> ceedings. These are supplemented by seven invited papers and
> by the reports of five working groups, each of which included a
> summary of research recommendations.

Meyer, Beat. SULFUR, ENERGY, AND ENVIRONMENT. Amsterdam: Elsevier
Scientific Publishing Co., 1977. xi, 448 p. Appendix; Bibliog.; Indexes.

> Meyer has prepared a guide to the extensive body of knowledge
> about sulfur. In fifteen chapters he reviews the history of sulfur,
> its chemical properties and analysis; occurrence and sources; cycles;
> production and recovery from combustion gases; control; medical
> uses and health effects; uses in agriculture, food and industry;
> polymers, occurrence in other materials such as asphalt, concrete,
> wood products, and batteries; and future trends. In the appendix,
> there are conversion factors for the metric system and a SO_2 emis-
> sion nomogram.

National Research Council. Advisory Committee on the Biological Effects of
Ionizing Radiations. THE EFFECTS ON POPULATIONS OF EXPOSURE TO
LOW LEVELS OF IONIZING RADIATION. Washington, D.C.: National
Academy of Sciences, 1972. xiii, 217 p. Paperbound. Tables; Figures;
Glossary; Bibliog.

> This report deals with the scientific basis for the establishment of
> radiation protection standards, and encompasses a review and re-
> evaluation of existing scientific knowledge of radiation exposure

of human populations. Following the summary and recommendations, the report covers sources of ionizing radiation; environmental transport and effects of radionuclides; genetic effects of
ionizing radiation; somatic effects; and effects on growth and development.

National Research Council. Committee for the Working Conference on Principles
of Protocols for Evaluating Chemicals in the Environment. PRINCIPLES FOR
EVALUATING CHEMICALS IN THE ENVIRONMENT. Washington, D.C.:
National Academy of Sciences, 1975. xiii, 454 p. Paperbound. Appendixes;
References.

This report brings together discussions of panels and participants
of a working conference held in 1973 to provide guidance on how
best to evaluate the impact of environmental chemicals on the
health of animals and man. Among the topics discussed are evaluative schemes; benefits and risks from environmental chemicals;
evidence of effects on health of man and nonhuman systems, and
on inanimate systems; and analysis and monitoring.

National Research Council. Committee on Medical and Biologic Effects of
Environmental Pollutants. Subcommittee on Ammonia. AMMONIA. Baltimore:
University Park Press, 1979. xiv, 384 p. Paperbound. Bibliog.

The subcommittee has prepared a comprehensive review of the
benefits and potential risks from environmental ammonia. Topics
are: properties, chemical interactions, monitoring, sources and
sinks, transport, toxicology, and effects on materials and human
health. Recommendations are made for future investigation.

National Research Council. Committee on Medical and Biologic Effects of
Environmental Pollutants. Subcommittee on Arsenic. ARSENIC. Washington,
D.C.: National Academy of Sciences, 1977. vii, 332 p. Paperbound.
Appendixes; Glossary; References.

This report concerns the chemistry of arsenic: its distribution in
the environment; metabolism; biologic effects on plants, animals,
and man; a summary and conclusions, with recommendations for
further research. Three appendixes give data on the arsenic content of plants, plant products, and animals, also on determining
traces of arsenic in natural materials.

National Research Council. Committee on Medical and Biologic Effects of
Environmental Pollutants. Subcommittee on Iron. IRON. Washington, D.C.:
National Academy of Sciences, 1977. v, 359 p. Paperbound. Appendix;
Bibliog.

Made at the request of the Environmental Protection Agency, this
study covers iron in the environment; microorganisms and iron; iron
and plants; iron metabolism in mammals; iron deficiency; acute and

chronic iron toxicity; inhalation of iron; summary and recommendations.

National Research Council. Committee on Medical and Biologic Effects of Environmental Pollutants. Subcommittee on Selenium. SELENIUM. Washington, D.C.: National Academy of Sciences, 1976. xi, 203 p. Paperbound. Bibliog.

> Part of a series prepared at the request of the Environmental Protection Agency. This report assembles, organizes, and interprets present-day information on selenium and its compounds and the effects of these substances on man, animals, and plants. It tells where selenium is found and how it is measured; describes its physical and chemical nature, its biologic effects, its relation to other pollutants, and dose-response relations; and discusses margins of safety. Recommendations are made for further research.

National Research Council. Committee on Medical and Biologic Effects of Environmental Pollutants. Subcommittee on Zinc. ZINC. Baltimore: University Park Press, 1979. xi, 471 p. Paperbound. Appendixes; Bibliog.

> A series under contract with the Environmental Protection Agency. This report covers the properties and uses of zinc; its natural and man-made sources; zinc in plants, aquatic animals, and humans; zinc in the diet; zinc in metalloproteins; clinical aspects of zinc metabolism; toxicity; standards for zinc in air and water; sampling and measurement techniques; and a summary and recommendations. Two appendixes are concerned with zinc content of various foods and with methods of zinc analysis.

National Research Council. Coordinating Committee for Scientific and Technical Assessments of Environmental Pollutants. Panel on Nitrates. NITRATES: AN ENVIRONMENTAL ASSESSMENT. Washington, D.C.: National Academy of Sciences, 1978. xxv, 723 p. Appendixes; Tables; Figures; Bibliog.

> This is a comprehensive assessment of the environmental problems associated with nitrates. After a summary of principal findings, the following topics are discussed: (1) nitrogen cycle, (2) environmental transport, (3) analysis and measurement of critical compounds, (4) mass-balance studies, (5) nitrate pollution, (6) nitrogen fixation and stratospheric ozone, (7) ecological effects, (8) health effects, (9) environmental control, (10) economic issues, and (11) policy issues. Four appendixes are devoted to (1) mass-balance studies, (2) dietary nitrate and cancer, (3) risk of cancer, and (4) research needs.

Nriagu, Jerome D., ed. THE BIOGEOCHEMISTRY OF LEAD IN THE ENVIRONMENT. Part A. ECOLOGICAL CYCLES. Part B. BIOLOGICAL EFFECTS. Topics in Environmental Health, no. 1. Amsterdam: Elsevier and North Holland Biomedical Press, 1978. xi, 422 p.; xi, 397 p.

This volume is a comprehensive review of lead. In part A, the
discussions include: (1) "Properties and the Biogeochemical Cycles
of Lead," J.O. Nriagu; (2) "Lead in Soils, Sediments and
Major Rock Types," J.O. Nriagu; (3) "Economic Lead Deposits,"
S.E. Kesler; (4) "Lead as a Factor in the World Economy," I.M.
Robinson; (5) "Biogeochemical Cycling of Lead in the New Lead
Belt of Missouri," B.G. Wixon; (6) "Lead in the Atmosphere," J.O.
Nriagu; (7) "Lead in Natural Waters," T.J. Chow; (8) Aqueous
Environmental Chemistry of Lead," D.T. Rickard and J.O. Nriagu;
(9) "Geochemical and Geophysical Applications of Radioactive
Lead," J.A. Robbins; and (10) "Biogeochemical Prospecting for
Lead," H.V. Warren. In part B, the discussions include (11)
"Environmental Exposure to Lead," K.R. Mahaffey; (12) "Appli-
cation of Radiolead to Metabolic Studies," R.B. Holtzman; (13)
"Distribution and Storage of Lead in Human Tissues," P.S.I. Barry;
(14) "The Metabolism and Subclinical Effects of Lead in Children,"
J.F. Rosen and M. Sorell; (15) "Human Health Effects of Lead,"
H.S. Posner, T. Damstra, and J.O. Nriagu; (16) "Lead Toxicity
in Domestic Animals and Wildlife," R.M. Forbes and G.C. Saun-
derson; (17) "Lead and the Aquatic Biota," P.T.S. Wong, B.A.
Silverberg, Y.K. Chan, and P.V. Hodson; (18) "Lead and Ter-
restrial Microbiota," P. Doelman; and (19) "Lead and Vegetation,"
P.J. Peterson.

_____. SULFUR IN THE ENVIRONMENT. Part 1: THE ATMOSPHERIC
CYCLE. New York: John Wiley and Sons, 1978. xii, 464 p. Bibliog.

This is the first part of a two-part monograph dealing with envi-
ronmental sulfur pollution. Essays are: "Production and Uses of
Sulfur," J.O. Nriagu; "Sources of Sulfur in the Environment:
The Global Sulfur Cycle," M.R. Moss; "Organosulfur Emissions
from Industrial Sources," S.P. Bhatia; "Sulfur Dioxide-Emission
Control: Costs and Benefits," L.R. Babcock, Jr.; "Dispersal Models
for Sulfur Oxides around Chimneys and Tall Stacks," U. Hogstrom;
"Dispersal Models for Sulfur Oxides in Urban Environments," K.L.
Brubaker and D.M. Rote; "Long-Range Transport and Deposition of
Sulfur Oxides," B.E.A. Fisher; "Atmospheric Chemistry of Sulfur-
Containing Pollutants," P. Urone and W.H. Schroeder; "Acid
Precipitation," J.R. Kramer; and "Determination of Atmospheric
Gaseous and Particulate Sulfur Compounds," R.L. Tanner, J. Forrest,
and L. Newman.

_____. SULFUR IN THE ENVIRONMENT. Part 2: ECOLOGICAL IMPACTS.
New York: John Wiley and Sons, 1978. xii, 482 p. Bibliog.

Essays are: "Deteriorative Effects of Sulfur Pollution on Materials,"
J.O. Nriagu; "Effects of Sulfur Oxices on Animals," M.O.
Amdur; "Health Consequences of Human Exposure," C.M. Shy;
"Effects of Air-Borne Sulfur Pollutants on Plants," S.N. Lizon;
"Physiological and Biochemical Effects of Sulfur Dioxide on Plants,"

J.E. Hallgren; "Chemistry of Pollutant Sulfur in Natural Waters,"
J.O. Nriagu and J.D. Hem; "Sulfur Pollution and the Aquatic
Ecosystem," B. Almer, W. Dickson, C. Ekstrom, and E. Hornstrom;
"The Acid Mine Drainage," P. Barton; "Sulfur Pollution and Soil,"
M. Nyborg; "Naturally Occurring Organosulfur Compounds in
Soil," J.W. Fitzgerald; and "Microbial Transformations of Sulfur
in the Environment," S.H. Zinder and T.D. Brock.

Oehme, Frederick W., ed. TOXICITY OF HEAVY METALS IN THE ENVI-
RONMENT. 2 parts. New York: Marcel Dekker, 1978. x, 907 p. Tables;
Figures; Bibliog.

The contributors discuss the basic concepts and principles of heavy
metal pollution, their course through the food chain, and mechanisms of toxicity. Several common toxic heavy metals are dealt
with in some detail: lead, cadmium, mercury, arsenic, selenium,
copper and molybdenum, fluoride, and beryllium as well as trace
heavy metals. Then they consider teratogenicity, interactions of
trace elements, regulation of metal pollution, beneficial effects
of trace elements, and their qualitative analysis in the environment and organisms. The concluding chapter considers chelation
therapy with British antilewisite.

Public Health Service. SYMPOSIUM ON ENVIRONMENTAL LEAD CON-
TAMINATION. Public Health Service Publications, no. 1440. Washington,
D.C.: U.S. Department of Health, Education, and Welfare, 1966. iii, 176 p.
Paperbound.

At the symposium, 13-15 December 1965, there were panel discussions presented both in detail and in summary on major sources
of lead pollution, risk of exposure and absorption of lead, toxicity
of lead, and control of lead pollution.

Ramel, C., ed. CHLORINATED PHENOCY ACIDS AND THEIR DIOXINS:
MODE OF ACTION, HEALTH RISKS AND ENVIRONMENTAL EFFECTS. Ecological Bulletins, no. 27. Swedish Natural Science Research Council. Stockholm: Royal Swedish Academy of Sciences, 1978. 302 p. Paperbound. Figures;
Tables; Bibliog.

The papers in this volume are developed from a conference organized by the Environment Committee of the Academy, 7-10 February 1977. The principal topics are: chemistry of phenoxy acids
and their dioxins, their herbicidal effects, their toxicology, their
genetic effects on plants and animals, and the ecological and
economic consequences of their application. This report includes
conclusions and recommendations.

Singer, S. Fred, ed. GLOBAL EFFECTS OF ENVIRONMENTAL POLLUTION.
Dordrecht, Holland: D. Riedel Publishing Co., 1970. xii, 218 p. References.

This volume contains papers from a symposium organized by the American Association for the Advancement of Science, Dallas, Texas, December 1968. The speakers addressed four broad sets of problems: (1) chemical balance of gases in the earth's atmosphere; (2) nitrogen compounds in soil, water, atmosphere, and precipitation; (3) effects of atmospheric pollution on climate; and (4) worldwide ocean pollution by toxic wastes. Other unsolved problems were also discussed.

United Nations. Conference on the Human Environment. REPORT. Stockholm, 5–16 June 1972. New York: 1973. vi, 77 p. Paperbound.

Included in the report are actions taken at the conference, constitution of the conference, and proceedings. There are a list of abbreviations and five annexes including draft declaration on the human environment and general principles for assessment and control of marine pollution.

Waldbott, George L. HEALTH EFFECTS OF ENVIRONMENTAL POLLUTANTS. 2d ed. St. Louis, Mo.: C.V. Mosby Co., 1978. x, 350 p. Paperbound. Appendixes; Glossary; Indexes.

Revised since the first edition of 1973, Walbott presents a balanced overview of the environmental pollutants in three sections. The first deals with the sources and actions of the pollutants; the second, with the health effects; and the third, with special situations, for example, economic pollutants, radiation, water, noise, fire, and smoking. The threshold limits set by the conference of governmental industrial hygienists in 1977 are recorded in an appendix.

C. AIR POLLUTION

Ad Hoc Task Group on Air Pollution Research Goals. NATIONAL GOALS IN AIR POLLUTION RESEARCH. Public Health Service Publication, no. 804. Washington, D.C.: U.S. Department of Health, Education, and Welfare, 1960. v, 38 p. Paperbound.

The task group identifies ten specific goals in research on the problems of air pollution. Accompanying each goal, there is a statement about the financial support that should be allocated to achieving the goal.

Air Pollution Control Association. THE NATIONAL CONFERENCE ON THE CLEAN AIR ACT. Pittsburgh: 1974. v, 203 p. Paperbound.

This volume contains the proceedings of a conference held 31 October–2 November 1973. The panelists and participants discussed the strengths and weaknesses of the Clear Air Act as amended in 1970. Among the topics considered were state, federal, and local responsibilities; agency discretion; problems of enforcement; the heating process; land use and transportation planning; air quality standards; and control of mobile and stationary sources.

Carr, Donald E. THE BREATH OF LIFE. New York: W.W. Norton and Co., 1965. 175 p.

The author discusses the problems of air pollution and examines strategies for the control of the pollution of the atmosphere, both existing and potential programs.

Cooper, Anna Grossman, comp. CARBON MONOXIDE: A BIBLIOGRAPHY WITH ABSTRACTS. Public Health Service Publication, no. 1503. Washington, D.C.: U.S. Department of Health, Education, and Welfare, 1966. viii, 440 p. Paperbound.

The annotated bibliography contains 983 selected references and several pages devoted to state, city-county, and interstate reports, and miscellaneous references drawn from the literature of 1880-1966.

Kneip, Theodore Joseph, and Lippmann, Morton, eds. "The New York Summer Aerosol Study, 1976." ANNALS OF THE NEW YORK ACADEMY OF SCIENCES 322 (14 May 1979): 1-164. Paperbound.

The papers were presented at a meeting held 20 April 1977. The objectives of the study had been to characterize the aerosol existing in New York City and background aerosol transported into the city. Among the topics reported were number, size, and distribution of atmospheric particles, light scattering, aerosols upwind of New York, trace element concentrations, sulfates, inorganic nitrogen, nature of organic fraction, and halogens. It was concluded that considerable total suspended particulates and sulfates were being transported into New York City.

Lave, Lester B., and Seskin, Eugene P. AIR POLLUTION AND HUMAN HEALTH. Baltimore: Johns Hopkins University Press, 1977. xx, 368 p.

Lave and Seskin undertook a comprehensive study of the relationship between air pollution and human health to develop data for cost-benefit analyses of pollution control programs. In the first section, they discussed the background theoretical framework for their study. In the second, there was a discussion of cross-sectional analyses of U.S. Standard Metropolitan Areas, 1960-1961, 1969. Section three was devoted to annual and daily time-series analysis. The last section dealt with policy implications. Considering the assumptions needed to complete this study, the authors correctly concluded that much more detailed information would be necessary for a realistic cost-benefit analysis to be made.

Lee, Douglas H.K., ed. ENVIRONMENTAL FACTORS IN RESPIRATORY DISEASE. Fogarty International Center Proceedings, no. 11. New York: Academic Press, 1972.

The papers in this monograph examine the relationship between environmental quality and respiratory disease. Part 1 deals with lung and its basic reactions to insult. In Part 2, the authors examine the influence of environmental factors such as air pollutants and airborne microorganisms on the lung. The third part focuses on smoking, air pollution, and lung cancer; occupational lung disease; epidemic and bronchial asthma; and the question of an optimum environment. The real problem requiring serious attention is the best way to implement rational and understandable programs of environmental control based on somewhat fragmentary knowledge of man-environment interactions.

Machta, L. AIR CONCENTRATION AND DEPOSITION RATES FROM UNIFORM AREA SOURCES. MARC Report, no. 10. London: Monitoring and Assessment Research Centre, Chelsea College, University of London, 1978. 12 p. Paperbound. Charts.

The Research Centre functions under the Scientific Committee on Problems of the Environment of the International Council of Scientific Unions. The author discusses a theory for predicting the national contribution to the air concentration or deposition of contaminants.

Matthews, William Henry; Kellogg, William; and Robinson, George D., eds. MAN'S IMPACT ON THE CLIMATE. Cambridge: MIT Press, 1971. xvii, 594 p.

This volume is one of a series emerging from the Study of Critical Environmental Problems held in July 1970. Here are detailed technical papers which deal with nine different aspects of man-climate interactions: (1) the nature of climate changes and the atmosphere effects of pollution; (2) concepts of modelling climate; (3) concepts of monitoring and surveillance; (4) carbon dioxide and atmospheric heating; (5) particles and trubidity; (6) particles and clouds; (7) contaminants of the upper atmosphere; (8) monitoring techniques; and (9) implications of climatic change, particularly decision making. There are also working group reports which contain conclusions and numerous recommendations.

May, Daryl N. HANDBOOK OF NOISE ASSESSMENT. Environmental Engineering Series. New York: Van Nostrand Reinhold Co., 1978. xiv, 400 p. Figures; Tables; Appendixes.

The text addresses two main topics: assessment of psychological effects, and assessment of physical effects. Five appendixes provide (1) basic acoustics, (2) acoustic standards, (3) regulating agencies, (4) useful acoustics periodicals, and (5) glossary of acoustical terms.

Mohr, U.; Schmahl, D.; and Tomatis, L., eds. AIR POLLUTION AND CANCER IN MAN. IARC Scientific Publications, no. 16. Lyon, France: International Agency for Research on Cancer, 1977. xvii, 331 p.

These are the proceedings of the second Hanover International Carcinogenesis meeting held 22–24 October 1975. They are a series of papers from the Working Group for Investigations on the Carcinogenic Burden from Air Pollution in Man. These papers focus on experimental design and studies of carcinogenicity of air pollutants for laboratory animals. Other groups of papers deal with monitoring and registration of carcinogenic substances in the air; epidemiology of lung cancer in man, with special reference to air pollution; and significance of experimental animal results for man.

National Conference on the Clean Air Act. PROCEEDINGS. Pittsburgh: Air Pollution Control Association, 1974. v, 203 p. Paperbound.

The 1973 National Conference on the Clean Air Act was held 31 October to 2 November at Chapel Hill, North Carolina, under the sponsorship of the Triangle Universities Consortium on Air Pollution, the Air Pollution Control Association, and the American Petroleum Institute. The proceedings consist of ten papers presented there, plus summaries of nine sessions, all directed toward possible revision and improvement of the Clean Air Act as amended, in the light of over two years' experience with its enforcement.

National Institute for Occupational Safety and Health. OCCUPATIONAL EXPOSURE TO FIBROUS GLASS. DHEW (NIOSH) Publication, no. 77-152. Washington, D.C.: U.S. Department of Health, Education, and Welfare, 1977. xii, 189 p. Paperbound. Bibliog.; Appendixes.

This volume was developed to guide the Department of Labor in setting standards to protect the health of workers exposed to potential hazards at their workplace. It establishes criteria for controlling employee exposure to fibrous glass. It covers biologic effects of exposure; environmental data and engineering controls; development of the standard; work practices; and needs for further research.

National Research Council. Climatic Impact Committee. ENVIRONMENTAL IMPACT OF STRATOSPHERIC FLIGHT. BIOLOGICAL AND CLIMATIC EFFECTS OF AIRCRAFT EMISSIONS IN THE STRATOSPHERE. Washington, D.C.: National Academy of Sciences, 1975. xiii, 348 p. Paperbound. Appendixes.

The committee assessed the implications of emissions from aircraft flying in the stratosphere on climate, agriculture, and human health, particularly skin cancer. Four problems were considered: (1) effects of nitrogen oxides on ozone and ultraviolet light; (2) biological and medical effects of nitrogen oxide emissions; (3) effects of exhaust effluents on surface climate; and (4) climate effects on agriculture and the biosphere. Possible solutions included engine design and operation and aircraft fuels to reduce emissions as well as economic analyses of alternate solutions. Even though it was concluded that aircraft emissions did increase terrestrial ultraviolet radiation, there were not sufficient data to spell out fully the biological and climatic consequences.

National Research Council. Committee on Appraisal of Societal Consequences of Transportation Noise Abatement. NOISE ABATEMENT: POLICY ALTERNATIVES FOR TRANSPORTATION. Vol. 8. Analytical Studies for the U.S. Environmental Protection Agency. Washington, D.C.: National Academy of Sciences, 1977. xiii, 206 p. Paperbound. Tables; Figures; References.

The committee attempted to assist the Environmental Protection Agency in formulating legislation to control noise from transportation. The main topics addressed were: policy and legal issues, measurement and sources of transportation noise, and costs and benefits of transportation noise abatement.

National Research Council. Committee on Biologic Effects of Atmospheric Pollutants. Panel on Asbestos. ASBESTOS: THE NEED FOR AND FEASIBILITY OF AIR POLLUTION CONTROLS. Washington, D.C.: National Academy of Sciences, 1971. vii, 40 p. Paperbound. References.

The panel reviewed pathogenicity of asbestos, evidence of human nonoccupational exposure, estimation of risk of nonoccupational exposure, sources of asbestos fibers in ambient air, principles of control, and research needs. The conclusion was that control was necessary and feasible.

National Research Council. Committee on Biologic Effects of Atmospheric Pollutants. Panel on Fluorides. FLUORIDES. Washington, D.C.: National Academy of Sciences, 1971. xi, 295 p. Paperbound. References.

This volume is an interpretive review of fluorides: environmental sources, forms, fate, and transformation; environmental analysis; nutritional role; metabolism; effects on vegetation, animals, and human health; and population hazards. There are recommendations for future research.

National Research Council. Committee on Biologic Effects of Atmospheric Pollutants. Panel on Manganese. MANGANESE. Washington, D.C.: National Academy of Sciences, 1973. viii, 191 p. Paperbound. Appendix; References.

The volume covers manganese in the ecosystem and in plants, its input and disposition in man, its metabolic role, toxicity, and epidemiology, permissible air concentrations, neurobiological effects of deficiency and toxicity, and manganese tricarbonyl compounds as well as recommendations for future research.

National Research Council. Committee on Biologic Effects of Atmospheric
Pollutants. Panel on Polycyclic Organic Matter. PARTICULATE POLYCYCLIC
ORGANIC MATTER. Washington, D.C.: National Academy of Sciences, 1972.
xiii, 361 p. Paperbound. Appendixes; References.

> This volume centers on: chemistry, sources, atmospheric physics,
> carcinogenicity, metabolism, and effects on vegetation and human
> health as revealed in clinical and epidemiological studies. In
> addition to recommendations for future research, there are four
> appendixes: (1) collection of airborne particles for chemical analysis;
> (2) separation methods; (3) detection, identification, and quantifi-
> cation; and (4) regression analysis.

National Research Council. Committee on Biologic Effects of Atmospheric
Pollutants. Panel on Vanadium. VANADIUM. Washington, D.C.: National
Academy of Sciences, 1974. vii, 117 p. Paperbound. Appendixes; References.

> In this interpretive review on vanadium, there are discussions of
> its industrial sources and uses, sources in ambient air, vanadium
> in the environment, and biological effects on man and laboratory
> animals as well as recommendations. There are two appendixes:
> (1) desulfurization of residual fuel oils, and (2) detection and
> measurement of vanadium.

National Research Council. Committee on Fire Research. AIR QUALITY AND
SMOKE FROM URBAN AND FOREST FIRES. Washington, D.C.: National
Academy of Sciences, 1976. xi, 381 p. Paperbound. Tables; Graphs; References.

> The volume contains the proceedings of an international symposium,
> 24-26 October 1973, in Fort Collins, Colorado. In the first ses-
> sion, there are papers on the nature of combustion products from
> fires. Laws, standards, and regulations for smoke abatement are
> discussed in the second session. Smoke management is the topic
> of the third session. At the fourth session on research and oper-
> ational programs for the protection of environmental quality, there
> are two panel discussions: (1) priorities for smoke research, and
> (2) government and industry programs for smoke control.

National Research Council. Committee on Impacts of Stratospheric Change.
HALOCARBONS: ENVIRONMENTAL EFFECTS OF CHLOROFLUOROMETHANE
RELEASE. Washington, D.C.: National Academy of Sciences, 1976. ix,
125 p. Paperbound. Appendixes.

> Opening with a summary of findings, conclusions, recommendations,
> the problem of regulation, and background information, this report
> covers suggestions for further research; phenomena in the strato-
> sphere; balancing losses and gains; expected changes in ozone;
> impacts of increased CFMs on climate; nonhuman biological effects;
> and health effects. There are four appendixes, devoted chiefly
> to control actions and prevention of melanoma.

National Research Council. Committee on Impacts of Stratospheric Change.
Panel on Atmospheric Chemistry. HALOCARBONS: EFFECTS ON STRATO-
SPHERIC OZONE. Washington, D.C.: National Academy of Sciences, 1976.
xv, 352 p. Paperbound. Appendixes.

> The Panel on Atmospheric Chemistry was charged with assessing
> the extent to which man-made halocarbons, particularly chloro-
> fluoromethanes, and potential emissions from the space shuttle
> might inadvertently modify the stratosphere. The present report
> considers the extent to which catalysis by halogen atoms reduces
> the amount of stratospheric ozone. It provides a summary of the
> problem and the panel's findings, also detailed discussion of the
> sources and amounts of pollutants; removal processes suggested;
> transport and measurement of the halogen compounds; the extent
> to which stratospheric ozone will be affected as a result of re-
> leasing the pollutants into the atmosphere; and the space shuttle
> and other considerations.

National Research Council. Committee on Medical and Biologic Effects of Environmental Pollutants. Panel on Nickel. NICKEL. Washington, D.C.: National Academy of Sciences, 1975. vii, 277 p. Paperbound. Appendixes;
Bibliog.

> This is a study of the biologic effects of nickel, describing its
> sources, physical and chemical nature; measurement; relation to
> other pollutants; biologic effects and margins of safety; and dose-
> response relations. Recommendations are offered for monitoring
> and controlling nickel in the environment and for further research.
> Two appendixes list the National Air Surveillance Networks am-
> bient nickel concentrations and analytical methods for nickel.

National Research Council. Committee on Medical and Biologic Effects of
Environmental Pollutants. Panel on Vapor-Phase Organic Pollutants. VAPOR-
PHASE ORGANIC POLLUTANTS. Washington, D.C.: National Academy of
Sciences, 1976. xiii, 411 p. Paperbound. Appendixes; Bibliog.

> This report, a companion to PARTICULATE POLYCYCLIC ORGANIC
> MATTER (see p. 114), concerns vapor-phase substances likely to be
> produced as community pollutants in sufficient amounts to affect
> health. There are four major parts. The first part deals with the
> sources of vapor-phase organic pollutants; it is supported by two
> appendixes on collection and sampling techniques and analytic
> methods. The second section is a thorough treatment of the pos-
> sible mechanisms of formation of oxygenated organic hydrocarbon
> compounds in the atmosphere and of atmospheric reactions of or-
> ganic molecules with oxides of nitrogen and sulfur, hydroxyl radicals,
> and oxygen atoms. The third section deals with the toxicologic,
> pathophysiologic, and epidemiologic information on vapor-phase
> organic pollutants, their metabolism and effects on the total en-
> vironment. There are two other appendixes on airborne contami-
> nants and on toxicity data on occupational exposure to selected
> substances.

National Research Council. Committee on Medical and Biologic Effects of Environmental Pollutants. Subcommittee on Airborne Particles. AIRBORNE PARTICLES. Baltimore: University Park Press, 1979. xi, 343 p. Bibliog.

This volume summarizes the knowledge on atmospheric particles arising from man's activities; not included are special particles such as lead, arsenic and asbestos, bacterial and viral particles, and vegetable particles. Topics are characteristics and size distribution; cycles and trends; and effects on atmospheric processes, human respiratory functions, human health, vegetation, and building materials.

National Research Council. Committee on Medical and Biologic Effects of Environmental Pollution. Subcommittee on Nitrogen Oxides. NITROGEN OXIDES. Washington, D.C.: National Academy of Sciences, 1977. vii, 333 p. Paperbound. References.

This volume reviews nitrogen oxides: their properties, sources, analytical methodology, atmospheric concentrations, chemical interactions in the atmosphere, and effects on natural ecosystems, materials, vegetation, and health of man and laboratory animals. There are summary, conclusions, recommendations for future research.

National Research Council. Committee on Medical and Biologic Effects of Environmental Pollutants. Subcommittee on Ozone and Other Photochemical Oxidants. OZONE AND OTHER PHOTOCHEMICAL OXIDANTS. Washington, D.C.: National Academy of Sciences, 1977. vii, 719 p. Paperbound. Figures;. Tables; Bibliog.

This report, one of a series requested by the Environmental Protection Agency, deals primarily with the origins and effects of ozone and other photochemical oxidants, and is limited to the problem of urban pollution and closely related topics. The first third of the report concerns the origins and measurement of ozone and other photochemical oxidants, and the relationship of atmospheric concentrations to emissions. The middle third deals with toxicologic studies and effects on humans, and the last with effects on plants, ecosystems, and materials. Each chapter is accompanied by a summary and/or a set of recommendations.

Nuttonson, N.Y., ed. A COMPILATION OF TECHNICAL REPORTS ON THE BIOLOGICAL EFFECTS AND PUBLIC HEALTH ASPECTS OF ATMOSPHERIC POLLUTANTS. AICE Survey of USSR Air Pollution Literature. Silver Spring, Md.: American Institute of Crop Ecology, 1971. xi, 152 p. Paperbound. Maps.

There are translations of eleven papers published in the Soviet Union by public health agencies and institutions. The papers deal with low-level chemical air pollutants around major petrochemical complexes, chemical plants manufacturing raw material for nylon production and organic syntheses plants, and methods for measuring low levels of air pollutants.

116

Stern, Arthur Cecil, ed. AIR POLLUTANTS, THEIR TRANSFORMATION AND TRANSPORT. Vol. 1 of AIR POLLUTION. 3d ed. Environmental Sciences. New York: Academic Press, 1976. xviii, 715 p.

Volume 1 of this five-volume set covers two major areas: the nature of air pollution and the mechanism of its dispersal by meteorological factors and from stacks. Each volume is aimed at scientifically advanced readers: engineers, chemists, physicists, physicians, meteorologists, lawyers, economists, sociologists, agronomists, and toxicologists.

_____. AIR QUALITY MANAGEMENT. Vol. 5 of AIR POLLUTION. 3d ed. Environmental Sciences. New York: Academic Press, 1977. xix, 700 p.

The problems of air quality management are considered on the local, state, and regional levels, as well as the national and worldwide. Air quality standards are discussed, including emission standards for mobile sources and for stationary sources.

_____. THE EFFECTS OF AIR POLLUTION. Vol. 2 of AIR POLLUTION. 3d ed. Environmental Sciences. New York: Academic Press, 1977. xix, 684 p.

Volume 2 is divided into three parts. Part A concerns the effects of air pollution on the physical properties of the atmosphere, on indoor air quality, and on economic materials and structures. In part B, its effects on biological systems, including human health, are surveyed. Part C is devoted entirely to the literature on air pollution, listing primary, secondary, and tertiary resources; newsletters; translations; audiovisual materials; bibliographies, directories, and guides.

_____. ENGINEERING CONTROL OF AIR POLLUTION. Vol. 4 of AIR POLLUTION. 3d ed. Environmental Sciences. New York: Academic Press, 1977. xxii, 946 p.

The fourth volume in this set includes part A, dealing with control concepts; part B, with control devices; and part C, with process emissions and their control. Of the twenty-one chapters, most are found in part C, dealing in detail with fuels; space heating and steam generation; power generation; incineration; motor vehicle emissions; and with problems found in specific industries: agriculture, forest products, mineral products, chemicals, petroleum refining, and metallurgical operations, both ferrous and nonferrous.

_____. MEASURING, MONITORING, AND SURVEILLANCE OF AIR POLLUTION. Vol. 3 of AIR POLLUTION. 3d ed. Environmental Sciences. New York: Academic Press, 1976. xx, 799 p. References.

Volume 3 has three sections: part A deals with sampling and

analysis; part B with ambient air surveillance, including global monitoring; and part C concerns source surveillance.

"Symposium on Statistics and the Environment." JOURNAL OF THE WASH-INGTON ACADEMY OF SCIENCES 64 (June 1974): 29-190. Paperbound.

The focus of this third symposium is toxicity of chemicals in the environment. There are three working sessions: (1) "Carcinogens--Safe Doses?" (2) "Air Pollutants--Safe Concentrations?" and (3) "Occupational Exposures--Threshold?" The problems were presented by health professionals and statisticians and there was a panel discussion.

SYMPOSIUM ON STATISTICS AND THE ENVIRONMENT, 4TH, 1976. Washington, D.C.: American Statistical Association, 1977. 124 p. Paperbound. Tables; Figures; References.

Air pollution is the central theme. Five sessions include: (1) scientific uncertainty and judicial assessment of uncertainty; (2) air pollution and human health: an overview; (3) air pollution and human health: some specific problems; (4) study of ozone in Northeast U.S.A.; and (5) analysis of environmental time. The papers presented are reproduced, but there is only a summary of the discussions.

U.S. Congress. Senate. Committee on Public Works. PROCEEDINGS OF CON-FERENCE ON HEALTH EFFECTS OF AIR POLLUTANTS. Serial No. 93-15. Washington, D.C.: Government Printing Office, 1973. 709 p. Paperbound. Tables; Figures; References.

At the conference sponsored by the National Academy of Sciences held 3-5 October 1973, there were five sessions devoted to pre-sentations by experts: (1) carbon monoxide, (2) sulfur oxides and particulates, (3) nitrogen oxides, (4) hydrocarbons and oxidents, and (5) general problems. Discussions of papers are included.

Whelpdale, D.M. ATMOSPHERIC PATHWAYS OF SULFUR COMPOUNDS. MARC Report, no. 7. London: Monitoring and Assessment Research Centre, Chelsea College, University of London, 1978. 39 p. Paperbound. References.

In a report prepared under the auspices of the Research Center, Special Committee on Problems of the Environment, International Council of Scientific Unions, Whelpdale reviews the literature dealing with atmospheric pathways of sulfur: production and emissions, distribution and deposition, modelling and programs for monitoring. Recommendations for future work are made.

D. WATER POLLUTION

Carr, Donald E. DEATH OF THE SWEET WATERS. New York: W.W. Norton Co., 1966. 257 p.

> The author focuses on the problems of man's use and abuse of water as a renewable natural resource. The need for a rational strategy of water resource management is stressed.

Degler, Stanley E., ed. OIL POLLUTION: PROBLEMS AND POLICIES. Washington, D.C.: Bureau of National Affairs, 1969. iii, 142 p. Paperbound.

> Oil spills at sea are considered, especially as to legal problems involved and as to the state of the art of spillage prevention, control, and restoration. Also included are a 1967 report to the president from the Secretaries of Transportation and the Interior, a national multiagency pollution contingency plan, and the complete texts of the Oil Pollution Acts of 1924 and 1961.

Giam, C.S., ed. POLLUTANT EFFECTS ON MARINE ORGANISMS. Lexington, Mass.: Lexington Books and D.C. Heath and Co., 1977. xi, 213 p.

> Covers the proceedings of a workshop held at Texas A & M University, College Station, 16-19 May 1976. The objective was to discuss research conducted under the Biological Effects Program of the International Decade of Ocean Exploration. Included are recommendations for future research, abstracts of presentations, and selected workshop papers dealing with marine pollutants and their effects of ocean animals.

Jeung, Rodney A. URBAN STORMWATER POLLUTION: AN INVESTIGATION OF THE PROBLEM AND ITS CONTROL. Ithaca, N.Y.: Cornell University, Program in Urban and Regional Studies, 1978. xi, 211 p. Paperbound. Figures; Tables; References.

> This work is one of a series on "Discussions in Environmental Health Planning." Jeung reviews the literature dealing with contaminants in stormwater runoff and discusses and evaluates alternative actions to prevent and control this major source of pollution. He also suggests a methodology by which a community may assess the magnitude of stormwater pollution.

McKee, Jack Edward, and Wolf, Harold W., eds. WATER QUALITY CRITERIA. 2d ed. Pasadena: California, State Water Resources Control Board, 1963. xiv, 548 p. Paperbound. Tables; Figures; Appendixes.

> This is a revision of the first edition of a 1960 report reviewing the technical and legal literature pertaining to water-quality criteria. Over thirty-eight hundred references are cited and summarized or abstracted. Although intended originally for the use of the California Water Pollution Control Board in promulgating

guidelines of water quality, the report has been used throughout the United States and in many other countries. It was prepared, with the assistance of the U.S. Public Health Service, by a team at the California Institute of Technology. Contents include the following: general considerations; water-quality criteria promulgated by state and interstate agencies; judicial expression; quality criteria for the major beneficial uses of water; potential pollutants; biological pollutants; radioactivity; pesticides; surface active agents.

THE MARINE ENVIRONMENT. Edited by John Lenihan and William W. Fletcher. Man and the Environment, vol. 5. New York: Academic Press, 1976. xiv, 170 p.

The authors examine the marine environment which man exploits as a source of power, food and water, and as a deposit for his wastes. The several contributions deal with marine production, biological consequences of oil spills, inorganic wastes, power from tides and waves, and desalination.

National Association of Manufacturers. THE FEDERAL WATER POLLUTION CONTROL ACT AMENDMENTS OF 1972: WHAT ARE THE EFFECTS? NATIONAL POLLUTANT DISCHARGE ELIMINATION SYSTEM (NEPDES): AN EVALUATIVE REPORT. Prepared by Paul S. Minor. Washington, D.C.: 1974. 68 p. Paperbound. Bibliog.; Glossary.

This report summarizes the background of PL 92-500 of 1972; its basic features; implications for U.S. manufacturers; and a policy for cost-effective implementation of this law.

_____. OVERVIEW OF PUBLIC LAW 92-500: THE FEDERAL WATER POLLUTION CONTROL ACT AMENDMENTS OF 1972. NATIONAL POLLUTANT DISCHARGE ELIMINATION SYSTEM (NEPDES): LEGISLATIVE OVERVIEW. Prepared by Congressional Research Service of Library of Congress. Washington, D.C.: 1974. 11 p. Paperbound.

This is a description of PL 92-500, enacted by Congress in 1972 to establish a National Pollutant Discharge Elimination System. It summarizes the law's provisions, with the congressional intent behind each.

National Research Council. Committee on Medical and Biologic Effects of Environmental Pollutants. Subcommittee on Chlorine and Hydrogen Chloride. CHLORINE AND HYDROGEN CHLORIDE. Washington, D.C.: National Academy of Sciences, 1976. vii, 282 p. Paperbound. Appendixes; Bibliog.

The purpose of this document is to present a balanced and comprehensive survey of knowledge about chlorine and hydrogen chloride in relation to health, for the information of the scientific community and the public, and for the guidance of standard-setting and regulatory agencies. The report describes sources, physical and chemical properties, measurements, biologic effects, and

interrelationships of a number of pollutants, and offers recommendations for further research. There is one appendix on analytic
determination of chlorine and hydrogen chloride, and a second
appendix on common and scientific names of plants.

National Research Council. Coordinating Committee for Scientific and Technical
Assessments of Environmental Pollutants. Panel on Kepone/Mirex/Hexachlorocy-
colopentadiene. KEPONE/MIREX/HEXACHLOROCYCOLOPENTADIENE: AN
ENVIRONMENTAL ASSESSMENT. Washington, D.C.: National Academy of
Sciences, 1978. xi, 73 p. Paperbound. Bibliog.

This report includes a discussion of environmental disperal and
fate, human exposure and health risks, and the ecological implications of environmental pollution by kepone, mirex, and hexa-
chlorocyclopentadiene. The findings are summarized.

National Research Council. Coordinating Committee for Scientific and Technical
Assessments of Environmental Pollutants. Panel on Low Molecular Weight Ha-
logenated Hydrocarbons. CHLOROFORM, CARBON TETRACHLORIDE, AND
OTHER HALOMETHANES: AN ENVIRONMENTAL ASSESSMENT. Scientific
and Technical Assessment Report. Washington, D.C.: National Academy of
Sciences, 1978. xi, 294 p. Paperbound. Appendixes; References.

This report was made by the National Research Council at the request of the Environmental Protection Agency. The study considers
the nonfluorinated halomethanes as to their sources, uses, behavior,
fate, and effects on human beings and the ecosystem, with special
attention to carcinogenic risks. The two final chapters cover control
techniques, options, and costs; also an economic analysis of selected
methods for removing chloroform from drinking water. Appendixes
include physicochemical properties of the nonfluorinated halomethanes;
their direct health effects; and a table of units of weight and
concentration.

National Research Council. Coordinating Committee for Scientific and Technical
Assessments of Environmental Pollutants. Panel on Mercury. AN ASSESSMENT
OF MERCURY IN THE ENVIRONMENT. Washington, D.C.: National Academy
of Sciences, 1978. ix, 185 p. Paperbound. Appendixes; References.

This document is designed to provide technical and scientific assessment of selected multimedia environmental pollutants. The
National Research Council wished also to study the methodological
problem of how such assessments should be done and how scientific
expertise could be best used to meet the expanding need for independent, critical scientific evaluation of pollutants. The report
includes sections on findings and overview; the global cycle of
mercury; forms and occurrence in the environment; chemical and
biochemical mechanisms for methylation and demetyhlation; ecological effects; environmental exposure and uptake by humans;
effects on human health.

National Research Council. Ocean Affairs Board. PETROLEUM IN THE MARINE ENVIRONMENT. Washington, D.C.: National Academy of Sciences, 1975. xi, 107 p. Paperbound. Appendixes; References.

> The participants of the Workshop on Inputs, Fates, and the Effects of Petroleum in the Marine Environment, 21-25 May 1975, examined the impact of petroleum hydrocarbons. The report summarizes their findings, discussions, and recommendations concerning magnitude of petroleum inputs, analytical methods, fates of petroleum, and effects on aquatic organisms and humans. One appendix characterizes U.S. statistics for petroleum accidently released into the sea.

National Research Council. Ocean Disposal Study Steering Committee. DISPOSAL IN THE MARINE ENVIRONMENT: AN OCEANOGRAPHIC ASSESSMENT. Washington, D.C.: National Academy of Sciences, 1976. viii, 76 p. Paperbound.

> This analytical study considers the scientific and technical aspects of problems in ocean disposal of waste materials as a basis for improving practices under existing regulations. The report describes the current legislation and regulations, as background of the disposal problem. It discusses the amount and properties of waste materials and the processes affecting their fate in the marine environment. The system under which the Environmental Protection Agency operates is then evaluated through examination of desirable practices for site selection and monitoring. Finally, recommendations are offered on the problem of incorporating existing scientific information into the management of ocean disposal.

National Research Council. Study Panel on Assessing Potential Ocean Pollutants. ASSESSING POTENTIAL OCEAN POLLUTANTS. Washington, D.C.: National Academy of Sciences, 1975. xx, 438 p. Paperbound. Tables; Figures; References.

> This volume summarizes a study which was conducted by the panel from 1972 to 1973. To select significant pollutants the criteria of production rate, environmental persistence, toxicity, and bioaccumulation were adopted. The report reviews methods for screening pollutants and then documents several categories of pollutants, transuranic elements, synthetic organic chemicals, ocean discharges, metallic wastes, medicinal wastes, and marine litter.

Nicholson, William Samison, and Moore, John Arthur, eds. "Health Effects of Halogenated Aromatic Hydrocarbons." ANNALS OF THE NEW YORK ACADEMY OF SCIENCES 320 (31 May 1979): 1-730. Paperbound. Tables; Figures; References.

> The papers were presented at an international symposium held 24-27 June 1978. They dealt with (1) production, chemistry, and distribution of halogenated aromatic hydrocarbons; (2) animal toxicity

and metabolism; (3) body clearance; (4) general human health effects; (5) neurological and behavioral abnormalities; (6) carcinogenicity; (7) reproductive effects; (8) immunological abnormalities and alterations; (9) a case study of the Hudson River; and (10) surveillance for future environmental contaminants.

Pettyjohn, Wayne A., ed. WATER QUALITY IN A STRESSED ENVIRONMENT: READINGS IN ENVIRONMENTAL HYDROLOGY. Minneapolis: Burgess Publishing Co., 1972. ix, 309 p. Paperbound.

Dealing mainly with ground-water and surface-water contamination, these readings are intended to provide background geologic and hydrologic information, and also to describe specific examples of significant occurrences of water pollution in the past twenty-five years. The six parts of the book are entitled: "The Water We Drink"; "Sources of Surface-Water Pollution"; "Geologic Controls and Ground-Water Pollution"; "Examples of Ground-Water Pollution"; "Trace Elements"; "Water Pollution and Legal Controls"; and "A Look into Future Environmental Monitoring."

Pickering, William F. POLLUTION EVALUATION: THE QUANTITATIVE ASPECTS. Environmental Science and Technology Series, vol. 2. New York: Marcel Dekker, 1977. vi, 199 p.

This book attempts to bridge the gap between quantitative chemical analysis, an exact science, and pollution evaluation, a complex problem involving socially relevant issues as well as scientific and technical data, and demanding many arbitrary decisions. The book therefore has been developed on a dual theme. Odd-numbered chapters discuss modes of evaluating typical forms of environmental pollution; procedures quoted are illustrative. Even-numbered chapters take up the fundamental principles of some of the techniques previously discussed, using an introductory approach rather than the rigor demanded by the dedicated teacher of chemical analysis. Consideration is given to pollution of the atmosphere, water, soil, plants, and food.

Purves, David. TRACE-ELEMENT CONTAMINATION OF THE ENVIRONMENT. Fundamental Aspects of Pollution Control and Environmental Science, 1. Amsterdam: Elsevier Scientific Publishing Co., 1977. xi, 260 p. Bibliog.

Purves examines the problems associated with the dispersal of trace elements from industrial activities into the air, water, and soil. Topics are trace-element contaminants, factors affecting the trace-element composition of soils, trace-element contamination of the atmosphere, sources of trace-elements in the soil, consequences of trace-element contamination of soils, availability of trace-elements in the soil, consequences of trace-element contamination of soils, trace-element contamination of the hydrosphere, and prevention of dispersal of metals in the environment.

Roels, Oswald A., ed. "Hudson River Colloquium." ANNALS OF THE NEW YORK ACADEMY OF SCIENCES 250 (24 May 1974): 1-185. Paperbound.

This monograph emerged from a colloquium series entitled "The Hudson Estuary" held at the City University of New York during the spring semester, 1972. The papers address the environmental problems of the estuary and their technical and legal management.

U.S. Department of the Interior. National Technical Advisory Committee on Water Quality Criteria. WATER QUALITY CRITERIA. Washington, D.C.: Federal Water Pollution Control Administration, 1968. x, 234 p. Appendix.

This report is a comprehensive document on water-quality requirements for use as a basic reference by those engaged in water-quality studies and standards-setting activities. The report also offers some recommendations. Sections are included on recreation and aesthetics, public water supplied, fish and wildlife, agricultural uses, and uses in industry.

U.S. Office of Water Planning and Standards. NATIONAL WATER QUALITY INVENTORY: 1974 REPORT TO THE CONGRESS. 2 vols. Washington, D.C.: Government Printing Office, 1974. Vol. 1: x, 305 p.; vol. 2: 362 p. Paperbound. Appendixes.

This report, required by Public Law 92-500 of 1972, as amended, is the first of an annual series. It was prepared by the Environmental Protection Agency through its Office of Water Planning and Standards, using data collected by federal and state agencies, and marks the first systematic analysis of the quantitative impact of water pollution on a national scale. Volume 1 contains three parts: water quality status; point source inventory; and water quality goals. Volume 2 contains eight appendixes; including a bibliography; a list of EPA monitoring stations; major sources of pollution (municipal, industrial, and federal); a gazetteer of individual waterway segments; and reference level rankings.

World Health Organization. SURVEILLANCE OF DRINKING-WATER QUALITY. WHO Monograph Series, no. 63. Geneva: 1976. 135 p.

This monograph provides information and guidelines for the development of national, state, or provincial water-supply surveillance programs. It is concerned only with operational activities of direct use in conventional programs for developing countries; it applies primarily to community water services. The guidelines presented originated from a study made for the WHO at the University of North Carolina in 1968, under the supervision of Dr. F.E. McJunkin.

E. ABUSE OF LAND AND WATER

Ackermann, William C; White, Gilbert F.; and Worthington, E.B., eds. MAN-MADE LAKES: THEIR PROBLEMS AND ENVIRONMENTAL EFFECTS. Geophysical Monograph, 17. Washington, D.C.: American Geophysical Union, 1973. xv, 847 p.

This publication brings together papers presented at the International Symposium on Man-Made Lakes organized by the Scientific Committee on Water Research of the International Council of Scientific Unions. The symposium was held in Knoxville, Tennessee, 3-7 May 1971. The contents are arranged into four sections: (1) case studies of major man-made lakes (world and national registers; Volta Lake, Ghana; Lake Kariba, Zambia and Southern Rhodesia; Lake of Bhakra, India; Lake Brokopondo; Kainiji Lake, Nigeria; Lake Mead; Lake Nassar; Ryinsk Reservoir; and TVA), (2) physical systems (hydrology and hydraulics, sedimentation, meteorology and hydrometeorology, and seismic effects), (3) biological systems (physical limnology and aquatic ecosystems), (4) man-made lakes in relation to man (fisheries, resettlement, marginal agriculture and wildlife, health, tourism, shoreline and terrestrial features, water transportation, archeological salvage, and engineering techniques). There are forty pages of recommendations. Because of the impact both on man and on the environment, these lakes require careful planning and interdisciplinary research.

Brady, Nyle C., ed. AGRICULTURE AND THE QUALITY OF OUR ENVIRONMENT. AAAS Publication, no. 85. Washington, D.C.: American Association for the Advancement of Science, 1967. xv, 460 p.

The papers were presented at a symposium during the 133d meeting of the American Association for the Advancement of Science, December 1966. Four main themes were addressed: (1) agriculture and air quality; (2) agriculture and water quality; (3) soil pollution in agriculture; and (4) human and animal waste. The several papers suggest that the benefit of increased productivity have come with a cost, namely pollution of air, water, and soil, which threatens that productivity. Much remains to be learned about this agroecosystem but it is clear that environmental quality is important for its functioning. To maintain that quality, society will have to make hard economic decisions.

Burton, Ian; Kates, Robert W.; Mather, John R.; and Snead, Rodman E. "The Shores of Megalopolis: Coastal Occuance and Human Adjustment to Flood Hazard." PUBLICATIONS IN CLIMATOLOGY 3, no. 3 (1965): 435-603. Available from C.W. Thornthwaite Associates Laboratory of Climatology, Elmer, N.J.

This is a discussion of the geographic approach to the problems of coastal occuance, the patterns of occuance, the climatology of damaging storms, human adjustment to coastal flooding, choice of adjustment, and the human use of the shore. In essence, the

authors evaluate the risks people take and the costs they are
willing to bear to live and play along the coastal zone.

Colson, Elizabeth. THE SOCIAL CONSEQUENCES OF RESETTLEMENT; THE
IMPACT OF THE KARIBA RESETTLEMENT ON THE GWEMBE TONGA. Kariba
Studies, 4. Manchester, Engl.: Manchester University Press, 1971. xi, 277 p.
Paperbound.

Colson studied the impact of forced resettlement imposed upon the
Gwembe Tonga of Central Africa in 1957 and 1958 as a consequence of the construction of a large hydroelectric dam across the
Zambesi River at Kariba Gorge. Because they had had no part
in the decision to build the dam, the need to relocate constituted
a crisis for the Gwembe Tonga. Colson traced the history of this
technological decision and the response of the natives, the move
and its aftermath, the disruptions of kinsmen and family, material
gains and losses, new political order which followed the move,
and effects of the move on ritual and security. Her report includes several case histories which illustrate aspects of the resettlement process.

Davis, Shelton H. VICTIMS OF THE MIRACLE: DEVELOPMENT AND THE
INDIANS OF BRAZIL. Cambridge: University Press, 1977. xviii, 205 p.
Notes; Bibliog.

Davis analyzes the economic development policies of the Brazilian
government in the past few years, and their human and ecological
consequences, especially to the Indian peoples in the Amazon
Basin. There are three parts: the first covering the economic
history of the Brazilian Amazon 1940-1970; the second, contemporary Indian policy in Brazil 1970-1975; the third, the social
and ecological effects of the Polamazonia Program 1975-1979.

EUTROPHICATION: CAUSES, CONSEQUENCES, CORRECTIVES: PROCEED-
INGS OF A SYMPOSIUM. Washington, D.C.: National Academy of Sciences,
1969. vii, 661 p. References.

Organized by the National Academy of Sciences, an international
symposium was held in Madison, Wisconsin, 11-15 June 1967, with
about six-hundred persons present, representing eleven foreign
countries and the United States. The proceedings appear in this
volume in six parts, covering introduction, summary, and recommendations; eutrophication, past and present; geographical concepts of eutrophication; detection and measurement; preventive
and corrective measures; contributions to science from the study
of eutrophication.

GEOGRAPHICAL PERSPECTIVES AND URBAN PROBLEMS: A SYMPOSIUM.
Washington, D.C.: National Academy of Sciences, 1973. vii, 107 p. Paperbound.

This symposium, organized by the Committee on Geography of the National Academy of Sciences, Division of Earth Sciences, was held in Washington, D.C., 20-21 September 1971. The proceedings include the seven papers presented, all intended to inform planners, policymakers and decision makers about some of the problems of urban geography and their possible solutions.

Gillett, James W., ed. THE BIOLOGICAL IMPACT OF PESTICIDES IN THE ENVIRONMENT: A SYMPOSIUM ASSESSING THE SIGNIFICANCE OF PESTICIDES IN RELATION TO ECOLOGICAL PROBLEMS AND HEALTH. Environmental Health Sciences Series, no. 1. Corvallis: Oregon State University, 1970. xi, 210 p. Paperbound. Appendixes.

This symposium, held 18-20 August 1969 at Corvallis, Oregon, assesses the impact of pesticides on nontarget species and biological systems by determining: (1) the extent of pesticide-related damage to health; (2) if this damage is significant; and (3) is this is a direct or contributory effect of the pesticide involved. The study areas are birds, fish, and mammals. Factors affecting the choice of possible remedies to impacted environments are also considered. Six appendixes include a pesticide glossary, a pesticide index, and a plant and animal index.

Gonzalez, Nancie L., ed. SOCIAL AND TECHNOLOGICAL MANAGEMENT IN DRY LAND. PAST AND PRESENT, INDIGENOUS AND IMPOSED. American Association for Advancement of Science, Selected Symposium 10. Boulder, Colo.: Westview Press, 1978. xvi, 199 p.

In the dry lands, management of water, plants, and animals is crucial for survival. By various stratagems, human social groups attempt to maintain an ecological balance. When they fail, there is desertification. This volume contains case histories which illustrate how man has attempted to achieve an ecological balance in arid regions: (1) "An Empirical Approach to Prehistoric Agrarian Collapse: The Case of the Moche Valley," by M.E. Moseley; (2) "Farmers and Technical Experts: Information Flow in Irrigated Agriculture," S.H. Lees; (3) "Human Use of the Pre-Saharan Ecosystem and Its Impact on Desertification," W.H. Bedoian; (4) "Utilization of Surface Water by North Arabian Bedouins," F.S. Vidal; (5) "Agroecosystem Diversity: A Model from the Sonoran Desert," R.S. Felger and G.P. Nabhan; (6) "A Rational-Choice Model of Agricultural Resource Utilization and Conservation," J.W. Bennett; (7) "Drouth versus Desertification: The Case of Sahel," S.E. Nicholson; and (8) "Some Observations on Adaption to Semi-arid Environments," P.C. Reining.

Hewitt, Kenneth, and Burton, Ian. THE HAZARDOUSNESS OF A PLACE: A REGIONAL ECOLOGY OF DAMAGING EVENTS. Department of Geography, Research Publication 6. Toronto: University of Toronto Press, 1971. xiv, 154 p.

Hewitt and Burton report a study of the ways a community perceives

and adjusts to both natural and man-made hazards. The community
studied was London in southwestern Ontario. They review the
natural and man-made hazards of London and their characteristics,
and the nature of the human response. The response involves
perception, adjustment, and institutional arrangements. They conclude that the mental framework of persons is a key element in
the human ecology of hazards.

Lowe-McConnell, R.H., ed. MAN-MADE LAKES. Symposia of the Institute
of Biology, no. 15. London: Academic Press, 1966. xiv, 218 p.

This volume contains the proceedings of a symposium held at the
Royal Geographical Society, London, 30 September to 1 October
1965. Nineteen engineers and scientists contributed working
papers which dealt with the natural history of man-made lakes
in the tropics and in the temperate zone. The topics considered
ranged widely across biological, economic, and human problems.

National Research Council. Committee on Agriculture and the Environment.
Subcommittee on Chemical Additives. DEGRADATION OF SYNTHETIC OR-
GANIC MOLECULES IN THE BIOSPHERE: NATURAL, PESTICIDAL, AND
VARIOUS OTHER MAN-MADE COMPOUNDS. Washington, D.C.: National
Academy of Sciences, 1972. xi, 349 p. Paperbound. References.

This volume comprises the proceedings of a conference held in
San Francisco, 12-13 June 1971. The focus of the papers presented was disposal of wastes and their environmental consequences.
The authors and participants discussed microbial and photochemical
degradation of various man-made chemicals and their toxicity.

National Research Council. Committee on Nitrate Accumulation. ACCUMU-
LATION OF NITRATE. Washington, D.C.: National Academy of Sciences,
1972. vii, 106 p. Paperbound. References.

The task of this committee was to examine various problems associated with the accumulation of nitrate nitrogen and related ni-
trogenous compounds in the environment, and to recommend courses
of action to mitigate these problems. Its report covers nitrogen
compartments in the biosphere; sources of nitrogen; fertilizer and
soil nitrogen; hazards of nitrate, nitrite, and nitrosamines to man
and livestock; and eutrophication. Conclusions and recommendations follow each chapter along with a summary.

National Research Council. Committee on the Effects of Herbicides in Vietnam.
THE EFFECTS OF HERBICIDES IN VIETNAM: PART A--SUMMARY AND CON-
CLUSIONS. Washington, D.C.: National Academy of Sciences, 1974. xxvi,
372 p. Paperbound. Photos.; Maps.

This report, prepared pursuant to Public Law 91-441 of 1970, presents the findings of the committee which investigated the ecological and physiological effects of the widespread military use of

herbicides in South Vietnam between 1962 and 1971. There is a listing of the herbicides used, an inventory of the operations, and an assessment of the effects on vegetation, soils, animals, and human beings.

National Research Council. Study on Problems of Pest Control. Environmental Studies Board. CONTEMPORARY PEST CONTROL PRACTICES AND PROSPECTS. Vol. 1 of PEST CONTROL: AN ASSESSMENT OF PRESENT AND ALTERNATIVE TECHNOLOGIES. Washington, D.C.: National Academy of Sciences, 1975. xxviii, 506 p. Paperbound. Appendixes; Bibliog.

This volume focuses on the social and institutional factors important to conduct pest control. The pests studied did not include human pathogens, but organisms that were detrimental in human affairs—insects and other arthropods, weeds, bacteria, fungi, viruses, nematodes, and some vertebrates. Topics discussed were achievements and problems in pest control; contemporary practices; institutions in pest control; production of materials for pest control; transportation; storage, and accidents; information; use of pesticides; the law; monitoring research on effects of pesticides; future of pest control enterprise; and status of selected control strategies. Extensive recommendations are discussed.

_____. CORN/SOYBEANS PEST CONTROL. Vol. 2 of PEST CONTROL: AN ASSESSMENT OF PRESENT AND ALTERNATIVE TECHNOLOGIES. Washington, D.C.: National Academy of Sciences, 1975. xi, 169 p. Paperbound.

The Corn and Soybeans Study Team reported a case study of pest control of the corn and soybean crops, crops which comprise the backbone of U.S. agriculture. Among the topics addressed were productivity and pests in the corn and soybean sector, current practices in pest control, and future strategies in pest control. The study team concluded that more emphasis was needed on monitoring, research on alternate control technologies, and public education.

_____. COTTON PEST CONTROL. Vol. 3 of PEST CONTROL: AN ASSESSMENT OF PRESENT AND ALTERNATIVE TECHNOLOGIES. Washington, D.C.: National Academy of Sciences, 1975. ix, 139 p. Paperbound.

The Cotton Study Team reported a case study of pest control of cotton. Among the topics addressed were effect of market, social, and institutional factors on cotton production practices; contemporary practices in pest management; current trends and future alternatives in pest management; impact of developments in cotton industry on pest management; integrated pest management programs; effects of adopting alternative pest control practices; relative environmental implications of producing either synthetic fibers or crops. The study team concluded that future government policies should aim at reducing the use of pesticides and emphasize management rather than control.

_____. FOREST PEST CONTROL. Vol. 4 of PEST CONTROL: AN ASSESS-MENT OF PRESENT AND ALTERNATIVE TECHNOLOGIES. Washington, D.C.: National Academy of Sciences, 1975. xi, 170 p. Paperbound. Appendixes.

> The Forest Study Team reported a case study of pest control in forests. Among the topics addressed were major forest land uses; nature of the forest pest problem; contemporary pest control practices; impact of public policy on forest pest management; trends in forest pest management. The study team concluded that future research should emphasize alternate control strategies and better ways of informing users of forest land about pest management practices. Five appendixes provide information on diseases in forest areas, insect and vertebrate pests in forest areas, and the use of pesticides, 1945-1974.

_____. PEST CONTROL AND PUBLIC HEALTH. Vol. 5 of PEST CONTROL: AN ASSESSMENT OF PRESENT AND ALTERNATIVE TECHNOLOGIES. Washington, D.C.: National Academy of Sciences, 1975. xiii, 288 p. Paperbound.

> The Public Health Study Team focuses on the implications for human health of programs aimed at controlling arthropod vectors. Topics are contemporary public health practices and use of pesticides in the United States; public health arthropods as international problems; alternative tactics and strategies; and consequences of diffusion of more intensive agricultural technologies. The study team antici-pates that in the future there would be a gradual return to inte-grated control programs each appropriate to the local ecology and behavior of pest species, the epidemiology of the disease, and environmental values.

Perring, Franklin Hugh, and Mellanby, Kenneth, eds. ECOLOGICAL EFFECTS OF PESTICIDES. Linnean Society Symposium Series, no. 5. London: Academic Press, 1977. xi, 193 p.

> The papers were presented at a symposium sponsored by the Linnean Society of London and the Institute of Biology London, 23-24 September 1976. Papers were: "Changes in Use of Pesticides since 1945," J.M.A. Sly; "Pesticides on Crops--Some Benefits and Problems," H.C. Glough; "Recent Developments in the Agricul-tural Use of Herbicides in Relation to Ecological Effects," J.D. Fryer; "Recent Developments in the Chemical Control of Agricul-tural Pests and Diseases in Relation to Ecological Effects," I.J. Graham-Bryce; "Pesticides in Forestry: An Introduction," J. Hobart; "Ecological Effects of Military Use of Herbicides," A.H. Westing; "Dilemmas in Forest Pest and Disease Management," M.J. Way and D. Bevan; "Review of Effects of Aquatic Herbicides," T.O. Robeson and P.R.F. Barrett; "Aquatic Herbicides: Possible Future Developments," C. Newbold; "The Onchocerciasis Control Pro-gramme and the Monitoring of Its Effects on the Riverine Biology of the Volta River Basin," C. Leveque, M. Odei, and M. Pugh Thomas; "The Control of Trypanosomiasis," J.R. Busvine; "Some

Problems in the Control of Malaria," M.W. Service; "Prediction of Ecological Effects by Pesticides," F. Moriarty; "The Future Prospect for Wildlife," N.W. Moore; and "The Future Prospect for Man," K. Mellanby.

Pimentel, David, ed. INSECTS, SCIENCE, AND SOCIETY. New York: Academic Press, 1975. xxv, 284 p.

Containing ten papers presented at the 1974 symposium at Cornell celebrating the centennial of entomology, this book covers five topics: insects and their social implications; communication among insects; patterns and processes in insect interactions; insect population dynamics; and insect-pest management.

_____. WORLD FOOD, PEST LOSSES, AND THE ENVIRONMENT. American Association for the Advancement of Science, Selected Symposium 13. Washington, D.C.: AAAS, 1978. xxv, 206 p.

The nine papers were presented at a symposium on "World Food, Pest Losses, and the Environment," convened during the meeting of American Association for the Advancement of Science, Denver, February 1977. The authors discuss the magnitude of food losses from pests and laternative strategies for controlling the pests: (1) "Dimensions of the World Food Problem and Losses to Pests," D. and M. Pimentel; (2) "Insect Pest Losses and the Dimensions of the World Food Problem," R.F. Smith and D.J. Calvert; (3) "Impact of Plant Disease on World Food Production," J.L. Apple; (4) "Weeds and World Food Production," W.R. Furtick; (5) "Animal Pests and World Food Production," R.O. Drummond, R.A. Bram, and N. Konnerup; (6) "Post-Harvest Food Losses: The Need for Reliabie Data," J.R. Pedersen; (7) "Of Millet, Mice and Men: Traditional and Invisible Technology Solutions to Post-Harvest Losses in Mali," H. Guggenheim; (8) "Environmental Aspects of World Pest Control," D. Pimentel; and (9) "Post-Harvest Losses: A Priority of the UN University," M. Milner, N.S. Scrimshaw, and H.A.B. Parpia.

Scientific Committee on Problems of the Environment. Working Group on Man-Made Lakes. MAN-MADE LAKES AS MODIFIED ECOSYSTEMS. SCOPE Report 2. Paris: International Council for Scientific Unions, 1972. 76 p. Paperbound.

The Working Group describes the man-made lake as a human experience in modification of ecosystems. The ecological characteristics of the man-made lake are first described. This type of lake is then considered as a socio-cultural system and the focus is on the impact of the new lake on human communities. A third section deals with water management. In the fourth section, the development of the biological systems in and around the lake is discussed. Finally, three areas of policy are addressed: public policy, intergovernmental support, and scientific cooperation.

Secretary's Commission on Pesticides and Their Relationship to Environmental Health. REPORT OF THE SECRETARY'S COMMISSION ON PESTICIDES AND THEIR RELATIONSHIP TO ENVIRONMENTAL HEALTH. Parts 1 and 2. Washington, D.C.: U.S. Department of Health, Education, and Welfare, 1969. xvii, 677 p. Paperbound.

> The members of the commission and its subcommittees and panels reviewed the evidence regarding the hazards of pesticides for the health of man and the environment. Part 1 comprises the recommendations and summary reports of subcommittees. Part 2 provides details of a review of more than five thousand references dealing with uses and benefits of pesticides, environmental contamination, effects of pesticides on nontarget organisms including man, and carcinogenicity, interactions, mutagenicity and teratogenicity of pesticides.

Small, William E. THIRD POLLUTION: THE NATIONAL PROBLEM OF SOLID WASTE DISPOSAL. New York: Praeger Publishers, 1970. xiii, 173 p. Bibliog.

> Covering both the technical and the political problems involved in solid waste disposal, this book discusses the overall situation; the urban problems; fallout from agriculture; mineral resources and energy wastes; the automobile as polluter; resource recovery; present technologies of collection and disposal; legal and political action; and the future outlook.

Stanley, N.F., and Alpers, Michael P., eds. MAN-MADE LAKES AND HUMAN HEALTH. London: Academic Press, 1975. xvi, 495 p.

> This book focuses on the impact of the man-made lake on human health, a problem frequently neglected in planning, constructing, and filling the man-made lake. The diseases which receive particular attention are malaria, illnesses caused by arboviruses, schistosomiasis, filariasis, and leptospirosis. Reports are given concerning several different dams: Kariba, Aswan, Ord River, Ubolratana, Central California Basin, Brokopondo, Kisumu, Kainji, and Volta Lake. There are several chapters devoted to ecological factors: nutrient cycles, fish, waterfowl, aquatic plants, mosquitoes, mollusks, and insect vectors. Among the human ecological problems discussed are changing patterns of disease; migration and resettlement; and irrigation. Effective planning for these dams and monitoring their biological and social effects demand interdisciplinary work and coordination of governmental and nongovernmental agencies.

Vogt, William. ROAD TO SURVIVAL. New York: William Sloane Associates, 1948. xvi, 335 p.

> The problems of population and exploitation of natural resources are addressed. The principal focus is abuse of the land through improper management. Because soil is a crucial factor in agricultural productivity, Vogt urges that we act to conserve the land and control the growth of the population.

F. AGRICULTURE AND FOOD

Brown, Lester Russell. THE SOCIAL IMPACT OF THE GREEN REVOLUTION.
Comments by L.K. Jha, Sterling Wortman, and Stanley Please. International
Conciliation, no. 581. New York: Carnegie Endowment for International Peace,
1971. 61 p. Bibliog.

> The introduction of fast-growing crops into agriculture has greatly
> augmented productivity of rice and wheat, the so-called Green
> Revolution. Brown examines the implications of this revolution
> for relief of hunger, malnutrition, and poverty. He discusses
> diverse social consequences: employment opportunities, rural de-
> velopment and the urban crisis, export of cereal grains, and crop
> diversity. There are policy implications for land reform, rural
> cooperative arrangements, regional economic disparities, and price
> supports. Appended are comments by L.K. Jha, Sterling Wortman,
> and Stanley Please.

Brown, Lester Russell, with Eckholm, Erik P. BY BREAD ALONE. New York:
Praeger Publishers, 1974. xvi, 272 p.

> Brown and Eckholm analyze the world food situation. They sum-
> marize the dimensions of the problem, focusing on population
> growth, environmental degradation, unevenly distributed agricul-
> tural productivity, and climatic vulnerability. In the second part,
> they discuss the four basic resources of agricultural productivity:
> land, water, energy, and fertilizer. In the third part, they evaluate
> the Green Revolution, oceanic harvests, and nonconventional
> sources of food. The fourth part focuses on areas of social policy:
> population control, simplified diets, employment, and research and
> development. The authors also emphasize the need for strong and
> imaginative leadership. They suggest that augmenting agricultural
> productivity in the developing countries will reap the most benefits
> at the least cost.

Crosson, Pierre R., and Frederick, Kenneth D. THE WORLD FOOD SITUATION;
RESOURCES AND ENVIRONMENTAL ISSUES IN THE DEVELOPING COUNTRIES
AND THE UNITED STATES. Research Paper R-6. Washington, D.C.: Re-
sources for the Future, 1977. v, 230 p. Paperbound.

> Crosson and Frederick make a systematic analysis of the interrela-
> tions among demand for food, agricultural productivity, and the
> resultant environmental problems with a view of clarifying the policy
> options for adequately feeding future generations at acceptable
> costs. The principal topics addressed include the growing food
> gap; strategies for increasing agricultural productivity; the environ-
> mental impacts of agriculture and food production in the developing
> countries; and resource and environmental implications of increasing
> food production in the United States. Because of limited data, extra-
> polations into the future are difficult to make. The authors conclude
> that soil erosion may become a far more serious environmental prob-
> lem than fertilizer and pesticide pollution or salinization from irrigation.

Day, Peter R., ed. "The Genetic Basis of Epidemics in Agriculture." AN-
NALS OF THE NEW YORK ACADEMY OF SCIENCES 287 (27 February
1977): 1–400. Paperbound.

> The papers were presented at a Conference on the Genetic Basis
> Epidemics in Agriculture held by the New York Academy of
> Sciences, 5–8 April 1976. The principal topics addressed were:
> (1) the global aspect of genetic vulnerability; (2) genetic models
> of crop and parasite populations; (3) genetic and physiological
> causes and mechanisms of epidemics; (4) examples of epidemics;
> (5) examples of breeding and agronomic programs; and (6) sources
> of genetic diversity in plants.

Dumont, Rene, and Rosier, Bernard. THE HUNGRY FUTURE. Translated from
French by Rosamund Linell and R.B. Sutcliffe. New York: Praeger Publishers,
1969. 271 p.

> The theme is the threat posed to man of a failure by agriculture
> to supply the food to meet the demand of the human population.
> The amelioration of this threat is complex. Increased aid and
> trade are involved, but the root of the problem lies in the more
> effective use of resources already available through restructuring
> of social institutions, including agrarian reform. The first part
> of the book examines the food and population problems in the
> Third World. The second part focuses on the agriculture in Western
> countries. In the third part, agricultural problems in the Soviet
> bloc are discussed, and in the fourth, problems in the Third World.
> The authors offer suggestions and recommendations for solving these
> agricultural problems by social and economic processes.

Eckholm, Erik P. LOSING GROUND: ENVIRONMENTAL STRESS AND WORLD
FOOD PROSPECTS. New York: W.W. Norton and Co., 1976. 223 p. Bibliog.

> Eckholm reviews the ecological deterioration that has been the
> consequence of over-grazing, desert encroachment, deforestation,
> soil erosion, increased flooding, and silting of irrigation systems.
> This deterioration seriously threatens the productivity of the world's
> agricultural systems. Because efforts to retard this deterioration,
> or even reverse the trends, have not been successful, Eckholm is
> not optimistic about the future.

Etheridge, Elizabeth W. THE BUTTERFLY CASTE: A SOCIAL HISTORY OF
PELLAGRA IN THE SOUTH. Westport, Conn.: Greenwood Publishing Co.,
1972. ix, 278 p.

> Etheridge traces the story of the social and economic factors which
> contributed to epidemic pellagra in the southern United States and
> which were crucial in the conquest of the disease. She explains
> how Joseph Goldberger and his colleagues unravelled the etiology
> of this disease and then the difficulties they faced in trying to
> make their case with the medical profession and to implement in-
> tervention programs in the afflicted regions.

Hall, Ross Hume. FOOD FOR NOUGHT; THE DECLINE OF NUTRITION.
New York: Harper and Row, 1974. xii, 292 p. Paperbound.

Modern man is being increasingly nourished on fabricated products,
not wholesome natural agricultural products. The effects of this
transformation are subtle and pervasive in the social fabric and
are responsible for many illnesses of peoples in technological societies. This general theme carries through chapters devoted to
"Lifeless Bread," "Crops as Raw Material," "A Surrogate for the
Senses," "Consumerism," "Animal as Machine," "Perverted Sexu-
ality," "Chemical Warfare against Insects," "Fertility," "Global
Greening," "Agribusiness," "Fabrication of Technologic Man,"
"Chemistry Abhors Nature," "Negative Nutrition," "Infantile Nutrition," and "The Polyunsaturated Heart."

Marei, Sayed Ahmed. THE WORLD FOOD CRISIS. 2d ed. London: Longman
Group, 1978. xii, 134 p.

Marei, president of the World Food Council, discusses the causes
and implications of the current imbalance between population and
agricultural productivity. He illustrates the problems and alternate solutions by focusing on the Arab world. There is a summary
of the 1974 World Conference for which the author served as secretary-
general. Marei proposes that regional economic cooperation might
provide an avenue toward increasing agricultural productivity and
improving human welfare; this he identifies as the Arab Marshall
Plan.

National Research Council. Committee on Genetic Vulnerability of Major Crops.
Agricultural Board. GENETIC VULNERABILITY OF MAJOR CROPS. Washington, D.C.: National Academy of Sciences, 1972. vii, 307 p.

The committee reviewed epidemics of plant diseases, then examined
the vulnerability of individual crops (corn, wheat, sorghum, pearl
millet, rice, potato, sugar beet, sweet potato, soybeans, vegetable
crops, and cotton), and finally addressed the challenges of genetic
vulnerability. It concluded that genetic uniformity in crops was
the basis of vulnerability to epidemic disease and that the major
crops were impressively uniform genetically.

Poleman, Thomas T., and Freebairn, Donald K., eds. FOOD, POPULATION,
AND EMPLOYMENT: THE IMPACT OF THE GREEN REVOLUTION. New
York: Praeger Publishers, 1974. xiv, 272 p.

Poleman and Freebairn report on a workshop held at Cornell University,
2-4 June 1971, which was sponsored by the Program on Science,
Technology, and Society. The first set of papers deals with "Parameters of Change" and focuses on the scientific bases of increased
productivity from rice and wheat, food needs and demands, fertility patterns, and population distribution. The theme of the
second set "Emerging Imbalances," is particularly income disparities,

politics of peasant participation, industrialization and unemployment, problems of urbanization, trade balances, and politics of agricultural development. It is concluded that although the Green Revolution has disrupted economic, social, and political institutions and values, social mechanisms will emerge.

Power, Jonathan, and Holenstein, Anne-Marie. WORLD HUNGER; A STRATEGY FOR SURVIVAL. London: Temple Smith, 1976. 202 p.

Power and Holenstein review the current food-population problem. They show that there is a food shortage in the developing countries, that in these regions there are hunger and malnutrition. They review the problems created by urbanization and discuss the feasibility of rural development. They consider the benefits and costs of the Green Revolution and suggest that combining land reform and wider use of high-yield plants might solve not only the food problem but the unemployment problem. The authors discuss how Japan, Tanzania, Brazil, Eire, Bangladesh, the Philippines, and China have moved to solve their problems of food shortage and unemployment. They also review the outcomes of the World Food Conference. Although pessimistic about the long-term future, they suggest that rural development projects underway might provide a model that would relieve the growing imbalance between demand for and availability of food.

"Principal Hazards in Food Safety and Their Assessment." FEDERATION PROCEEDINGS (Federation of American Societies of Experimental Biology) 37 (October 1978): 2575-97.

At a symposium sponsored by the American Institute of Nutrition, 10 April 1978, objectives were to examine the principal hazards in food safety and draw conclusions about the assessment of relative risks for human health. Five papers were presented: "Introductory Remarks," H.R. Roberts; "Foodborn Hazards of Microbial Origin," E.M. Foster; "Environmental Contaminants," I.C. Munro and S.M. Charbonneau; "Food Hazards of Natural Origin," J.V. Rodricks; and "Assessment of Food Safety," D. Doull.

Roe, Daphne A. PLAGUE OF CORN; THE SOCIAL HISTORY OF PELLAGRA. Ithaca, N.Y.: Cornell University Press, 1973. xiii, 217 p.

Roe describes the natural history of pellagra and the association of the disease with the consumption of corn. The eating of corn provides the link between socioeconomic conditions and pellagra. The conquest of pellagra is then discussed and it is shown that pellagra is still endemic in several regions of the world, particularly Central America and South Africa.

THE ROLE OF ANIMALS IN THE WORLD FOOD SITUATION. Working Papers, Rockefeller Foundation. New York: Rockefeller Foundation, 1976. 101 p. Paperbound. Tables.

This volume contains papers presented at a conference held at the Rockefeller Foundation in 1975. Emphasizing the problems of demand for food by the growing world population and providing an adequate supply through agriculture, the topics discussed are regional and global use of animals as food; nonfood uses of animals; competition between animals and man; food needs in the future; comparative efficiency of animals; potentials of ruminants and non-ruminants; alternative uses of land; and potential for developing range lands.

Smith, Philip E.L. FOOD PRODUCTION AND ITS CONSEQUENCES. Menlo Park, Calif.: Cummings Publishing Co., 1976. x, 120 p. Bibliog.

Smith develops the thesis that the invention of food production some ten thousand years ago is the basis for today's population, environmental, and energy problems. He discusses the elements of food production, demography, the development of settlements, environmental degradation, technical innovations, changes in social and political organization, and various aspects of intergroup interaction.

Steele, F., and Bourne, Arthur, eds. THE MAN/FOOD EQUATION. London: Academic Press, 1975. xv, 289 p.

The volume comprises the proceedings of a symposium held at the Royal Institution, London, September 1973. The theme is food and population. Papers of the first session focus on food resources. In the second session, the natural and economic constraints to increasing food supplies are discussed. Papers of the third session deal with alternative sources of food, such as protein and various wastes. In the fourth session, several health problems are considered: nutrition requirements, food additives and hyperkinesis, protein myth, and diseases related to fiber-depleted diets.

U.S. Department of Agriculture. Economic Research Service. THE WORLD FOOD SITUATION AND PROSPECTS FOR 1985. Foreign Agricultural Economic Report, no. 98. Washington, D.C.: 1974. ix, 90 p. Paperbound.

The authors of this economic report examine recent developments and the short-term trends in food production, consumption, trade, and stocks; trends in food prices and price policy; projected world food supply and demand; world food security and grain stocks; nutrition; food aid; factors affecting the supply of food; factors affecting the demand for food; production diversity among developing countries; and the resolutions adopted by the World Food Conference of the Food and Agricultural Organization in 1974.

G. POPULATION

Borgstrom, Georg. THE FOOD AND PEOPLE DILEMMA. North Scituate, Mass.: Duxbury Press, 1973. xiv, 140 p. Paperbound. Tables.

> Borgstrom examines the problems arising from the disparities between food production and population and between food consumption among the developed and the undeveloped nations. He brings out the fact that when domesticated animals are converted to human equivalents, the population to be fed is far greater than is usually considered in studies on food and population. He argues that more efficient use of wastes and environmental controls must be included in strategies for providing adequate diets for all people.

Brown, Lester Russell. IN THE HUMAN INTEREST: A STRATEGY TO STABILIZE WORLD POPULATION. New York: W.W. Norton and Co., 1974. 190 p.

> It is Brown's concept that a workable world order can only be achieved when the interdependence of peoples, nations, and ecosystem is taken into account. Within this framework, he considers such topics as population growth, affluence, economic growth, food resources, environmental perturbations, natural resources, and social conditions. Finally, he discusses problems of population policy and concludes that the population must be stabilized.

Feinberg, Gerald. CONSEQUENCES OF GROWTH: THE PROSPECTS FOR A LIMITLESS FUTURE. Tree of Life Series. Continuum Book. New York: Seabury Press, 1977. xx, 157 p. References.

> Feinberg envisions the possibilities of major changes in man and society through the application of science and technology. He discusses social implications of space colonization, control of aging, a long-term future materials policy, post-modern science, long-range goals and environmental problems, and the limitation of human aspirations.

Fraser, Dean. THE PEOPLE PROBLEM: WHAT YOU SHOULD KNOW ABOUT GROWING POPULATION AND VANISHING RESOURCES. Bloomington: Indiana University Press, 1971. 248 p. Bibliog.

> This book deals with the worldwide problem of exponential expansion of population. It considers the factors which classically limit population growth (space, food, water, mineral resources and energy, pollution, and competitors or predators), and how effective they are for human beings. The last section discusses the possibility of regulating the birth rate and hence controlling population at the expense of the unborn.

International Union for the Scientific Study of Population. INTERNATIONAL

POPULATION CONFERENCE, MEXICO 1977. Vol. 1. Liege, Belgium: 1977. xxi, 522 p. Paperbound.

This volume contains invited papers presented at the Conference in Mexico, 8-13 August 1977. The general topics are (1) fertility (natural fertility, analyses of world fertility survey data, value and cost of children to parents, effect of child mortality on fertility, and mathematical models of conception and birth); (2) nuptiality and family (new developments in the analysis of nuptiality and family formation and dissolution, and methods in measuring the family life cycle); and (3) mortality (influence of nutrition on mortality, and effects of development on mortality differentials).

_____. INTERNATIONAL POPULATION CONFERENCE, MEXICO 1977. Vol. 2. Liege, Belgium: 1977. xi, 527 p. Paperbound.

This volume contains invited papers presented at the conference in Mexico, 8-13 August 1977. The general topics are: (1) population and economics (population growth and agrarian change, household models of economic-demographic decision making, and the role of demographic variables in the formulation of development policies and plans); (2) migration and urbanization (demographic aspects of human settlements, the demography of metropolitan growth and planning, and international migration and national population policies); (3) population policies (conditioning factors of the success or failure of explicit population policies, formulation and implementation of the world population plan of action by region, and relationship between changes in the economic, social and political structures of society and population change).

_____. INTERNATIONAL POPULATION CONFERENCE, MEXICO 1977. Vol. 3. Liege, Belgium: 1977. xi, 516 p. Paperbound.

This volume contains invited papers presented at the conference in Mexico, 8-13 August 1977. The general topics are: (1) population growth (self-regulation mechanisms of traditional populations before the demographic revolution, socio-demographic conditions and implications of a stationary or declining population, and food supply and its demographic implications); (2) family planning and abortion (family planning programs and fertility changes, and demographic aspects of abortion); (3) data and methods of analysis (data collection and demographic analysis, population genetics, and woman's status).

McKeown, Thomas. THE MODERN RISE OF POPULATION. New York: Academic Press, 1976. 168 p.

The "modern rise" of the human population began in the eighteenth century. The European evidence examined suggested that this upward swing was caused primarily by a reduction in mortality from infectious diseases, diseases which probably began to afflict man ten thousand years ago at the time of the agricultural revolution. The birth rate did not begin to decline until the nineteenth century. A review of the several possible causes for this decrement of mortality--changes in infective organisms or resistance of human hosts; immunization, chemotherapy, and medical care; exposure to infection; nutritional state; and noninfective conditions--suggests that the primary causes were improved nutriture through increased agricultural productivity and better environmental sanitation. Only recently have medical procedures had significant impacts on mortality.

National Academy of Sciences. National Research Council. Office of the Foreign Secretary. IN SEARCH OF POPULATION POLICY: VIEWS FROM THE DEVELOPING WORLD. Washington, D.C.: 1974. ix, 108 p. Paperbound.

Prepared for the Office of Population, Bureau for Population and Humanitarian Assistance, Agency for International Development, this report covers five regional seminars held in 1973, with over one hundred individuals from thirty-seven countries participating. The areas covered include: South Asia, Middle East, Latin America, Africa, and Southeast Asia. The seminar reports are followed by the steering committee's summary and reflections.

Singer, S. Fred, ed. IS THERE AN OPTIMUM LEVEL OF POPULATION? New York: McGraw-Hill Book Co., 1971. xiv, 426 p. Appendixes.

Published under the auspices of the Population Council, this book is the outgrowth of a symposium held in Boston in December 1969 as a part of an annual meeting of the American Association for the Advancement of Science. It includes twenty-eight papers by various authors, organized into three parts to address the question of optimum population considering (1) natural resources and environmental factors; (2) education, health, and welfare services; and (3) life-styles and human values. The emphasis throughout is on the quality of life, with suggestions as to the strategy to be adopted by all nations, rich and poor, in order to face the population problem.

Uedo, Masao. POPULATION PROBLEMS IN JAPAN: CHANGING JAPAN. Tokyo: International Society for Educational Information, 1975. 112 p. Paperbound. Illus.; Tables; Graphs; Maps.

Uedo discusses changes which have occurred in the numbers and distribution of people in Japan since the late nineteenth century. In particular, he considers population trends, changes in population distribution, prospects for population change, population problems, measures for population control, and comparisons between world population and Japan.

Section VI

COMMUNITY HEALTH
(DEVELOPED AND DEVELOPING COUNTRIES)

Though we have not come across a concise definition of community health by Dr. Sargent, he chose Ralph Audy and Frederick Dunn to write the chapter on the subject in his volume. It seems likely, then, that the concepts presented in section VI are closely related to those of Drs. Audy and Dunn as quoted in the following paragraphs.

> The term community health is generally used somewhat narrowly to mean 'health in the community'. In practice this really means 'disease and disorder in the community', since health is commonly assessed by presence or absence of disease or disability.

> We suggest that community health can also mean health of the community itself, taken as an organized system of people interacting with each other, with the biotic and abiotic environment, and with the culture, including political, economic, religious, and other systems by which that community tries to govern itself. Community or societal health (or ill health) . . . is influenced by disorders of whole groups, communities or societies. This conception is akin to that of Ryle[1], one of the pironee physicians who drew attention to the pathology of society. He regarded society as a system within which social processes can evoke diseases. In fact the term 'social pathology' dates back to the turn of the century, but the sociologists of that time merely used it as a label for those behaviors by individuals that would be labelled 'bad' by social reformers. . . . Throughout life the individual is protected by 'cocoons', which may succeed each other (as when the uterine cocoon is replaced by an equally essential maternal cocoon in the period of extrauterine gestation) or enclose each other (as a family-cocoon is enclosed by the cultural cocoon). However, while the primary purpose of a cocoon is to be protective, it may give rise to insults to the individual, one of the most common examples being stresses within the family.

---

1. J.A. Ryle, CHANGING DISCIPLINES (London: Oxford University Press, 1948).

Attempted adaptation to a new social environment with unfamiliar cues for behavior and without accustomed warmth of communion, whether this be on transfer to a foreign assignment, migrating from country to city, or entering a big college from a little school, may lead to a lowering of social health called 'culture shock'. This in turn lowers physiological health. Social health reflects the efficiency (not necessarily comfort) with which the psyche fits into the group, society, or culture--cocoons to which the individual may not be preadapted by training. However, the very security that comes with familiarity may permit nonconformity. Some socially approved behavior is psychopathological. He who perceives this must rebel or, however reluctantly, conform. If one's own cultural cocoon changes rapdily enough, its demands for speedy adaptation resemble transfer to an alien environment. The resulting form of culture shock is one element in the 'generation gaps'. The demand for rapid change is an insult that will particularly affect the socioculturally rigid members of society, but it is usually these same people who are powerful enough to resist rapid changes. Nevertheless, since the change is likely to accelerate, most people are likely to become involved. This is what Toffler[2] calls 'future shock' already with us.[3]

A. CHANGING PATTERNS OF ILLNESS AND DEATH

American Medical Association. Committee on Public Hygiene. THE FIRST AMERICAN MEDICAL ASSOCIATION REPORTS ON PUBLIC HEALTH IN AMERICAN CITIES. New York: Arno Press, 1977.

This volume contains a reprint of a report from the Transaction of American Medical Association, volume 2, 1849. This report was also published under the title FIRST REPORT OF THE COMMITTEE ON PUBLIC HYGIENE OF AMERICAN MEDICAL ASSOCIATION, by T.K. and P.G. Collings, Philadelphia, 1849. Contained in the volume are separate reports on the sanitary conditions of Concord, New Hampshire; Portland, Maine; New York City; Philadelphia; Massachusetts, particularly Boston and Lowell; Baltimore; Charleston, South Carolina; New Orleans; Louisville; and Cincinnati. See especially pages 431-634.

American Medical Association. Congress on Environmental Health. HUMAN HABITAT AND HEALTH. DHEW Publication, no. (HSM) 73-1005. Bureau of

---

2. A. Toffler, FUTURE SHOCK (New York: Random House, 1970).

3. J. Ralph Audy, and Frederick L. Dunn, "Community Health," in HUMAN ECOLOGY by Frederick Sargent, II (Amsterdam: North Holland Publishing Co., 1974), pp. 345-46.

Community Environmental Management. Health Services and Mental Health Administration. U.S. Department of Health, Education, and Welfare, Washington, D.C.: Government Printing Office, 1973. iv, 211 p. Paperbound.

This volume represents the proceedings of a Congreess held 24-25 April 1972 in Los Angeles. The papers presented were (1) "The Human Habitat: From Inoptimum to Optimum?: F. Sargent II; (2) "The Future of the Urban Habitat," J. Friedman; (3) "Urbanization--Social and Psychological Consequences," E. M. Gruenberg; (4) "Health Consequences of Population Density and Crowding," J. Cassel; (5) "The Environment We See--A Photographic Presentation," H.H. Swinburne; (6) "Potentialities of Metropolitan Planning for Human Needs," H.L. Blum; (7) "The City in 1980--Friend or Foe?" D.H. Lutes; and (8) "Design for Optimal Living," I.L. McHarg. Comments by invited reactors are included.

American Medical Association. Department of Environmental Health. POPULATION AND ENVIRONMENTAL HEALTH. Proceedings of 2d A.M.A. Congress on Environmental Health Problems. Chicago: 1965. 118 p. Paperbound.

The participants of this congress, held in Chicago 26-27 April 1965, sought to evaluate the interrelationships betwen changing environmental conditions and changing disease patterns and to define the role of the physician in the necessarily interdisciplinary approach to the complex environmental problems. The specific topics include changing environmental influences, changing disease patterns, control and prevention of environmentally related disease, and urban planning for healthful living.

Bain, Sheila M., and Herbertson, M., eds. "Aspects of Medical Geography." JOURNAL OF BIOSOCIAL SCIENCE 6 (April 1974): 183-292. Paperbound.

Published as Symposium Report, no. 5, this issue contains proceedings of a symposium held 23 August 1973 at the Canterbury meeting of the British Association for the Advancement of Science. The principal papers were: "Medical Geography: A Theory of Medicine," J.M. May; "A Geographer's Approach in the Epidemiology of Psychiatric Disorder," S.M. Bain; "Environmental Lead: A Survey of Its Possible Physiological Significance," H.V. Warren; "Air Transport and Disease," L.J. Bruce-Chwatt; "Geography and the Organization of Medical Services," W.B. Fisher; "Changes in the State of Infectious Diseases in South and South-East Asia," H.J. Jusatz; and "Fallacies in Comparing International Disease Trends," D.A. Robinson, A.J. Radford, and N.R.E. Fendall.

Basch, Paul F. INTERNATIONAL HEALTH. New York: Oxford Press, 1978. vii, 380 p. Tables; Figures; References.

Basch examines the health of mankind and provides a general discussion of selected topics of current interest. His first two chapters

contain background information on man, environment, diseases,
and sociocultural evolution. The major topics include development, culture, sources of information on health, health policy,
health care systems, and organizations dealing with community
health.

Bruhn, John G., and Wolf, Stewart George. THE ROSETO STORY: AN
ANATOMY OF HEALTH. Norman: University of Oklahoma Press, 1979. xvi,
158 p. 158 p.

Bruhn and Wolf report the results of continuing health surveys begun in 1961 among the residents of three urban communities in
eastern Pennsylvania: Roseto, Bangor, and Nazareth. They sought
an answer to the question, why so few deaths from myocardial infarction among the Italian residents of Roseto? They examined
the histories of the three communities, made detailed clinical ex-
aminations, and conducted dietary and sociological interviews.
Residents of the three communities exhibited equally all the usual
clinical and dietary risks to coronary heart disease. The striking
finding was a strong sense of social cohesion among the people of
Roseto. Bruhn and Wolf concluded that this factor probably protected against coronary heart disease. Supporting the conclusion
was the fact that as traditional family culture was disrupted by
the adoption of an American life-style by young people, the incidence of myocardial infarction increased.

Carter, Cedric O., and Peel, John, eds. EQUALITIES AND INEQUALITIES
IN HEALTH. London: Academic Press, 1976. x, 170 p.

In the proceedings of the twelfth Annual Symposium of the Eugenics
Society held in London, September 1975, the contributions were
"The Global Incidence of Genetic Illness," C.O. Carter; "Sex
Differences in Disease and Mortality," D.F. Roberts; "Single Factor
Predisposition to Disease," J.H. Edwards; "The Geography of Dis-
ease," G. Melvyn Howe; "The Assessment of Risks to Health at Work,"
W.R. Lee; "The Galton Lecture, 1975: Inequality, Is It Necessary?"
John Brotherston; "How Doctors Generate Disease," Donald Gould;
"Social Class and Health Inequalities," Mildred Blaxter; "Urban and
Suburban Differentials," R.J. Donaldson; "Comparisons in Care of
the Disabled," D.M. Prinsley; "Problems and Solutions in De-
veloping Countries," D.M. Potts; and "Health as Aid: The Need
for Medical Advisors," P.J. Huntingford.

Crosby, Alfred W., Jr. THE COLUMBIAN EXCHANGE; BIOLOGICAL AND
CULTURAL CONSEQUENCES OF 1492. Westport, Conn.: Greenwood Press,
1972. xv, 268 p.

The discovery and subsequent colonization of the New World by
peoples from the Old World had profound biological, demographic,
and cultural impacts throughout the world. Epidemic diseases
brought by the colonists played a significant part in the subjugation

of the American Indian. In fact, the demographic impact was sufficiently great to provoke the slave trade to provide manpower. Crosby also discusses epidemic syphilis in Europe in the sixteenth century. More intriguing, however, is his hypothesis that the introduction and adoption of food plants from the New World, particularly maize, potato, bean, and manioc, supported a rapid increase in the population of the world commencing about 1600. The history of this exchange of cultigens is traced insofar as the fragmentary sources allow documentation and the emergent story is most suggestive.

Cruikshank, Robert; Standard, Kenneth L.; and Russell, Hugh B.L., eds. EPIDEMIOLOGY AND COMMUNITY HEALTH IN WARM CLIMATE COUNTRIES. Edinburgh: Churchill Livingstone, 1976. xv, 492 p.

This work, which contains thirty-nine chapters written by twenty-eight contributors, aims to refocus attention on the need for an emphasis on preventive and community medicine in warm climate countries in medical education and practice. The first nineteen chapters are devoted to the epidemiology and control of communicable diseases common to warm climates. Chapters 20-27 deal with noninfectious diseases (malaria, schistosomiasis, filariasis, onchoceriaciasis, amebiasis, trypanosomiasis, leishmaniasis, and nematode infections). Chapters 28-33 examine the problems of malnutrition, cardiovascular disease, cancer of uterine cervix and breast, sickle cell hemoglobinopathies, mental retardation, and accident. A final group (chapters 34-39) deals with health interventions such as health planning and administration, maternal and child health, family planning, hygiene of food and water, factors contributing to malnutrition and gastroenteritis, and training health auxiliaries.

Dickey, Lawrence D., ed. CLINICAL ECOLOGY. Springfield, Ill.: Charles C Thomas, 1976. xvi, 807 p. Appendixes.

This book presents the fundamental concepts and techniques of clinical ecology, a branch of medicine concerned with illnesses provoked by environmental insults. The text, prepared by a large group of authors is arranged into seven sections: basic concepts of clinical ecology; basic therapeutic and diagnostic concepts and techniques; manifestations and levels of reaction; environmental hazards of excitants in air, water, food, drugs, and habitat; diagnostic concepts and techniques; therapeutic concepts and techniques; and ecological orientation as applied to various fields of medical practice. Appendix 1 summarizes the history of the Society of Clinical Ecology and three other appendixes give detailed forms, questionnaires, and directions useful in clinical ecology.

Dubos, Rene. MAN ADAPTING. New Haven: Yale University Press, 1971. xxii, 527 p. Paperbound.

Man's successes and failures in coping with environmental challenges can be measured in terms of health and disease. Dubos examines man's nature, his physical and biological world, and his food; nutrition and infection; the evolution of microbial disease; environmental pollution; changing patterns of disease; human adaptability; the population problem; and the tasks of disease control and environmental management.

_____. MIRAGE OF HEALTH; UTOPIAS, PROGRESS, AND BIOLOGICAL CHANGE. Reprint from World Perspective Series, vol. 22. New York: Harper Bros., 1959. Reprint. Garden City, N.Y.: Anchor Books and Doubleday and Co., 1961. 235 p. Paperbound.

Dubos discusses many facets of the interplay between man and his environment: biological and social adaptation, coexistence with microbial organisms, environmental factors in disease, curative medicine, social patterns of health and disease, effects of disease on populations and civilization, and utopian ideas about man's health and disease.

Eckholm, Erik P. THE PICTURE OF HEALTH; ENVIRONMENTAL SOURCES OF DISEASE. New York: W.W. Norton and Co., 1977. 256 p.

Eckholm discusses the influence of environment on human health. The topics include malnutrition (both under and overnutrition), cancer, smoking, air pollution, occupational hazards, schistosomiasis, and family planning. Improvement in health would follow from a better standard of living, reduction in environmental pollution, and change in human behavior.

Fisher, K.D., and Nixon, A.V., eds. THE SCIENCE OF LIFE; CONTRIBUTIONS OF BIOLOGY TO HUMAN WELFARE. Federation of American Societies of Experimental Biology Monograph, vol. 1. New York: Pleunum Press, 1972. xxiv, 358 p. Paperbound ed., 1977.

The six chapters, originally published in FEDERATION PROCEEDINGS 31, no. 6, Pt. 2, November-December 1972, were reports of panels which reviewed some of the recent findings in biology and indicated how they had contributed to improving human welfare. The several panels included basic biomedicine, clinical medicine, dental science, food, population biology, environmental hazards, marine sciences, and natural resources.

HEALTH AND THE ENVIRONMENT. Edited by John Lenihan and William W. Fletcher. Environment and Man Series, vol. 3. New York: Academic Press, 1976. x, 166 p.

The authors examine the effects of a variety of environmental factors on human health: G.M. Howe, "Environmental Factors in Disease"; R. Murray, "Health and the Working Environment"; P.C.C. Gornham, "Arthropods and Disease"; and C.S. Muir,

"Evidence from Epidemiology"; M. Gardner, "Soft Water and Heart Disease"; and T.S. Wilson, "Clearing the Air." Even though the evidence that much of man's current illness has an environmental origin, e.g., cases showing the relations between heart disease and soft water, there is "an abundance of answers and a dearth of good questions."

Henry, James Paget, and Stephens, Patricia M. STRESS, HEALTH, AND THE SOCIAL ENVIRONMENT: A SOCIOBIOLOGIC APPROACH TO MEDICINE. Topics in Environmental Physiology and Medicine. New York: Springer-Verlag, 1977. xii, 282 p. Glossary; References; Indexes.

Henry and Stephens develop the theme that disease can result from the disruption of protective affiliative social networks. They discuss the historical development of the theoretical concept, basic patterns of social interaction, inherited behavioral patterns as social assets, early experience and programming behavior, monitoring behavioral disturbances in experimental systems, neocortex and limbic system in social interaction, neuroendocrine responses to social interaction, functional and structural changes in response to psychosocial stimulation, production of disease in animals by psychosocial stimulation, pathophysiologic consequences of human social disturbance, and prevention and treatment of detrimental effects of psychosocial environment.

Hinkle, Lawrence E., Jr., and Loring, William C., eds. THE EFFECT OF THE MAN-MADE ENVIRONMENT ON HEALTH AND BEHAVIOR. DHEW Publication, no. (CDC) 77-8318. Atlanta: Center for Disease Control, Public Health Service, U.S. Department of Health, Education, and Welfare, 1977. xlvi, 315 p. Paperbound.

This volume is the product of several years of a collaborative effort by an interdisciplinary group to examine the impact of the residential environment on human health and behavior. The several chapters critically review the literature and suggest designs for productive research. Particular attention is given to measuring the environment, the organism, and the outcomes of the interaction between the environment and the organism in terms of health and behavior.

Howe, G. Melvyn, ed. A GEOGRAPHY OF HUMAN DISEASES. London: Academic Press, 1977. xxviii, 621 p. Glossary; References.

In this multiauthored volume, the editor discusses environmental influences on and hazards to health, and he and his colleagues describe what is known about the geography of schistosomiasis, filariasis, malaria, amoebiasis, cholera, diarrheal diseases, tuberculosis and leprosy, diphtheria, venereal diseases, measles, smallpox, yellow fever, dengue and dengue hemorrhagic fever, bronchitis, influenza, industrial lung disease, illnesses associated with drug abuse, cardiovascular disease, mental disorders and mental subnormality, malignant neoplasms, and deficiency diseases.

Howe, G. Melvyn, and Loraine, John A., eds. ENVIRONMENTAL MEDICINE. London: William Heinemann Medical Books, 1973. xii, 271 p.

This book, consisting of twenty chapters by contributors from various disciplines, is intended to show how environmental conditions are or may be causatively related to man's health or diseases. It begins with introductory chapters on certain selected natural and man-made aspects of the environment, followed by contributions showing, for a selection of diseases, the importance of environmental hazards in both developed and developing countries. A chapter on the geography of genes is included along with chapters more concerned with external environmental conditions and with disease relationships. A final chapter gives information useful to the researcher, on conventional and computerized methods for the retrieval of published materials relevant to the field of environmental medicine.

Hunter, John Melton, ed. THE GEOGRAPHY OF HEALTH AND DISEASE. Studies in Geography, no. 6, Department of Geography. Chapel Hill: University of North Carolina, 1974. 193 p. Paperbound.

The papers presented at the First Carolina Geographical Symposium held in 1974 included: "The Challenge of Medical Geography," J.M. Hunter; "The Geography of Nutrition," J.M. May; "The Geography of Vectored Diseases," C.G. Knight; "The Geography of Non-Vectored Infectious Diseases," J.C. Girt; "The Geography of Chronic Diseases," M.A. Murray; "The Geography of Psychosocial Stress," J.M. Hunter and S.D. Brunn; and "The Geography of Health Care," G.F. Pyle. Comments are summarized.

Learmonth, Andrew. PATTERNS OF DISEASE AND HUNGER. Newton Abbot and London: David and Charles, 1978. 256 p. Bibliog.; Figures.

The principal topics are infectious disease in the developed and underdeveloped world, cancer and bronchitis, and the geography of medical care. One chapter is devoted to case studies.

Levi, Lennart, ed. SOCIETY, STRESS, AND DISEASE. Vol. 1: THE PSYCHOSOCIAL ENVIRONMENT AND PSYCHOSOMATIC DISEASES. London: Oxford University Press, 1971. xvi, 485 p. Bibliog.

This volume represents the proceedings of an Interdisciplinary Symposium held in Stockholm in April 1970 sponsored by the University of Uppsala and the World Health Organization. Six general topics were addressed: (1) definition of problems and objectives, and review of methods; (2) review of potentially pathogenic psychosocial stressors, and mechanisms for their actions in today's society; (3) review of experimental, clinical and epidemiological evidence concerning psychiatric and psychosomatic diseases provoked by psychosocial stressors; (4) review of experimental, clinical and epidemiological evidence concerning specific diseases provoked by psychosocial stressors; (5) possible ways of modifying or preventing psychiatric and psychosomatic diseases through social actions; and (6) objectives and methodology for future research.

_____. SOCIETY, STRESS, AND DISEASE. Vol. 2: CHILDHOOD AND ADOLESCENCE. London: Oxford University Press, 1975. xxii, 551 p. Bibliog.

This volume contains the updated and expanded proceedings of an International Interdisciplinary Symposium held in Stockholm, June and July 1971, sponsored by University of Uppsala and the World Health Organization. The principal topics were: (1) the well-adapted child-definitions, objectives, methodological considerations; (2) potentially pathogenic psychosocial stressors, intervening variables, mechanisms and precursors, in childhood and adolescence; (3) psychiatric and psychosocial disease processes provoked by psychosocial stressors; (4) specific diseases provoked by psychosocial stressors; and (5) prevention, primary, secondary; and future research.

_____. SOCIETY, STRESS, AND DISEASE. Vol. 3: THE PRODUCTIVE AND REPRODUCTIVE AGE--MALE/FEMALE ROLES AND RELATIONSHIPS. Oxford: Oxford University Press, 1978. xvi, 295 p.

This volume contains the proceedings of the Third Interdisciplinary Symposium on Society, Stress, and Disease sponsored jointly by the World Health Organization and the University of Uppsala. There were four sessions: (1) the concept of normality: male-female roles and relationships; (2) potentially pathogenic psychosocial stimuli originating from male-female roles and relationships; (3) psychiatric and psychosomatic diseases possibly associated with male-female roles and relationships; and (4) the prevention (primary and secondary) of stress originating from male-female relationships.

Levi, Lennart, and Anderson, Lars. PSYCHOSOCIAL STRESS: POPULATION, ENVIRONMENT AND QUALITY OF LIFE. New York: Spectrum Publications, 1975. 142 p. Bibliog.; Glossary.

A limited version of this volume was published by the Royal Swedish Ministry of Foreign Affairs as a contribution to the UN World Population Conference held in 1974. Levi and Anderson discuss the psychosocial stresses on individuals and societies generated by population pressures and processes such as urbanization, ruralization, and migration. They consider high risk groups, complex interacting environmental variables, outcomes in terms of quality of life, and monitoring and research for an integrated world plan of action.

Levy, Robert I.; Dennis, Barbara H.; Rifkind, Basil M.; and Ernst, Nancy, eds. NUTRITION, LIPIDS, AND CORONARY HEART DISEASE: A GLOBAL VIEW. Nutrition in Health and Disease, vol. 1. New York: Raven Press, 1979. x, 566 p. Bibliog.

The contributing authors present a comprehensive review of the
relation between diet and coronary heart disease. The principal
topics are: (1) "Epidemiology of Diet, Lipids, and Heart Disease";
(2) "Role of Dietary Components in Lipid Metabolism"; (3) "Use
of Diet in Preserving Health and Treating Disease"; (4) "Methods
for Changing Dietary Habits"; (5) "The Changing Food Supply and
Consumption Patterns"; and (6) "Nutrition in Relation to Other
Aspects of Cardiovascular Disease."

McGlashan, N.D., ed. MEDICAL GEOGRAPHY: TECHNIQUES AND FIELD
STUDIES. London: Methune and Co., 1972. xii, 336 p. Illus.; Bibliog.

McGlashan has brought together original articles and a few previously published papers which provide a survey of the ways to
analyze the geographical patterns of disease and activities associated with health planning and care. There are five chapters
dealing with the nature of medical geography and cartographic
applications. Four illustrate use of medical geography in public
health administration. Five focus on spatial definition, four on
associative occurrences, and four on disease diffusion.

McKeown, Thomas. THE ROLE OF MEDICINE: DREAM, MIRAGE, OR NEMESIS?
Rock Carling Fellowship 1976. London: Nuffield Provincial Hospitals Trust,
1976. xv, 180 p.

McKeown presents a critical assessment of medicine. It is his
view that medical science and services, because they assume that
the body is a machine to be protected from disease by internal
intervention, have been misdirected. He demonstrates that the
determinants of health are primarily external influences such as
nutrition and hygiene and personal behavior. In contrast, the
impact of iatrotechnology (immunization and therapy) has been
relatively small. He argues that in the future medicine will have
to become increasingly involved in the prevention of disease by
personal and nonpersonal measures and care of the sick who are
not now thought to require active intervention.

McLaren, Donald S., ed. NUTRITION IN THE COMMUNITY. New York:
John Wiley and Sons, 1976. xxv, 393 p.

The book is designed for students of public health and medicine.
The topics deal with description of communities and assessment of
their nutriture, epidemiology of over and undernutrition, intervention strategies to combat malnutrition and the role of various
agencies, private, governmental, and academic, in programs of
community nutrition.

McNeill, William H. PLAGUES AND PEOPLES. Garden City, N.Y.: Anchor
Press and Doubleday, 1976. 369 p.

McNeill traces the impact of infectious disease on the course of

human history from ancient times (where the record is sketchy and
the interpretation necessarily speculative) down to modern times
(where the record is definitive). The infectious diseases are generally the consequences of man's disturbances of the ecological
balance through the food quest, migration, transportation, urbanization, and warfare. The outcomes are constantly changing
patterns of disease among various peoples and perturbations in their
demography.

May, Jacques M. THE ECOLOGY OF HUMAN DISEASE. Studies in Medical
Geography, vol. 1. New York: MD Publications, 1958. xxiv, 327 p. Bibliog.

The first in a series of books on the relationship between disease
and the geographical environment, intended for use by physicians,
geographers, and anthropologists, this volume expounds the author's
concept of the nature and ecology of disease; stimuli and responses;
the terrain; races or populations; the changing map of diseases;
and cultural factors. Next it discusses the ecology of the principal infectious, nutritional, and behavioral diseases, with a chapter
devoted to each: cholera, brucellosis, poliomyelitis, tuberculosis,
leprosy, bacillary dysentery, salmonelloses, amebiasis, yaws, certain two-factor nematode infections, scarlet fever, measles, and
trachoma.

_____. THE ECOLOGY OF MALNUTRITION IN CENTRAL AND SOUTH-
EASTERN EUROPE: AUSTRIA, HUNGARY, RUMANIA, BULGARIA, CZECHO-
SLOVAKIA. Studies in Medical Geography, vol. 6. New York: Hafner
Publishing Co., 1966. xv, 290 p. Maps; Tables; Bibliog.

This volume continues the inquiry into the ecological problems involved in man's struggle to feed himself. It analyzes the geographical aspects of food resources in the five countries of South
Central Europe linked by the Danube River.

_____. THE ECOLOGY OF MALNUTRITION IN FIVE COUNTRIES OF EASTERN
AND CENTRAL EUROPE: EAST GERMANY, POLAND, YUGOSLAVIA, AL-
BANIA, GREECE. Studies in Medical Geography, vol. 4. New York: Hafner
Publishing Co., 1963. xvii, 292 p. Maps; Tables; References.

Another in the series focusing on dietary adequacy of whole peoples
associated with specific parts of the earth, this study analyzes the
food geography of east-central Europe, with a total population of
over seventy-five million.

_____. THE ECOLOGY OF MALNUTRITION IN MIDDLE AFRICA: GHANA,
NIGERIA, REPUBLIC OF THE CONGO, RWANDA, BURUNDI, AND THE
FORMER FRENCH EQUATORIAL AFRICA. Studies in Medical Geography, vol.
5. New York: Hafner Publishing Co., 1965. xvi, 255 p. Maps; Tables;
Bibliog.

This volume is concerned with the food geography of Middle Africa,
involving primitive tropical agriculture and limited livestock economy.

_____. THE ECOLOGY OF MALNUTRITION IN NORTHERN AFRICA: LIBYA, TUNISIA, ALGERIA, MOROCCO, SPANISH SAHARA, AND IFNI, MAURITANIA. Studies in Medical Geography, vol. 7. New York: Hafner Publishing Co., 1967. xv, 275 p. Tables; Maps; Diagrams; Bibliog.

The five countries and two territories studied in this book have similar geography and patterns of history, religion, and culture, and all suffer from a scarcity of water resources. Also all face the problems of conflict between the modern Western world and the old-world social structure involving four-fifths of their population.

_____. THE ECOLOGY OF MALNUTRITION IN THE FRENCH SPEAKING COUNTRIES OF WEST AFRICA AND MADAGASCAR: SENEGAL, GUINEA, IVORY COAST, TOGO, DAHOMEY, CAMEROON, NIGER, MALI, UPPER VOLTA AND MADAGASCAR. Studies in Medical Geography, vol. 8. New York: Hafner Publishing Co., 1968. xiii, 433 p. Tables; Maps; Bibliog.

The unifying factors among these ten countries are their common culture, reflecting their former status as French colonies and their common African ethnic base. They also have common basic problems, including monostaple diets, lack of skilled personnel, financing and storing of crops, and poor agricultural technology. This study emphasizes the role of governments in providing adequate diets for people most of whom can do little for themselves because of poverty, ignorance, poor health, and superstitious tradition.

_____, ed. STUDIES IN DISEASE ECOLOGY. Studies in Medical Geography, vol. 2. New York: Hafner Publishing Co., 1961. xx, 613 p. Bibliog.

The second in a series of fourteen treatises based on study of the ecological approach to transmissible, degenerative, and behavioral disease, the present volume contains chapters on the ecology of thirteen diseases, as follows, with each subject followed by the name of the contributing author: smallpox (Z. Deutschmann); dengue (Charles L. Wisseman, Jr., and Benjamin H. Sweet); filariasis (John F. Kessel); onchocerciasis (Thomas A. Burch); tularemia (Anna C. Gelman); relapsing fevers (Anna C. Gelman); hydatidosis (Thomas W.M. Cameron and G.A. Webster); malaria (Jacques M. May); African trypanosomiasis (Jacques M. May); schistosomiasis (Emile A. Malek); leishmaniasis (Abdel-Rahim Omran); scrub typhus (J. Ralph Audy); plague (R. Pollitzer and Karl F. Meyer).

May, Jacques M., and McLellan, Donna L. THE ECOLOGY OF MALNUTRITION IN EASTERN AFRICA AND FOUR COUNTRIES OF WESTERN AFRICA: EQUATORIAL GUINEA, THE GAMBIA, LIBERIA, SIERRA LEONE, MALAWI, RHODESIA, ZAMBIA, KENYA, TANZANIA, UGANDA, ETHIOPIA, THE FRENCH TERRITORY OF THE AFARS AND ISSAS, THE SOMALI REPUBLIC AND SUDAN. Studies in Medical Geography, vol. 9. New York: Hafner Publishing Co., 1970. xii, 675 p. Maps; Tables; Bibliog.

The fourteen countries studied form a heterogeneous group as to
habitat and culture, yet all are rapidly changing as they develop
from a subsistence to a money economy. None is a true nation,
but is comprised of many tribes, and none is really independent,
being forced to rely on foreign capital and assistance.

_____. THE ECOLOGY OF MALNUTRITION IN EASTERN SOUTH AMERICA.
Studies in Medical Geography, vol. 13. New York: Hafner Publishing Co.,
1974. x, 558 p. Bibliog.

This volume covers Venezuela, Guyana, Surinam and the Netherlands Antilles, French Guiana, Brazil, Uruguay, Paraguay, and
Argentina. It supplies background information for each country;
discusses food resources and their adequacy, diets, and nutritional
disease patterns; and lists conclusions.

_____. THE ECOLOGY OF MALNUTRITION IN MEXICO AND CENTRAL
AMERICA. Studies in Medical Geography, vol. 11. New York: Hafner
Publishing Co., 1972. xiii, 395 p. Maps; Tables; Bibliog.

This volume covers Mexico, Guatemala, British Honduras, El Salvador,
Nicaragua, Costa Rica, and Panama. For each area, background
information is given on physical setting, climate, population, history and government, agricultural policies, and foreign aid. This
is followed by discussion of food resources and their adequacy,
diets, nutritional disease patterns, and conclusions.

_____. THE ECOLOGY OF MALNUTRITION IN SEVEN COUNTRIES OF
SOUTHERN AFRICA AND IN PORTUGUESE GUINEA: THE REPUBLIC OF
SOUTH AFRICA, SOUTH WEST AFRICA (NAMIBIA), BOTSWANA, LESOTHO,
SWAZILAND, MOZAMBIQUE, ANGOLA, PORTUGUESE GUINEA. Studies
in Medical Geography, vol. 10. New York: Hafner Publishing Co., 1971.
xi, 432 p. Maps; Tables; Bibliog.

The problems of these African countries are similar in that they
are all poor, living on a continent with poor soil and inadequate
water resources. Also, they are attempting to move from a subsistence economy to one of productivity and high consumption,
and must deal with the economic facets of the transition, most
importantly with food production and distribution. Based on their
historical backgrounds, the various countries are following different
systems in dealing with their problems, some relying on an African
elite for leadership, others on a European elite, and a third group
on creating a bicultural elite.

_____. THE ECOLOGY OF MALNUTRITION IN THE CARIBBEAN. Studies
in Medical Geography, vol. 12. New York: Hafner Publishing Co., 1973.
viii, 490 p. Maps; Tables; Bibliog.

Covering the Bahamas, Cuba, Jamaica, Haiti, the Dominican

Republic, Puerto Rico, the Lesser Antilles, and Trinidad and Tobago, this volume follows the established practice of giving for each country first background information, then a discussion of food resources and their adequacy, diets, nutritional disease patterns, and finally conclusions.

_____. THE ECOLOGY OF MALNUTRITION IN WESTERN SOUTH AMERICA. Studies in Medical Geography, vol. 14. New York: Hafner Press, 1974. xii, 365 p. Bibliog.

This volume covers Colombia, Ecuador, Peru, Bolivia, and Chile. It supplies background information for each country, then discusses food resources and their adequacy, diets, nutritional disease patterns, and lists conclusions.

May, Jacques M., with the collaboration of Irma S. Jarcho. THE ECOLOGY OF MALNUTRITION IN THE FAR AND NEAR EAST: FOOD RESOURCES, HABITS, AND DEFICIENCIES. Studies in Medical Geography, vol. 3. New York: Hafner Publishing Co., 1961. xv, 688 p. Maps; Figures; Tables.

This report concerns the various factors responsible for deficiency diseases in Asia, each chapter being devoted to one country. These factors include the land and water environment governing food production; purchasing power and means of exchange; and traditions and traits promoting survival. Each chapter includes discussion of the diet types prevailing; the adequacy of food resources; and nutritional disease patterns.

National Research Council. U.S. National Committee for Geochemistry. Subcommittee on the Geochemical Environment in Relation to Health and Disease. GEOCHEMISTRY AND THE ENVIRONMENT. Vol. 1: THE RELATION OF SELECTED TRACE ELEMENTS TO HEALTH AND DISEASE. Washington, D.C.: National Academy of Sciences, 1974. ix, 113 p. Paperbound. References.

At the workshop held at Pacific Grove, California, 7-12 February 1972, the trace elements discussed were fluorine, iodine, chromium, lithium, cadmium, zinc, lead, selenium, tellurium, copper, and molybdenum. In addition to considering evidence of health effects, there were discussions of analytical methods, sampling and sample preparation, and experimental design and epidemiological considerations. The needs and priorities were summarized.

_____. GEOCHEMISTRY AND THE ENVIRONMENT. Vol. 2: THE RELATION OF OTHER SELECTED TRACE ELEMENTS TO HEALTH AND DISEASE. Washington, D.C.: National Academy of Sciences, 1977. xi, 163 p. Paperbound. References.

The other trace elements discussed at the workshop held at Capon Springs, West Virginia, 6-12 May 1973, were beryllium, magnesium, manganese, nickel, silicon, strontium, tin, and vanadium.

There were also discussions of interaction of trace elements, consequences of soil imbalances, disease patterns among southwestern Indians, the Missouri Study, study of geochemistry and health by World Health Organization, problems of cartographic display of patterns, and a National Environmental Specimen Index System.

_____. GEOCHEMISTRY AND THE ENVIRONMENT. Vol. 3: DISTRIBUTION OF TRACE ELEMENTS RELATED TO CERTAIN CANCERS, CARDIOVASCULAR DISEASES, AND UROLITHIASIS. Washington, D.C.: National Academy of Sciences, 1978. xi, 200 p. Paperbound. Appendixes.

This volume reports the third workshop convened by the Subcommittee on the Geochemical Environment in Relation to Health and Disease at Captiva Island, Florida, 6–11 October 1974. There are three parts: (1) trace element pathways to man (e.g., rocks, water, soils, and foods); (2) trace elements and certain diseases, (e.g., gastrointestinal cancer, cardiovascular diseases, and urolithiasis); and (3) data collection, manipulation, display, and analysis. The report contains a summary and recommendations and three appendixes with descriptive comments on (1) Atlas of Cancer Mortality for U.S. Counties: 1950–1969, (2) National Environmental Specimen Bank Survey, and (3) National Center for Health Statistics.

Nestor, Joanne P. TOWARDS AN INTERNATIONAL MALNUTRITION MAP. INP Discussion Papers 76-7. International Nutrition Planning Program. Center for International Studies. Cambridge: MIT, 1976. vii, 86 p. Paperbound. Tables; Graphs; Bibliog.

Detailed data on the nutrition, health, economic and social status and availability of resources for twenty-one nations were assembled and carefully evaluated for accuracy and comparability. The report contains a discussion of these data, country-specific tables, and graphs of the relative status among the nations.

Randolph, Theron G. HUMAN ECOLOGY AND SUSCEPTIBILITY TO THE CHEMICAL ENVIRONMENT. Springfield, Ill.: Charles C Thomas, 1962. vii, 148 p.

Randolph limits human ecology to the study of the effects of the chemical environment on man. Specifically, he focuses on the problems of physical allergy. He examines air pollution, chemical contamination of ingestants, and drugs, cosmetics, and so on. His experience with these etiological agents is drawn from the clinical management of patients with physical allergy.

Sakamoto-Moniyama, Masako. SEASONALITY IN HUMAN MORTALITY: A MEDICO-GEOGRAPHICAL STUDY. Tokyo: University of Tokyo Press, 1977. xx, 181 p. Bibliog.

Sakamoto-Moniyama summarizes twenty years of research on the changing seasonal pattern of human mortality, particularly among

the developed countries. In seven chapters she discusses morbidity, mortality, and environment; the seasonal disease calendar
as a tool of analysis, international comparison of total and infant
deaths; deseasonality of mortality in the United States; comparison
of cerebrovascular mortality by country; time-series analysis of
mortality; and signs of deseasonality in Japanese mortality. Deseasonality is attributed to sociocultural advance, especially heating
and air-conditioning.

Spink, Wesley William. INFECTIOUS DISEASES: PREVENTION AND TREAT-
MENT IN THE NINETEENTH AND TWENTIETH CENTURIES. Minneapolis:
University of Minnesota Press, 1978. xx, 577 p. References; Bibliog.; Indexes.

The history of the prevention and treatment of infectious diseases
is arranged in three sections. In the first, Spink discusses early
concepts of contagion and methods of control; the development of
bacteriology, immunology and virology; and the evolution of public
health. The second part is devoted to twentieth-century developments in chemoprophylaxis and therapy. The third part focuses
on evolution of knowledge about specific infectious diseases; for
example, communicable diseases, respiratory diseases, enteric
diseases, venereal infections, and zoonoses. Appended are Shattuck
Report of Massachusett, 1850, and Constitution of World Health
Organization.

World Health Organization. Working Group on the Role of Geographical
Factors with the Planning of Health Programmes. THE ROLE OF GEOGRAPHIC
FACTORS IN THE PLANNING OF HEALTH PROGRAMMES. Copenhagen:
Regional Office for Europe, WHO, 1975. 15 p. Paperbound. Available from
Regional Office. Diagrams.

In this report, formulated in Heidelberg, 22-25 April 1975, the
members of the working group examine the role of geographical
or location-specific factors in health planning and review the
availability of appropriate information on environmental factors
and measures of health status.

B. HEALTH INDICATORS (HEALTH STATISTICS)

Anderson, K. Lange; Masironi, R.; Rutenfranz, J.; and Seliger, V. HABITUAL
PHYSICAL ACTIVITY AND HEALTH. World Health Organization, Regional
Publications, European Series, no. 6. Copenhagen: Regional Office for Europe,
WHO, 1978. 188 p. Paperbound. Bibliog.; Appendixes.

The authors have prepared a handbook on the assessment of habitual
physical activity and health. The first part contains a brief discussion of physiological principles and summarizes some of the
known relationships between habitual physical activity and age,
sex, ethnicity, occupation, climate and altitude, industrialization,
and health status. The second part describes various methods for

measuring physical activity in individuals and populations. There
are three appendixes: (1) caloric value of foods; (2) energy costs
of specified activities; and (3) examples of activity questionnaires.

Geller, Harvey, and Steele, Gregory. THE 1974 PROBABILITY TABLES OF
DYING IN THE NEXT TEN YEARS FROM SPECIFIC CAUSES. Indianapolis:
Methodist Hospital, 1977. Unpaged. Paperbound.

Geller and Steele have prepared a series of tables which contain
the probability of dying from specific causes for white males and
females and black males and females between ages 5 and 80. The
probabilities are based on 1974 data from National Center of Health
Statistics. These tables were prepared for use in the Health Risk
Appraisal.

Symposium of Measurement of Ill Health. INTERNATIONAL JOURNAL OF
EPIDEMIOLOGY 1 (Winter 1972): 315-68; 2 (Spring 1973): 5-46.

The invited contributions deal with various health status indexes
that can be used to measure the health of communities and evaluate
intervention programs: "The Implications of Health Indicators: A
Comment," by B.S. Hetzel; "A Meaningful Measure of Health for
Epidemiology," S. Fanshel; "Interventions and Outcomes: Notes
on Designing and Implementing an Experiment in Health Care,"
G.L. Maddox; "A Quantitative Approach to the World Health
Organization Definition of Health: Physical, Mental and Social
Well-Being," L. Breslow; "Problems in the Definition of Ill Health,"
G. Lamm; "The Measurement of Hospital Output," R.M. Rosser
and V.C. Watts; "Measurement of Ill Health: A Comment," A.
W. Grogono; "How to Measure Health: A Stochastic Model for
an Index of Health," C.L. Chiang and R.D. Cohen; "Approaches
to Health and Personal Social Services Planning in the National
Health Service and the Place of Health Indices," C. Himatsingani;
"The Use of Outcome Measures in Health Service Planning," J.
D. Pole; and "An Analysis of Variations in Perinatal Mortality
Amongst Local Authorities in England and Wales," J.R. Ashford,
K.L.G. Read, and V.C. Riley.

C. SOCIAL INDICATORS

Andrews, Frank M., and Withey, Stephen B. SOCIAL INDICATORS OF WELL-
BEING; AMERICANS' PERCEPTIONS OF LIFE QUALITY. New York: Plenum
Press, 1976. xxii, 455 p. Appendixes.

Social indicators measure the conditions of society. The indicators
may be subjective, for example, record perceptions, or they may
be objective and derive from diverse statistical information. Andrews
and Withey report a study of more than five thousand Americans.
The principal aims were to conceptualize and then to measure the
perception of well-being. Part 1 is devoted to developing indi-

cators of perceived well-being. In part 2, the perceptions of
well-being of Americans are described. Future applications of
the instrument designed and tested in these studies are discussed
in part 3.

Galnoor, Itzhak, ed. "Social Information for Developing Countries." ANNALS
OF THE AMERICAN ACADEMY OF POLITICAL AND SOCIAL SCIENCE 393
(January 1971): 1-121.

The authors of this collection of nine articles address the meaning
of social information, the collection of such information, and its
application in the developing countries: "Social Information for
What?" I. Galnoor; "Uses of Information: When Social Infor-
mation Becomes Desires," Z. Bauman; "Crisis Prediction," P. Wiles;
"Social Problem Indicators," L. Guttman; "Information Systems and
Inter-Organizational Space," A.J.N. Judge; "Analysis of Socio-
Economic Development through a System of Indicators," D.B. Mc-
Granahan; "The Practical Significance of Social Information," J.
Drewnowski; "Social Information and Government-Sponsored De-
velopment: A Case Study of West Pakistan," Z. Shariff; and
"Progress in Health: What Index of What Progress?" W. Malenbaum.

Gross, Bertram M., ed. "Social Goals and Indicators for American Society."
ANNALS OF THE AMERICAN ACADEMY OF POLITICAL AND SOCIAL SCIENCES
371 (May 1967): 1-177; 373 (September 1967): 1-218.

The contributions survey the developing subject of social indicators,
their relation to appraising the state of society and their application to social planning. Essays are: "A New Orientation in
American Government," B.M. Gross and M. Springer; "Indi-
vidual and Group Values," R.M. Williams, Jr.; "Civil Liberties,"
M.R. Konvitz; "Electoral Participation," R.M. Scammon; "The
Mass Media--A New for Greatness," A. Fontaine; "Discrimination
against Negroes," O.D. Duncan; "National Goals and Indicators
for the Reduction of Crime and Delinquency," D. Glaser; "The
Natural Environment," J.L. Fisher; "Urban Conditions: New York
City," D. Gottehrer; "Urban Conditions: General," D.P. Moynihan;
"Some Dangers in 'Valid' Social Measurement," A. Etzioni and
E.W. Lehman; "Poverty, Inequality, and Conflict," S.M. Miller,
M. Rein, P. Roby, and B.M. Gross; "Democratic Participation,"
S. Verba; "Education and Learning," W.J. Cohen; "Employment
and the 'New Economics,'" L.H. Keyserling; "Science, Technology,
and Change," R.A. Bauer; "Health and Well-Being," P.R. Lee;
and "New Goals for Social Information," B.M. Gross and M.
Springer.

Japan. Council on National Living. Research Committee. SOCIAL INDI-
CATORS OF JAPAN. Tokyo: Printing Bureau, Ministry of Finance, 1975.
270 p. Paperbound.

The members of the research committee discuss how social indicators are processed and calculated, the general system of social concerns measured by these indicators, and their particular application in studies of health, education, leisure, and the material environment.

Tacuber, Conrad, ed. "America in the Seventies: Some Social Indicators." ANNALS OF THE AMERICAN ACADEMY OF POLITICAL AND SOCIAL SCIENCE 435 (January 1978): 1-294.

In 1973 and 1976, the Office of Management and Budget issued reports of statistical information entitled "Social Indicators." The authors of papers in this volume of the ANNALS were invited to discuss this information, the significance of trends, and the implications for policy. The topics addressed were "Social Indicators and Social Reporting," R. Parke and D. Seidman; "Getting and Spending," S.H. Danziger and R.J. Lampman; "Boom to Birth Dearth and Beyond," A.A. Campbell; "Finally the Family," M.S. Weitzman; "Changing Work Life Patterns: A Twenty-Five Year Review," A.R. Miller; "A Decent Home and Suitable Living Environment," D.B. Holleb; "Social Security and Social Welfare Indicators," I.C. Merriam; "Continuing Trends in Health and Health Care," D.W. Wilson, J.J. Feldman, and M.G. Kovar; "Trends in Education and Training," A.L. Ferriss; "Perceptions about Black Americans," B.L. Carter and D.K. Newman; "'Massification' and Democratization of the Leisure Class," J.P. Robinson; "Social Mobility and Social Participation," W.H. Sewell; "Public Safety: Crime Is Up, But What about Punishment?" D. Seidman; "SOCIAL INDICATORS '76 and PERSPECTIVE CANADA II: Elixirs of Reason or of Sleep," D.A. Brusegard; "Social Indicators and Congressional Needs for Information," E.A. Staats; and "Postlude: Past, Present, and Future," D.F. Johnston.

Section VII

HEALTH INTERVENTION STRATEGIES (DISEASE CONTROL)
DEVELOPED AND DEVELOPING COUNTRIES

One of the urgent tasks that man now faces is the development of an appropriate strategy for resource management. This process cannot be productive until there is a consensus about objectives. One fundamental objective that has not yet received adequate detailed study is the quality of the environment required to sustain the biosphere. Although there is much talk about environmental quality, it is not clear whether the strategy should subsume ecological adaptation or environmental control. Because the qualities of the environment will be widely different depending upon which course is followed, this decision must receive first attention. In view of the fact that ecological adaptation involves grave risks, environmental control is the course that should be followed.

The formulation of a strategy for environmental control involves four important elements: 1) environmental criteria which describe the effects which can be expected to occur whenever or wherever a given environmental quality or configuration of qualities deviate above or below a specific level for a specific period of time; 2) environmental monitoring which will provide for continuing surveillance of physical and chemical qualities of environments and sentinel organisms particularly sensitive to environmental alteration; 3) environmental planning and implementation to assure that a strategy will be formulated that will maintain the fitness of the ecosystem and the continuing productivity of that biological system; and 4) environmental education to enhance and broaden the public's awareness and understanding of environmental problems and the need for its involvement in formulation of the strategy.

Author's Abstract of Frederick Sargent, II. "Environmental Control or Ecological Adaptation: A Decision in Planning for Quality of Environment." AMERICAN METEOROLOGICAL SOCIETY A CENTURY OF WEATHER PROGRESS, pp. 130-36.

When the problems of environmental health are viewed in ecological perspective, their complexities become evident, and the short-sightedness of a fragmented approach to their solution becomes clear. Because our understanding of the concepts of ecology has not been general, our attack on these problems has been uncoordinated, and unsystematic. Separate federal, state, or local agencies have focused their work on only part of the ecosystem, e.g., land, water,

air, city, fish, and wildlife, and man. There is real need to
coordinate such focal approaches and explore their true ecological
dimensions. . . .[2]

A. ENVIRONMENTAL SURVEILLANCE AND MONITORING, IMPACT ANALYSIS

Barker, David. SOME METHODOLOGICAL ISSUES IN THE MEASUREMENT,
ANALYSIS AND EVALUATION OF PEASANT FARMERS' KNOWLEDGE OF THEIR
ENVIRONMENT. MARC Report, no. 9. London: Monitoring and Assessment Re-
search Centre, Chelsea College, University of London, 1977. 13 p. Paperbound.

Barker discusses the problem of measuring environmental attitudes
with specific reference to utilizing farmer's environmental knowledge in systems for monitoring ecological change. His memo-
randum was prepared under the auspices of the Research Centre
of the Special Committee on Problems of the Environment, International Council of Scientific Unions.

Barrett, Eric C., and Curtis, Leonard F., eds. ENVIRONMENTAL REMOTE
SENSING: APPLICATIONS AND ACHIEVEMENTS. London: Edward Arnold,
1974. vi, 309 p.

This volume records papers presented at the Bristol Symposium on Remote Sensing, Department of Geography, University of Bristol, 2
October 1974. The fifteen papers deal with rocks, soils and land
forms; land use, vegetation and crops; and water, weather and climate.

_____. ENVIRONMENTAL REMOTE SENSING 2: PRACTICES AND PROB-
LEMS. New York: Crane Russak, 1977. vi, 314 p.

This volume contains papers presented at the Second Bristol Symposium on Remote Sensing, Department of Geography, University of
Bristol. The fifteen papers are arranged in three groups: policymaking
for remote sensing, the processing and presentation of remote sensing
data, and in situ observation and the interpretation of remote sensing
data.

Canter, Larry W. ENVIRONMENTAL IMPACT ASSESSMENT. McGraw-Hill
Series in Water Resources and Environmental Engineering. New York: McGraw-
Hill Book Co., 1977. xiv, 331 p. Appendixes; References.

In a book written primarily for advanced undergraduate and graduate
students and professionals in science and engineering, Canter discusses the process of composing an environmental impact statement
as required under the National Environmental Protection Act of
1970. His text emphasizes several areas: (1) requirements and
implementation of the act, (2) the conduct of environmental studies,

2. Frederick Sargent, II, "Ecological Dimensions of Environmental Health Problems," ARCHIVES OF ENVIRONMENTAL HEALTH 18 (1969): 244-48.

(3) definition of environmental settings, (4) methods for predicting environmental change, (5) criteria for evaluating significance of predicted changes, (6) methodologies of environmental impact assessment, (7) techniques for public participation, and (8) writing impact statements. There are seven appendixes: (1) text of National Environmental Policy Act, (2) Council on Environmental Quality guidelines, (3) data sources for environmental factors, (4-6) three examples of study methodologies, and (7) environmental factors to be used in comparing alternative plant systems.

Cardenas, Raul; Golden, Jack; Greeley, Richard; and Sluyter, Deborah M., eds. ENVIRONMENTAL IMPACT STATEMENTS: PROTECTION OR PAPER WORK? 2 vols. A Symposium Report. New York: Metrek Division, Mitre Corp., 1978. vii, 105 p.; vii, 126 p. Paperbound.

The symposium, held 19-20 May 1975, was cosponsored by the Polytechnic Institute of New York and the Mitre Corporation. Volume 1 contains presentations and discussion of the first day. The chief topics addressed were role of Council of Environmental Quality, ways to improve preparation and use of environmental impact statements, approaches of federal agencies to preparing and using these statements, role of environmental groups, the approach of industry, and cost-benefit analysis. In volume 2, there is a panel discussion, held on the second day, on improving relevance and usefulness of environmental analyses.

Council on Environmental Quality and Federal Council for Science and Technology. Committee on Ecological Research. THE ROLE OF ECOLOGY IN THE FEDERAL GOVERNMENT. Washington, D.C.: 1974. xi, 78 p. Paperbound.

The committee examined the national needs for ecological knowledge and capability and the current status of ecological knowledge and efforts to meet the needs and made recommendations for short- and long-term national programs to meet national environmental quality goals, coordinating interagency ecological research, and strengthening the ecological basis for regulatory action in environmental control and resource and land use management.

Craik, Kenneth H., and Zube, Ervin H., eds. PERCEIVING ENVIRONMENTAL QUALITY: RESEARCH AND APPLICATIONS. New York: Plenum Press, 1976. xiii, 310 p. Bibliog.

The volume contains commissioned papers presented and discussed at workshops held during the spring and summer of 1975. The goals were to review methodological issues, analyze policy and procedural issues, and examine research needs related to perceived environmental quality indixes. There are five parts: (1) environmental quality indexes; (2) scenic and recreational environments; (3) residential and industrial environments; (4) air, water, and sonic environments; and (5) general summary and research strategies. Each section contains a summary.

Cross, Frank L., Jr. HANDBOOK ON ENVIRONMENTAL MONITORING. Westport, Conn.: Technomic Publishing Co., 1974. 242 p. Paperbound. Bibliog.

> Cross discusses the techniques and devices for monitoring air pollution, water pollution, meteorological factors, noise, industrial environments, solid wastes, radioactivity, and pesticides.

Dickert, Thomas G., and Domeny, Katherine R., eds. ENVIRONMENTAL IMPACT ASSESSMENT: GUIDELINES AND COMMENTARY. Berkeley: University of California, University Extension, 1974. xi, 238 p. Bibliog.

> This monograph contains papers presented at a conference on "Improving the Environmental Impact Assessment Process" held in September 1972 under the auspices of Continuing Education in City, Regional, and Environmental Planning, University Extension, and the College of Environmental Design, University of California, Berkeley. The topics addressed were "Linking the EIS to the Planning Process," R.H. Twiss; NEPA/CEOA; "Legal Aspects," I.M. Heyman; "The Use of Data in Environmental Impact Assessment," L.B. Leopold; "Some Suggestions on the Content and Organization of Environmental Impact Statements," T.G. Dickert and J.C. Sorensen; "Social Equity and Environmental Quality," M.H. Krieger; "The BART Residential Impact Study: An Empirical Study of Environmental Impact," D. Appleyard and F.M. Carp; "Concepts and Methods of Cost-Benefit Analysis," S.O. Andersen; "Uncertainty and the Evaluation of Environmental Impacts: A Case Study," R.C. Bishop; "The Berkeley Environmental Simulation Project: Its Use in Environmental Impact Assessment," D. Appleyard and K.H. Craik; and "Methods of Environmental Impact Assessment: A Comparison," T.G. Dickert. Appended are compendium of federal and state guidelines and legislation, California Environmental Quality Act of 1970, guidelines for content of environmental impact reports, and a bibliography on governmental reports and scientific papers dealing with environmental impact analyses.

Ditton, Robert B., and Goodale, Thomas L., eds. ENVIRONMENTAL IMPACT ANALYSIS: PHILOSOPHY AND METHODS. Madison: University of Wisconsin, Sea Grant Program, 1972. ix, 171 p. Paperbound.

> The volume comprises proceedings of a Conference on Environmental Impact Analysis held 4-5 January 1972. Participants included scientists and administrators from academic institutions and governmental agencies. The principal topics considered were (1) impact of National Environmental Policy Act; (2) early experiences with assessment; and (3) implementation, implications, and consequences of assessment.

Dogan, Mattei, and Rokkan, Stein, eds. QUANTITATIVE ECOLOGICAL ANALYSIS IN THE SOCIAL SCIENCES. Cambridge: MIT Press, 1969. xv, 607 p. Indexes.

This book brings together various styles and technologies used in
political analysis: sample survey, geographical-ecological analysis,
and biometric procedures which can be computerized. There are
six parts: (1) the logic of ecological inference; (2) individual
and group behavior; (3) multivariate analysis in political ecology;
(4) factor analysis and ecological typologies; (5) historical dimensions of ecological analysis; and (6) organization of ecological
data archives.

Holdgate, Martin W., and White, Gilvert Fowler, eds. ENVIRONMENTAL
ISSUES. SCOPE Report 10. London: John Wiley and Sons, 1977. xviii,
224 p. Paperbound. Appendixes.

Report 10 of the Scientific Committee on Problems of the Environment (SCOPE) summarizes evidence on global trends in the biosphere and considers the more important environmental issues requiring attention from the scientific community. There are three
parts. The first deals with environmental properties and processes
and science in policy formulation. In the second part, the current
program of SCOPE is reviewed, that program reflecting the urgent
concerns of scientists. Among its activities are investigations of
biogeochemical cycles, climate, environmental pollutants, and
ecosystem processes; and studies of environmental management including monitoring, modelling, risk estimation, evaluation and
communication, and standard setting. In the third part, specific
actions that might be taken in the future are discussed. There
are four appendixes: (1) bibliography; (2) summary statements of
activities of International Council of Scientific Unions; (3) names
of individuals who prepared Report 10 and chairman of current
SCOPE projects; and (4) report of an expert group on methyl mercury.

House, Peter W. TRADING OFF ENVIRONMENT, ECONOMICS, AND ENERGY.
Lexington, Mass.: Lexington Books and D.C. Heath and Co., 1977. xix,
137 p.

Models play an important role in policy formulation. House describes the construction of the Strategic Environmental Assessment
System of the Environmental Protection Agency. He provides
technical details about how the system was built and discusses its
use in decision making.

MARINE POLLUTION MONITORING (PETROLEUM): PROCEEDINGS OF A
SYMPOSIUM AND WORKSHOP HELD AT THE NATIONAL BUREAU OF STAN-
DARDS, GAITHERSBURG, MD., 13-17 MAY 1974. National Bureau of Standards Special Publication 409. Washington, D.C.: Government Printing Office,
1974. xvi, 316 p. Paperbound. Indexes.

This international symposium was sponsored by the Intergovernmental
Oceanographic Commission (IOC-UNESCO), the World Meteoro-
logical Organization, and the U.S. Department of Commerce.
The proceedings contain fifty-eight invited and contributed papers,

plus the recommendations of the topical discussion groups and a
report of an international workshop with specific recommendations
for setting up a pilot project on marine pollution (petroleum)
monitoring.

MEASURING AND MONITORING THE ENVIRONMENT. Environment and Man
Series, vol. 7. Edited by John Lenihan and William W. Fletcher. New York:
Academic Press, 1978. xii, 131 p. Bibliog.

The authors discuss some ways by which environmental variables
can be measured and monitored. Papers are: "Biological Methods
of Environmental Monitoring," K. Mellanby; "Analysis of Food,"
M.J. Saxby; "Some Aspects of Water Quality," D.B. James; "Hair
as a Mirror of the Environment," J. Lenihan; and "Drug Toxicity,"
J.P. Griffen.

National Research Council. Committee for International Environmental Programs.
INSTITUTIONAL ARRANGEMENTS FOR INTERNATIONAL ENVIRONMENTAL
COOPERATION. Washington, D.C.: National Academy of Sciences, 1972.
xiii, 74 p.

The committee's report, prepared for U.S. Department of State,
examines basic institutional choices, changes in the UN system,
an environmental science advisory and research board, monitoring
and surveillance networks, world environment fund, and ways to
strengthen transnational environmental capabilities.

National Research Council. Committee on National Statistics. Study Group
on Environmental Monitoring. ENVIRONMENTAL MONITORING. Analytical
Studies for the U.S. Environmental Protection Agency, vol. 4. Washington,
D.C.: National Academy of Sciences, 1977. xiii, 181 p. Paperbound.
Glossary.

The study group examines the monitoring program of EPA and its
associated state, local, and regional agencies. There are discussions of the purposes of monitoring, EPA's management of scientific data, and suggestions for a more effective national program
of environmental monitoring. There are several appendixes: (1)
monitoring genetic effects in man; (2) the Maumee Estuary: a
case study; (3) handling uncertainty in environmental guidelines;
and (4) directories of monitoring programs and monitoring information centers.

National Research Council. Committee on Remote Sensing for Agricultural
Purposes. REMOTE SENSING WITH SPECIAL REFERENCE TO AGRICULTURE
AND FORESTRY. Washington, D.C.: National Academy of Sciences, 1970.
xiii, 424 p.

The committee, whose work was supported by the National Aero-
nautics and Space Administration and the U.S. Department of
Agriculture, attempts to develop concepts, value judgments, and

background on potential uses of remote sensing in agriculture and forestry, and to give a technical appraisal of state of the art sensors and discrimination techniques. Subjects treated are: imaging with photographic and nonphotographic sensors; applications of remote sensing; physical and physiological properties of plants; soil, water, and plant relations; field spectroscopy; sampling and statistical problems; research needs.

Oppenheimer, Carl H.; Oppenheimer, Dorothy; and Brogden, William B., eds. ENVIRONMENTAL DATA MANAGEMENT. NATO Conference Series, Ecology, vol. 2. New York: Plenum Press, 1975. xvi, 244 p.

This is a verbatim record of a Conference on Environmental Data Management sponsored by NATO Special Program Panel on Eco-Sciences held in Houston, Texas, 8-11 August 1974. The objectives of the conference were to discuss the scope of world environmental data and consider whether a systematic approach to a total system of data management was feasible now or in the future. The chief topics included review of present computerized systems, existing bodies of data, statistical theory appropriate to environmental data, theoretical consideration of data management systems, and total information systems. The participants recommended that there was a need for providing a systematic set of procedures for organizing, storing, and retrieving environmental data.

Sabins, Floyd F., Jr. REMOTE SENSING: PRINCIPLES AND INTERPRETATION. San Francisco: W.H. Freeman and Co., 1978. xi, 426 p. Illus.; References; Glossary; Indexes.

Sabins discusses the fundamentals of remote sensing; particular techniques: aerial photography, manned satellite imagery, Landstat imagery, thermal infrared imagery, and rader imagery; digital imagery processing; and applications in resource exploration, environmental pollution, land use and natural hazards. He concludes with a comparison of techniques and discussion of limitations and precautions.

B. RESOURCE MANAGEMENT

Abler, Ronald; Janelle, Donald; Philbrick, Allen; Sommer, John. HUMAN GEOGRAPHY IN A SHRINKING WORLD. Belmont, Calif.: Duxbury Press, 1975. 307 p. Paperbound.

This is a collection of essays on the locations of events and people during the next century. Part 1 consists of four chapters that analyze current and future transportation and communication technologies in relation to locational decisions. Part 2 explores some consequences of hypermobility, such as future settlement patterns and alternative ways of organizing society, government, and cultural groups. In part 3, possible answers are given to the questions

and dilemmas previously raised; some scenarios and simulations
offer alternative futures. Emphasis is laid on the need to adjust
our institutions and ethics so as to choose wisely from the opportunities provided by technology, and to organize and manage our
journey toward the future.

Austin, James E., and Wallerstein, Mitchel B. TOWARD A DEVELOPMENT
FOOD AID POLICY. Discussion Paper, no. 11. International Nutrition
Policy and Planning Program. Cambridge: MIT, Center for International Studies,
1977. 93 p. Paperbound. References.

Austin and Wallerstein contribute ideas on how food and policy
for developing nations might be reformulated so as to stimulate
economic growth. The main policy elements discussed are rationale
for food aid, selection of recipients, quantity determination, use
of commodities, terms of assistance, mechanisms of delivery, alternate channels, and organization of program.

Ayres, Robert U. RESOURCE, ENVIRONMENT, AND ECONOMICS; APPLI-
CATIONS OF THE MATERIALS/ENERGY BALANCE PRINCIPLE. New York:
John Wiley and Sons, 1978. xii, 207 p.

Ayres's monograph brings together recent advances of large-scale
simulation modelling which should be useful to resource economists
and environmental systems analysts and demonstrates what can be
accomplished in the construction of realistic economic models for
policy analysis. The six chapters deal with economics and the
environment, dynamic optimizing models of resources and the environment, application of physical principles to economics, materials-
energy accounting and forecasting models, optimizing materials-
energy process models, and need for an integrated materials-energy
balance statistical system.

Bell, Gwen, ed. STRATEGIES FOR HUMAN SETTLEMENTS: HABITAT AND
ENVIRONMENT. Honolulu: University Press of Hawaii, 1976. xix, 172 p.

Bell has assembled contributions on proposed solutions for improving
the quality of life in human settlements with minimal disturbance
of the environmental systems. Many of the ideas expressed derived
from preparatory meetings for the UN Conference on Human Settlements (Habitat) held in 1976. The papers in the first part focus on
achieving a balanced existence between settlement systems and
natural systems; in the second part, with providing food, water,
and energy for settlements; and in the third, with housing and
transportation.

Berg, Alan; Scrimshaw, Nevin S.; and Call, David L., eds. NUTRITION,
NATIONAL DEVELOPMENT, AND PLANNING. Cambridge: MIT Press, 1973.
xiii, 401 p.

This volume comprises the proceedings of an International Conference on Nutrition, National Development, and Planning, held at MIT, 19-21 October 1971. Its objective was to explore the place of nutrition planning in national development, particularly in the developing countries. The participants addressed five topics: (1) effects of nutrition on the individual; (2) role of nutrition in national development; (3) diagnosis of food and nutrition problems and establishment of priorities; (4) determinants of nutrition and alternative intervention programs; and (5) conceptual approach to national nutrition program planning. Several case studies were reviewed: Czechoslovakia, Columbia, India, and Japan. The consensus was that nutrition played a central role in planning and there was a need for training nutrition planners.

BIOLOGICAL BALANCE AND THERMAL MODIFICATIONS. TOWARD A PLAN OF ACTIONS FOR MANKIND. Vol. 3. Edited by M. Marois. Oxford, Engl.: Pergamon Press, 1977. xv, 304 p.

This volume is one of five which contain the proceedings of a World Conference held in Paris, 9-13 September 1974, under the auspices of the Institut de la Vie. The several reports and papers, in either French or English, dealing with meteorological consequences and biological impact of thermal pollution, were arranged under four topics: (1) atmospheric and climatic changes due to a modification of the heat balance; (2) thermal discharges: biological consequences (brackish and marine water); (3) thermal discharges: biological consequences (fresh water); and (4) strategy for the future.

Bonsall, Peter; Dalvi, Quasim; and Hills, Peter J., eds. URBAN TRANSPORTATION PLANNING: CURRENT THEMES AND FUTURE PROSPECTS. Tunbridge Wells, Engl.: Abacus Press, 1977. 386 p.

The text comprises an edited version of papers originally contributed to a conference on urban transportation planning held at University of Leeds in the spring of 1976. The topics discussed included (1) estimation of demands for travel; (2) modelling the interaction between land-use and transport; (3) transport networks; (4) consistency, efficiency, and equity in evaluation; (5) application of strategic transportation planning techniques; (6) attitude-measurement and evaluation of environmental impact; and (7) future directions in transportation planning.

Brown, Lester Russell. WORLD WITHOUT BORDERS. New York: Random House, 1972; Vintage Books, 1973. xviii, 395 p. Paperbound.

Brown attempts to provide a global perspective to the problems of population, food, environmental quality, natural resources, and economics. The growing interdependence of nations calls for multinational approaches to the solution of these problems and a global infrastructure to provide the mechanisms for remedial action and management.

Brown, Peter G., and Shue, Henry, eds. FOOD POLICY: THE RESPONSI-
BILITY OF THE UNITED STATES IN THE LIFE AND DEATH CHOICES. New
York: Free Press and Macmillan Publishing Co.; London: Collier Macmillan
Publishers, 1977. viii, 344 p. Notes; References.

In this volume sponsored by the Academy for Contemporary Problems,
Brown, Shue and their colleagues examine the questions: What
should the U.S. policy be regarding world hunger? What are the
facts? What are the institutional constraints? The essays are
arranged into four parts: needs and obligations, responsibilities
in the public sector, responsibilities in the private sector, and
reducing dependence. Particular emphasis is placed on the developmental, economic, technological, political, and moral issues
of a food policy.

CONCLUSIONS AND PERSPECTIVES. TOWARD A PLAN OF ACTIONS FOR
MANKIND. Vol. 5. Edited by M. Marois. Oxford, Engl.: Pergamon Press,
1977. xviii, 194 p.

The fifth volume of the proceedings of a World Conference held
in Paris, 9-13 September 1974, under the auspices of the Institut
de la Vie is devoted principally to reports and the contents of a
plan of actions. There are eight chapters. The first two contain
speeches. The next five are devoted to reports, in either French
or English, from working groups on economic sciences and problems
of growth, long-range mineral resources and growth, long-range
energetic resources and growth, biological balance and thermal
modifications, and global system models. Each includes an extensive discussion. In the eighth chapter, general conclusions regarding a plan of action are presented and discussed. The conclusions are reported in both French and English.

DESIGN OF GLOBAL SYSTEMS MODELS AND THEIR LIMITATIONS. TOWARD
A PLAN OF ACTION FOR MANKIND. Vol. 4. Edited by M. Marois.
Oxford, Engl.: Pergamon Press, 1977. xiii, 247 p.

This volume is one of five which contain the proceedings of World
Conference held in Paris, 9-13 September 1974, under the auspices
of the Institut de la Vie. The several reports and papers, in either
French or English, dealing with modelling are arranged into four
groups: (1) the state of the art of modelling; (2) application and
applicability of known methods; (3) needs of new methods and
techniques for modelling; and (4) direction of research for the design
of major programs of action. The discussions are recorded and
some of the chapters are documented.

Deutsch, Karl Wolfgang; Fritsch, Bruno; Jaguaribe, Helip; and Mankovits, Andrei
S., eds. PROBLEMS OF WORLD MODELING: POLITICAL AND SOCIAL IM-
PLICATIONS. Cambridge, Mass.: Ballinger Publishing Co., 1977. xviii,
423 p. Tables; Figures; References.

The papers were first presented at a conference sponsored by the World University of the World Academy of Art and Science held at Harvard University in February 1976. The objectives of the conference were to review developing simulation models of major general trends in world economics, politics, and ecology and to examine their application to national and regional planning and policy formulation. Four major topics were considered: (1) general problems of world modelling; (2) politics and social classes; (3) the data question; and (4) more comprehensive models.

Enzer, Selwyn; Drobnick, Richard; and Alter, Steven. NEITHER FEAST NOR FAMINE: FOOD CONDITIONS TO THE YEAR 2000. Lexington, Mass.: Lexington Books and D.C. Heath and Co., 1978. xviii; 185 p. Appendixes; Tables; Graphs.

The authors, members of the Center for Futures Research at the University of Southern California, discuss various models and scenarios which might be used to forecast the world food and population balance for each year for the next twenty years. Among the topics considered are historical background of current food situation and socioeconomic, technologic, and environmental conditions which can influence future developments; models for exploring alternative food futures and relation of concept of self-reliance to these scenarios; and impacts of world food conditions on U.S. business and society. There are four appendixes: (1) Delphi inquiry; (2) world food model; (3) historical regional data on population and food production and consumption; and (4) regional projections.

Firey, Walter. MAN, MIND AND LAND. Glencoe, Ill.: Free Press, 1960. 256 p.

Firey develops a general theory which seeks to specify the necessary and sufficient conditions which may assist planning agencies in changing people's use of land and resources. He defines resources systems as any combination of resource processes by which man uses natural resources. His systematic theory of natural resources, deriving from a study of four different resource systems, two belonging to folk societies, one to a feudal society, and one to an industrial society, provides insights into universally true descriptions of human behavior toward resources in different physical and cultural contexts.

Gilliland, Martha W., ed. ENERGY ANALYSIS: A NEW PUBLIC POLICY TOOL. American Association for the Advancement of Science, Selected Symposium 9. Washington, D.C.: AAAS, 1978. xvii, 110 p.

There is a pressing need to develop effective tools for evaluating and choosing among energy alternatives. The five papers, presented at a national meeting of AAAS, consider the utility of energy analysis as a tool in policymaking: (1) "Energy Analysis;

The Kinds of Information It Provides Policymakers," M. W.
Gilliland; (2) "Energy and Employment Impacts of Policy Alternatives," C.W. Bullard III; (3) "Second Law Efficiencies and
Public Policy," M. Ross; (4) "Energy Analysis, Energy Quality,
and Environment," H.T. Odum; and (5) "Energy Analysis in Energy
RD&D: Planning and Decisionmaking," R.H. Williamson. Different
approaches to energy analysis are illustrated by these papers; their
strengths and weaknesses are considered. The best approach will
probably be determined by its ability to provide the most useful
policy information.

Gladstone, Francis. THE POLITICS OF PLANNING. London: Temple Smith,
1976. 128 p.

Gladstone identifies the urban crisis as one between suburban
(city users) and nonsuburban (city needers) elements of society.
Cities have been planned largely with the needs of the user in
mind. To resolve the crisis, the common man must understand
the planning process and must develop a net set of values about
cities. The planning for four English cities--Sheffield, Teeside,
South Hampshire, and Liverpool--is discussed. The challenge in
the politics of planning will come when city users adapt the values
about cities which the city needers hold.

Goodall, Brian, and Kirby, Andrew, eds. RESOURCES AND PLANNING.
Oxford, Engl.: Pergamon Press, 1979. xviii, 373 p. Maps; Figures; Tables;
References.

The fifteen authors discuss applications of geographical concept
and methods to environmental planning. Among the topics considered are scientific bases of planning system.

Hakim, Peter, and Solimano, Giorgio. DEVELOPMENT, REFORM AND MAL-
NUTRITION IN CHILE. International Nutrition Policy Series. Cambridge:
MIT Press, 1978. xvi, 91 p. Notes; Bibliog.

The interventions used by the Chilean government to remedy malnutrition over the period 1930 to 1970 are evaluated. Several
governmental programs are studied, but the authors focus on the
milk distribution program. Contrary to the general belief that
socioeconomic development will improve the nutritional status of
a population, these authors found that in Chile economic growth
and social reform perpetuated malnutrition and undermined the
effectiveness of the intervention programs.

Hardin, Garrett. EXPLORING NEW ETHICS FOR SURVIVAL. THE VOYAGE
OF THE SPACESHIP BEAGLE. Baltimore: Penguin Books, 1973. xii, 273 p.
Paperbound.

The author carries forward ideas first expressed in "Tragedy of the

Commons," SCIENCE 162 (1968): 1243-48. He examines the socioeconomic, political, and ethical origins of man's current problems, population, resources, food, and pollution. He concludes that the solutions will not be technological but behavioral, new organization of human institutions and revision of ethical values.

Hill, Dennis S. AGRICULTURAL INSECT PESTS OF THE TROPICS AND THEIR CONTROL. Cambridge: University Press, 1975. xii, 516 p. Appendix.

Hill has prepared a handbook on the biological and chemical control of insect pests of the tropics. There are six parts: (1) principles and methods; (2) biological control in Africa; (3) chemical control; (4) pest descriptions, biology and control measures; (5) major tropical crops and their pests; and (6) general bibliography (eleven pages). Appended are list of trade names for pesticides cited, glossary, and simple hints on preservation, shipment, and identification of insect specimens.

Hitch, Charles J., ed. MODELING ENERGY-ECONOMY INTERACTIONS: FIVE APPROACHES. Research Paper R-5. Washington, D.C.: Resources for the Future, 1977. v, 303 p. Paperbound.

The papers were presented at a Joint National Meeting of the Institute of Management Sciences and the Operations Research Society of America, San Francisco," May 1977. The five approaches were "ETA-MACRO: A Model of Energy Economy Interactions," by A.S. Manne; "The Long-Term Economic and Environmental Consequences of Phasing Out Nuclear Electricity," D.L. Behling, Jr., W. Marcuse, J. Lukachinski, and R. Dullien; "Economic, Energy and Environmental Consequences of Alternative Energy Regimens: An Application of the RFF/SEAS Modeling System," R.G. Ridker, W.D. Watson, Jr., and A. Shapanka; "A General Equilibrium Two-Sector Energy Demand Model," D.B. Reister and J.A. Edmonds; and "Energy-Economy Interactions: The Fable of the Elephant and the Rabbit," W.W. Hogan and A.S. Manne. L.B. Lave summarized the five models and concluded that it might be possible to approach a future much less demanding of energy than heretofore thought.

Ingman, Stanley R., and Thomas, Anthony E., eds. TOPIAS AND UTOPIAS IN HEALTH. POLICY STUDIES. The Hague: Mouton Publishers, 1975. xviii, 548 p.

This volume comprises the proceedings of a symposium on "Topias and Utopias in Health" held during the ninth International Congress of Anthropological and Ethnological Sciences, Chicago, 4 September 1973. The principal focus of the symposium was health systems in various social organizations. The papers were arranged in three groups. Those of the first group addressed the topic

"Interest Groups and the Allocation of Health Care." The authors
analyzed the functioning of health systems or components of health
systems. The papers of the second group, "Topias, Utopias," and
"Counter-Utopias in Health Care," examined experimental and
new Socialist systems of health care. The papers of the final
group dealt with "Social Sciences in Health Research and Action."
Although illness is a universal phenomenon, it was evident from
these papers that, depending upon the social organization and
political ideology, very different health systems were being tried
or planned.

LONG RANGE ENERGETIC RESOURCES AND GROWTH. TOWARD A PLAN
OF ACTIONS FOR MANKIND. Vol. 2. Edited by M. Marois. Oxford,
Engl.: Pergamon Press, 1977. xii, 168 p. Bibliog.

This volume is one of five which contain the proceedings of a
World Conference held in Paris, 9-13 September 1974, under the
auspices of the Institut de la Vie. The several reports and papers,
in either French or English, dealing with energy resources, are
arranged in four groups: (1) consumption of energy after the year
2000; (2) potential resources in the year 2000 from new techniques
and the problems of transport; (3) impact of energetic solutions on
nature (i.e., climate, ocean, and environment generally); and
(4) impact of energetic solutions on social, political, and economic life. The discussions are recorded.

LONG RANGE MINERAL RESOURCES AND GROWTH. TOWARD A PLAN
OF ACTION FOR MANKIND. Vol. 1. Edited by M. Marois. Oxford,
Engl.: Pergamon Press, 1977. xv, 314 p. Bibliog.

This volume is one of five which contain the proceedings of a
World Conference held in Paris, 9-13 September 1974, under the
auspices of the Institut de la Vie. The several reports, papers,
and communications in either French or English, dealing with
mineral resources, are arranged in four parts: (1) resources availability and depletion; (2) effects of recycling upon water and
agriculture; (3) effects of recycling of waste on nonrenewable resources; and (4) environmental effects of waste materials.

Mayer, Jean, and Dwyer, Johanna T., eds. FOOD AND NUTRITION POLICY
IN A CHANGING WORLD. New York: Oxford University Press, 1979. xii,
300 p. Appendix.

This book, addressing considerations involved in planning food and
nutrition policy for the young child of the developing countries,
is an abbreviated version of a five-volume report, "Priorities in
Child Nutrition in Developing Countries," submitted to UNICEF
in May 1975. There are five parts. In the first, there is a
general discussion of the complex problems in formulation food
policy and of child malnutrition. The second part addresses planning. The third considers various intervention strategies of a

short-term nature. In the fourth, two examples of problems and
programs in the health sector are discussed, and in the fifth, three
examples in the food industry sector. The appendix contains
"Nutrition Primer" by P. Araujo.

National Goals Research Staff. TOWARD BALANCED GROWTH: QUANTITY
WITH QUALITY. Washington, D.C.: Government Printing Office, 1970.
v, 222 p. Paperbound.

This staff report to the president seeks to identify emerging needs
and encourage discussion for a better framework of decisions about
social policy. The issues treated include population growth and
distribution, environment, education, basic natural science, technology assessment, consumerism, and economic choice and balanced
growth.

National Research Council. Commission on International Relations. Steering
Committee. NRC Study on World Food and Nutrition. WORLD FOOD AND
NUTRITION STUDY. THE POTENTIAL CONTRIBUTIONS OF RESEARCH. Washington, D.C.: National Academy of Sciences, 1977. xxvi, 192 p. Paperbound.

A steering committee and fourteen study teams prepared an assessment of the problem of world hunger and malnutrition and developed a series of recommendations on the contributions of research and development to the solution of the problem. The several
recommendations covered such topics as increasing food supply,
reducing poverty, stabilizing food supplied, slowing population
growth, and the roles of research and development of the United
States. The problem was seen as challenging, but there was
optimism.

_____. SUPPORTING PAPERS: WORLD FOOD AND NUTRITION STUDY.
Vol. 1. Washington, D.C.: National Academy of Science, 1977. vii,
318 p. Paperbound. Bibliog.

The research most likely to increase food production and reduce
hunger and malnutrition was identified and discussed by study team
1, crop productivity; study team 2, animal productivity; and study
team 3, aquatic food sources. The principal topics considered by
study team 1 were crop productivity by nonconventional technologies
and crop protection through pest control. Topics emphasized by
study team 2 were role of livestock and animal health, and by
study team 3, fish as food and long-term needs.

_____. SUPPORTING PAPERS: WORLD FOOD AND NUTRITION STUDY.
Vol. 2. Washington, D.C.: National Academy of Sciences, 1977, vii, 299 p.
Paperbound. Bibliog.

The research most likely to increase food production and reduce hunger and malnutrition was identified and discussed by study team 4, resources of agriculture, and study team 5, weather and climate. The principal topics considered by study team 4 were farming systems, land and water, fertilizer, and energy. Study team 5 focused on predictability of change of weather and climate and adaptability of agricultural practices to weather and climate variability.

_____. SUPPORTING PAPERS: WORLD FOOD AND NUTRITION STUDY. Vol. 3. Washington, D.C.: National Academy of Sciences, 1977. vii, 341 p. Paperbound. Bibliog.

The research most likely to increase agricultural productivity and reduce hunger and malnutrition was identified by study team 6, food availability to consumers; study team 7, rural institutions, policies, and social science research; study team 8, information systems; and study team 10, interdependencies. Study team 6 focused on marketing and distribution of food; study team 7, on institutional arrangements for education and research; study team 8, on information needs and information systems; and study team 10, on population and health, energy, resources, and environment, international trade policies, and national development policies.

_____. SUPPORTING PAPERS: WORLD FOOD AND NUTRITION STUDY. Vol. 4. Washington, D.C.: National Academy of Sciences, 1977. vii, 165 p. Paperbound. Bibliog.

The research most likely to increase food production and reduce hunger and malnutrition was identified and discussed by study team 9, nutrition and study team 12, new approaches to the alleviation of hunger. The principal topics discussed by study team 9 were functional significance of nutritional status and intervention strategies. Those considered by study team 12 were food, culture, and change and definition and measurement of nutritional success.

_____. SUPPORTING PAPERS: WORLD FOOD AND NUTRITION STUDY. Vol. 5. Washington, D.C.: National Academy of Sciences, 1977. vii, 195 p. Paperbound. Bibliog.

The research most likely to increase food production and reduce hunger and malnutrition was identified and discussed by study team 14, agricultural research organization. Three topics were emphasized: (1) research organization in the United States, (2) global agricultural research organization, and (3) training of research personnel.

National Research Council. Committee on Agriculture and Environment. PRO-DUCTIVE AGRICULTURE AND A QUALITY ENVIRONMENT: FOOD PRODUC-

TION, LIVING, RECREATION: THE RURAL-URBAN INTERFACE. Washington, D.C.: National Academy of Sciences, 1974. vii, 189 p. Paperbound. Appendix; Reference; Bibliog.

> The report considers three principal topics. Under the first, food and fiber production, there is a discussion of crop-protection chemicals, fertilizer, and by-product management. The second, the rural environment, deals with making the countryside livable. In the third, the allocation of resources--land, recreation and rural growth, water, and energy--is examined. An appendix contains a discussion of the effect of eliminating use of fragile lands for agricultural production.

National Research Council. Committee on Energy and the Environment. IM-PLICATIONS OF ENVIRONMENTAL REGULATIONS FOR ENERGY PRODUCTION AND CONSUMPTION. Analytical Studies for the U.S. Environmental Protection Agency. Vol. VI. Washington, D.C.: National Academy of Sciences, 1977. xvi, 233 p. Paperbound. Appendixes; Glossary.

> The committee studied the interrelations between environmental regulations and energy and suggested improvements in the cost-effectiveness of selected federal pollution control regulations, namely, the coal and uranium fuel cycles and automotive transportation. There are discussions of effects of these energy systems on health and the environment, major energy and environment issues, and challenges to management. Four appendixes deal with (1) a review of energy systems, fuel cycles, residuals, and effects; (2) the energy and environment matrix; (3) costs and benefits of effluent regulations; and (4) energy conversion factors.

National Research Council. Committee on Mineral Resources and the Environment. MINERAL RESOURCES AND THE ENVIRONMENT: SUPPLEMENTARY REPORT: RESOURCE RECOVERY FROM MUNICIPAL SOLID WASTES. Washington, D.C.: National Academy of Sciences, 1975. xiii, 416 p. Paperbound.

> One of the three supplements to the original committee report of February 1975, this report deals with a topic needing special attention. A summary of findings lists nine conclusions of the committee. Two chapters follow which discuss the technical aspects of resource recovery from municipal solid wastes and the systems approach to resource recovery and regional planning. Three appendixes are devoted to general, technical, and institutional problems; these consist of papers presented at a workshop on resource recovery from solid waste held at the National Academy of Sciences, 3-4 April 1975.

National Research Council. Committee on Radioactive Waste Management. Panel on Engineered Storage. INTERIM STORAGE OF SOLIDIFIED HIGH-LEVEL RADIOACTIVE WASTES. Washington, D.C.: National Academy of Sciences, 1975. vii, 82 p. Paperbound. Appendixes; References; Glossary.

The panel discusses the possibilities of interim retrievable storage (not exceeding one hundred years) of radioactive waste at or near the earth's surface. The main points considered include fuel processing and waste solidification, concepts of retrievable surface storage, environmental consequences, cost estimates, and reliability of materials. There are several appendixes in which technical details of various storage devices are summarized.

National Research Council. Committee on Water. ALTERNATIVES IN WATER MANAGEMENT. Publication no. 1408. Washington, D.C.: National Academy of Sciences, National Research Council, 1966. 52 p. Paperbound.

This report to the Division of Earth Sciences examines principles requiring more attention in decision making about the use of water. Among these principles are a focus upon the needs of people, new institutional arrangements, and better use of scientific and technological knowledge in formulation of water policy.

Ophuls, William. ECOLOGY AND THE POLITICS OF SCARCITY. San Francisco, Calif.: W.H. Freeman and Co., 1977. xi, 303 p. Bibliog.

There is no question that natural resources can long support the growing human population at traditional levels of expectations. Scarcity is already evident. The central problem, to which he devotes most of his attention, is that American political values and institutions cannot deal with scarcity. From his critique, general principles emerge, principles that might be incorporated into a society learning to live with scarcity.

Pariser, Ernst R.; Wallerstein, Mitchell B.; Corkery, Christopher J.; and Brown, Norman L. FISH PROTEIN CONCENTRATE: PANACEA FOR PROTEIN MALNUTRITION? International Nutrition Policy Series. Cambridge: MIT Press, 1978. xix, 296 p. References; Notes.

The authors analyze the history of fish protein concentrate as a technological fix to remedy the protein gap that did not succeed. Part 1 deals with history and cultural significance of fish as food; part 2, with policy issues related to development of fish protein concentrate in the United States; part 3, with international developments in Canada, Morocco, Chile, and Sweden; and part 4, with an analysis of the international experiences.

PROBLEMS IN GOVERNMENT PLANNING OF NUTRITION POLICY. Working Papers, Rockefeller Foundation. New York: Rockefeller Foundation, 1976. xi, 72 p. Paperbound.

The paper contains the transcription of a conference held 16 December 1976 in which the participants (nutritionists, agricultural scientists, and social scientists) considered the format and contents of a book which might be written to assist planners in governmental agencies to formulate nutrition policy.

Rogers, Paul, ed. FUTURE RESOURCES AND WORLD DEVELOPMENT. Frontiers in Human Ecology. New York: Plenum Press, 1976. xii, 268 p.

> The authors examine the long term applications of the use of global resources for development and on the relations between developed and less developed countries. In part 1, there are papers on resources, development, and producer power. Minerals and oil are emphasized. In part 2, various declarations, speeches, memoranda, and plans related to resources and development by government officials and agencies between 1973 and 1976 are reproduced.

Saarinen, Thomas Frederick. PERCEPTION OF THE DROUGHT HAZARD ON THE GREAT PLAINS. Department of Geography, Research Paper, no. 106. Chicago: University of Chicago, 1969. xi, 183 p. Paperbound. Bibliog.

> The resource manager's perception of drought hazard will condition his management strategies. This perception will vary according to the aridity of the region, the frequency of the drought actually experienced, and personality difference among managers. This hypothesis was tested in a study conducted in the central Great Plains (Nebraska, Colorado, Kansas, and Oklahoma) which utilized interview, questionnaire, and psychometric testing. Information collected focused on perception of drought hazard; perception of options in management strategies; perceptions, adoptions, and adaptations; and personality characteristics of farmers. The results tended to support the hypothesis. The report contains climatological information on the study area.

Sai, Fred T. POPULATION AND NATIONAL DEVELOPMENT--THE DILEMMA OF DEVELOPING COUNTRIES. Occasional Essay, no. 2. London: International Planned Parenthood Federation, 1977. 31 p. Paperbound.

> Sai examines the current issues and debates concerning population, resources, environment, and development. He concludes that the rational objective should be to bring about a balance among number of people, resources, and capabilities so that the people of each nation would be able to attain full genetic and social potential.

Sheperd, Jack. THE POLITICS OF STARVATION. New York: Carnegie Endowment for International Peace, 1975. xiii, 101 p.

> Sheperd documents the failure for international disaster relief to be provided to Ethiopia between 1973 and 1975 because it was not politically expedient in the view of the reigning governmental regimes. Although the existence of famine and starvation were known, conventions prevented intervention by international agencies. In an afterward, Stephen I. Green discusses questions of human rights raised by this experience and suggests that UN conventions should be altered so that more rapid and effective relief could be provided in future disasters.

Streeter, Carroll P. REACHING THE DEVELOPING WORLD'S SMALL FARMERS.
Working Papers, Rockefeller Foundation. New York: Rockefeller Foundation,
1975. vii, 48 p. Paperbound.

Streeter argues that given the resources of the new agriculture
(seeds, fertilizer, biocide, and water), the understanding of how
to use them, and access to credit and market, the small farmers
of the developing nations can increase agricultural productivity
substantially. Case histories from Latin America, Africa, and
India demonstrate that this process is practicable and economically
feasible.

United Nations. Conference on the Human Environment, Stockholm, 1972.
HUMAN SETTLEMENTS: THE ENVIRONMENTAL CHALLENGE. New York:
United Nations, 1974. xvi, 209 p.

One of the main themes of the Stockholm Conference, the planning
and management of human settlements for environment quality, included fifteen subject areas, each the topic of a background report. These reports, together with the related decisions of the
conference and the UN General Assembly, comprise the present
book. Some subjects are: the evolution of human settlements;
comprehensive development planning; the process of implementation;
housing; industry; recreation and leisure; transport and communication; infrastructure; and social and cultural aspects.

U.S. Environment and Resources Council. URBAN ALTERNATIVES: PROCEED-
INGS OF THE USERC ENVIRONMENT, RESOURCES, AND URBAN DEVELOP-
MENT WORKSHOP, NOVEMBER 1975. Edited by Edward A. Wolff. Oxford,
Engl.: Pergamon Press, 1976. vii, 110 p. Paperbound.

The workshop, held 12-14 November 1975, in Greenbelt, Maryland, had sixty participants organized into ten panels according
to disciplines: urban development, energy, communications, meteorology, water resources, public health, in-situ sensing, remote
sensing, socioeconomic problems, and science, technology, and
government. Its purpose was to obtain information on the technical implications of various possible urban development decisions,
for use at a UN Conference on Human Settlements in Vancouver,
31 May to 11 June 1976. After discussing various possible scenarios,
the panels considered their impact on the specific disciplines, and
made recommendations for altering the scenarios to improve environmental consequences.

Vann, Anthony, and Rogers, Paul, eds. HUMAN ECOLOGY AND DEVELOP-
MENT. Frontiers in Human Ecology. London: Plenum Press, 1974. xvi, 180 p.

This volume contains the proceedings of a Symposium on Human
Ecology and Development organized jointly by Commonwealth Human Ecology Council and Huddersfield Polytechnic held in Huddersfield in April 1973. The several papers included: "The Nature

and Extent of World Poverty," P. Kenyon; "Current and Future
Trends in Development Assistance," B. Dinwiddy; "World Trade
Patterns and the Developing Countries 1970-2000," A. Hone;
"The Global Ecosystem," P. Newbould; "Ecological Effects of
Current Development Processes in Less Developed Countries,"
K.A. Dahlberg; "Ecological Approaches to Agricultural Development,"
S. Holliman; "Development and Physical Resource Utilization,"
A. Tucker; and "The Implications of Ecological Limits to Develop-
ment in Terms of Expectations and Aspirations in Developed and
Less Developed Countries," E. Brooks. Discussion of each paper
was summarized. A position paper of the World Development
Movement entitled "Environmental Considerations for Development
in the Third World" was discussed in workshops.

Van Sickle, Dirck. THE ECOLOGICAL CITIZEN: GOOD EARTHKEEPING
IN AMERICA. New York: Perennial Library and Harper and Row, 1971. xix,
295 p. Paperbound.

Van Sickle addresses citizens as individuals and groups discussing
the consumption of resources and what can be done to lower the
drain on them. He recommends a new life-style aimed at conserving resources and protecting ecosystems.

Watt, Kenneth E.F. ECOLOGY AND RESOURCE MANAGEMENT: A QUAN-
TITATIVE APPROACH. New York: McGraw-Hill Book Co., 1968. xii, 450 p.

The author seeks to define the broad area of resource management
for not only graduate students and professionals but also undergraduates and laymen. The four parts deal with the problem,
theory, principles, and methods of resource management, respectively. Because modelling and simulation techniques are crucial
to decision making, the reader should have some mathematical
foundation.

Winikoff, Beverly, ed. NUTRITION AND NATIONAL POLICY. Cambridge:
MIT Press, 1978. xi, 580 p. Bibliog.; Appendix.

This volume records papers presented and discussions at a conference on Nutrition and Government Policy, sponsored by the
Rockefeller Foundation, held in Bellagio, Italy, 20-23 September
1975. The conference focused on relations between governmental
activity in health, agriculture, and economics and the nutritional
status of population and sought to understand why traditional intervention programs had proven ineffective. Case studies were
presented and discussed for eleven countries: Chile, Colombia,
Ghana, Nigeria, Indonesia, Jamaica, Panama, Philippines, Tanzania, United States, and Zambia. Commentaries on policy issues
such as planning and program implementation and nutrition and
culture, political process, agricultural policy, and economic policy
were presented and discussed. Finally the editor prepared two
chapters: "Political Commitment and Nutrition Policy" and "Program and Policy: Some Specific Questions."

Wolman, Abel. WATER, HEALTH, AND SOCIETY: SELECTED PAPERS. Edited by Gilbert F. White. Bloomington: Indiana University Press, 1969. xii, 400 p. Bibliog.

> These papers, selected from Wolman's writings of the past fifty years, show his expertise in water supply, sanitary engineering, public-works planning and construction, water resources, and environmental management. They reflect his activities at many levels—university, municipal, state, federal, foreign, and international. The papers are organized under six topics: water resources; water quality and treatment; the search for standards; water planning and policy; comprehensive planning for human environment; and the role of the engineer.

Wortman, Sterling. THE WORLD FOOD SITUATION: A NEW INITIATIVE. Working Papers, Rockefeller Foundation. New York: Rockefeller Foundation, 1976. 35 p. Paperbound.

> In a paper prepared for the Subcommittee on Science, Research and Technology and the Subcommittee on Domestic and International Scientific Planning and Analysis of the U.S. House of Representatives, Wortman presents a strategy for augmenting the agricultural productivity of the small farmers of the developing nations, and urges that the United States assume a leadership role through research and technical assistance.

C. ENVIRONMENTAL MANAGEMENT

Albertson, Peter, and Barnett, Margery, eds. "Environment and Society in Transition." ANNALS OF THE NEW YORK ACADEMY OF SCIENCES 184 (7 June 1971): 1-699. Paperbound.

> The volume comprises papers, reports of working groups, and discussions bearing on the general areas of scientific developments, social consequences, and policy implications during an International Joint Conference of the American Geographical Society and the American Division of the World Academy of Art and Science, 27 April-2 May 1970. To implement the conference objective, there would need to be greater involvement of the scientist in the formulation of public policy on the environment.

American Medical Association. Department of Environmental Health. CAN SOME DISEASES BE "ENGINEERED" OUT OF THE ENVIRONMENT? Proceedings of the AMA Congress on Environmental Health Problems. Chicago: 1964. iii, 108 p. Paperbound.

> The participants of the congress, held in Chicago, 1-2 May 1964, discussed the magnitude of the health problems created by air pollution, pesticides, ionizing radiation, and water pollution as well as the engineering control of these environmental contaminants.

Because there were more questions raised than could be answered, the main question of the congress was not answered either.

Argonne Universities Association. REPORT OF THE AUA SPECIAL COMMITTEE ON ENVIRONMENTAL PROGRAMS. Chicago: 1970. 27 p. Paperbound.

The report was produced by the special committee after the conference on "Universities, National Laboratories, and Man's Environment" (see next entry). The special committee recommended the Argonne National Laboratory and the Argonne Universities Association (AUA) undertake major environmental studies on waste management and settlement policies and land-use planning.

_____. UNIVERSITIES, NATIONAL LABORATORIES, AND MAN'S ENVIRONMENT. Washington, D.C.: U.S. Atomic Energy Commission, 1969. vii, 167 p. Paperbound. Available as CONF-690705 from Clearinghouse for Federal Scientific and Technical Information, National Bureau of Standards, U.S. Department of Commerce, Springfield, Virginia 92151.

Contains the proceedings of a conference held 27-29 July 1969. The participants, who came from academia, industry, and government, address the question, "How might the intellectual resources of mid-American universities, together with those of Argonne National Laboratory, be applied to the problems of improving man's environment?" Regional interinstitutional cooperation working in a consortial framework was viewed as a possible mechanism.

Ashby, Eric. RECONCILING MAN WITH THE ENVIRONMENT. Stanford, Calif.: Stanford University Press, 1978. ix, 104 p.

In his Leon Junior Memorial Lectures, Ashby discussed the process of identifying an environmental hazard and the political action taken to control the hazard. He identified the process as a chain reaction in which there are three steps: (1) arousal of public opinion, (2) objective scientific and economic examination of the hazard, and (3) formulation of a political discussion. At each stage there were numerous problems and need for value judgments. These problems were discussed with examples. Ashby concludes that there is a trend toward greater and more rational concern on the part of the public about environmental hazards and their control and was optimistic that, within the framework of the present political systems, man and environment can be successfully reconciled. He was, however, less optimistic that these political systems could cope with allocation of scarce natural resources and reconciliation of ideological differences.

Barnsey, Morris E., and Hibbs, James R., eds. SOCIAL SCIENCES AND THE ENVIRONMENT. CONFERENCE ON THE PRESENT AND POTENTIAL CONTRIBUTION OF THE SOCIAL SCIENCES TO RESEARCH AND POLICY FORMULATION IN THE QUALITY OF THE PHYSICAL ENVIRONMENT. Boulder: University of Colorado Press, 1967. vi, 249 p.

This monograph contains papers presented and discussed during a conference sponsored by the University of Colorado and the Environmental Sciences Service Administration. The topics considered by the participating social, life, and physical scientists included program decisions in the environmental sciences, ecology as a basis for synthesis among social sciences, geography, the case for the specialized generalist in a science of the environment, public policy implications of environmental control, weather modifications as an uncertain innovation, valuation of public goods, economics and environmental quality, applications of program budgeting to environmental problems, and environmental policy and management. Agreeing that man-environment interactions were most complex, the unresolved issue was how most effectively to institutionalize joint research programs by persons trained and experienced in diverse disciplines (so-called interdisciplinary research).

Bower, Blair T., ed. REGIONAL RESIDUALS ENVIRONMENTAL QUALITY MANAGEMENT MODELING. Research Report R-7. Washington, D.C.: Resources for the Future, 1977. xii, 230 p. Paperbound. Tables; Figures; References.

The papers in this report grew from a conference on regional residuals environmental quality management modelling held in Rotterdam, 22-25 October 1974. The seven papers were: (1) "The Why and What of Regional Residuals-Environmental Quality Management Modeling, "Blair T. Bower; (2) "Issues Surrounding Regional Residuals-Environmental Quality Management Modeling," Allen V. Kneese and Blair T. Bower; (3) "The Lower Delaware Valley Integrated Residuals Management Model: A Summary," Walter O. Spofford, Jr., Clifford S. Russell, and Robert A. Kelly; (4) "A Coordinated Set of Economic, Hydro-Salinity, and Air Quality Models of the Upper Colorado River Basin with Applications to Current Problems," Charles W. Howe; (5) "An Analysis for REQM in the Ljubljana, Yugoslavia, Area," Daniel J. Basta, Blair T. Bower, and James L. Loundsbury; (6) "Case Study on Using Systems Engineering Models in the Environmental Pollution Research Pilot Area of Ostrava, Czechoslovakia," B. Reznicek; and (7) "What the Rotterdam Session Hath Wrought," Blair T. Bower.

Boxer, Baruch, and Pramer, David, eds. ENVIRONMENTAL PROTECTION IN THE PEOPLE'S REPUBLIC OF CHINA. Rutgers: State University of New Jersey, 1978. xii, 84 p.

Here are seven papers presented by members of the Environmental Sciences Study Group visiting the United States in September 1976: "Environmental Work in China," C. Hsiao-ke; "Research Work on Environmental Protection," C. Pao-lin; "Hygienic Evaluation of Urban Garbage and Night Soil Composting Operations," W. Tzu-shih; "An Investigation of the Effect of Phenol and Arsenic on Crops and Their Accumulation in Plants," H. Yin-hsiao; "Toxic Elements in the Sediments of Water Bodies in China's Semi-arid Area and Their Environmental Chemical Behavior," C. Shen; "Experiment on the Removal of Ammonia Nitrogen by Algae," W. Te-ming; and "The Application of Aerylonitrile-Oxidizing Microorganisms for Polyacrylonitrile Wastewater Treatment," Y. Hui-fang.

Burberry, Peter. ENVIRONMENT AND SERVICES. 3d ed. London: B.T. Batsford, 1977. 350 p. Paperbound. Diagrams; Tables; Index.

Burberry has completed detailed information about environmental factors and services which are important in building design and construction. The book has been written so that it may be used as a reference in courses on building design and technology. The material is arranged under three main topics: environmental factors, environmental services, and utility services.

Caldwell, Lynton Keith. IN DEFENSE OF EARTH: INTERNATIONAL PROTECTION OF THE BIOSPHERE. Bloomington: Indiana University Press, 1972. x, 295 p. References; Appendixes.

Caldwell discusses the historical aspects of the environmental movement which today seeks to bring man's relation to the biosphere under rational control. He considers international conservation efforts, protection of resources, transnational structures, national programs for environmental protection, and various strategies for safeguarding the biosphere. One appendix gives a representative listing of international organizations and programs concerned with environmental issues, the other a list of international conferences and agreements of particular significance for protection of the biosphere, 1945-1972.

Chanlett, Emil T. ENVIRONMENTAL PROTECTION. New York: McGraw-Hill Book Co., 1973. xvi, 569 p.

Chanlett seeks to provide the rationale for managing resources, disposing of wastes, dealing with insect and animal pests, and protecting food supplies so that both human health and also natural ecosystems are protected. He emphasizes principles and objectives of design and practice. Among the specific topics discussed are water resources; disposal of domestic, industrial, and solid wastes; air pollution; vector control; food protection; ionizing radiation; various electromagnetic radiations (e.g., ultraviolet, laser and microwave); and heat and sound.

Charlesworth, James C., and Eggers, Alfred J., Jr., eds. HARMONIZING TECHNOLOGICAL DEVELOPMENTS AND SOCIAL POLICY IN AMERICA. Monograph no. 11. Philadelphia: American Academy of Political and Social Science, 1970. vii, 247 p. Paperbound.

The monograph contains six conference study papers: (1) "The Development of Social Policy in Technological America," J. C. Charlesworth; (2) "Recent Technological Developments Which Have Had an Impact, Good or Bad, on Our Society," R.L. Bisplingoff; (3) "Likely Technological Developments of the Future which May Significantly Affect Our Society," S. Ramo; (4) "Educating Technologists in Desirable Social Policy and Educating Social Scientists in Technological Capabilities," W.J. Haggerty; (5) "How to Achieve a Balance between Technological Progress and Control of Its Undesirable Side Effects," F. Seitz; and "Machinery Needed to Harmonize Technological Developments and Social Policy," J.J. Carson. The conference was held 6-7 May 1970.

Cooley, Richard A., and Wandesforde-Smith, Geoffrey, eds. CONGRESS AND THE ENVIRONMENT. Seattle: University of Washington Press, 1970. xix, 277 p.

The authors examine controversial environmental issues which were addressed by the U.S. Congress in the 1960s. The issues included land use policy, for example, the Wilderness Act; management of water quality and uses, for example, water quality standards; and wild and scenic rivers; solid waste management; noise abatement; control of ocean floor; and a national environmental policy. From these analyses it is evident that political and economic forces complicated an orderly response by government to a number of environmental problems.

Coomber, Nicholas H., and Biswas, Asit K. EVALUATION OF ENVIRONMENTAL INTANGIBLES: REVIEW OF TECHNIQUES. [Ottawa]: Environment Canada, Ecological Systems Branch, June 1972. 74 p. Paperbound.

Coomber and Biswas examine the historical and economic background of evaluatory techniques and their applicability to cost-benefit analysis and discuss techniques for both economic and also nonfinancial evaluation of environmental intangibles.

Daetz, Douglas, and Pantell, Richard H., eds. ENVIRONMENTAL MODELING: ANALYSIS AND MANAGEMENT. Stroudsburg, Pa.: Dowden, Hutchinson and Ross, 1974. xv, 407 p. Bibliog.; Indexes.

The articles illustrate the difficulties and applications of systems analysis for analysis and management of environmental problems. The papers are arranged in six groups: (1) ecosystems analysis, (2) management of ecological systems, (3) air quality, (4) water management, (5) waste management, and (6) coupled-systems analysis. Each group is introduced with editorial comments.

Darling, Frank Fraser, and Milton, John Potter, eds. FUTURE ENVIRONMENTS OF NORTH AMERICA. Garden City, N.Y.: Natural History Press, 1966. xviii, 767 p.

This is the record of a conference convened by the Conservation Foundation in April 1965, at Airlie House, Warrenton, Virginia. Participants examine the status of the human habitat and its future. The emphasis is on the need for careful, ecologically sensitive management. The papers of part 1 deal with the organic world and its environment. In part 2, the focus is the developmental history and future of regions, viz. highly productive lands, middle America, tundra and taiga, and arid lands. The papers of part 3 examine economic patterns and processes, and those of part 4, social and cultural pruposes. In part 5, the focus is regional planning and development, and part 6, organization and implementation. Discussion is also recorded.

Dunne, Thomas, and Leopold, Luna B. WATER IN ENVIRONMENTAL PLANNING. San Francisco: W.H. Freeman and Co., 1978. xxvii, 818 p. Bibliog.; Table.

This book is a textbook at the senior and graduate levels for planners and students concerned with solving or avoiding problems in environmental quality. Emphasis is on hydrology, geomorphology, and river quality; materials are also included on landscape architecture, physical geography, environmental geology, agricultural management, forestry, and engineering. Most chapters are followed by lists of typical problems; many chapters by bibliographies. A table of conversions and equivalents is included.

Edington, John M., and Edington, M. Ann. ECOLOGY AND ENVIRONMENTAL PLANNING. London: Chapman and Hall, 1977. vii, 246 p. References.

The Edingtons discuss the application of ecological concepts and principles to environmental planning at the regional level. In the first part, there are general discussions of rural land use, urban development, industrial development, man-made lakes, and transportation systems. In the second part, there are four case studies: coastal development area, national park, district industrial area, and tropical development area. The authors' objective is to demonstrate how to minimize disruption by human enterprises.

Ewald, William R., Jr., ed. ENVIRONMENT AND CHANGE: THE NEXT FIFTY YEARS. Bloomington: Indiana University Press, 1968. xvi, 397 p.

The editor and his colleagues were commissioned by the American Institute of Planners to prepare philosophical papers on "The Next Fifty Years," which aimed at defining the human environment, the forces of change, competence to cope with change, and future roles of individuals and society. Within this context, the papers are organized under five general topics: (1) creating the future environment; (2) future change; (3) planning for change; (4) the future society and the role of the individual; and (5) youth, technology and the world.

_____. ENVIRONMENT FOR MAN: THE NEXT FIFTY YEARS. Bloomington: Indiana University Press, 1967. ix, 308 p.

This book results from a two-year national consultation mounted by the American Institute of Planners and begins with a conference on optimum environment with man as the measure, held 14-18 August 1966 in Portland, Oregon. The papers are intended to begin the definition of optimum environment, its controllable variables, and its functions, in an attempt to understand both the present state of the art of city planning and the scope of the intellectual enterprise yet to be evolved to develop a truly human environment. Authors include René Dubos, John W. Dyckman, Christopher Alexander, Stephen Carr, William L.C. Wheaton, and John T. Howard.

Fitzpatrick, Malcolm S. ENVIRONMENTAL HEALTH PLANNING: COMMUNITY DEVELOPMENT BASED ON ENVIRONMENTAL AND HEALTH PRECEPTS. Cambridge, Mass.: Ballinger Publishing Co., 1978. xiii, 265 p.

Fitzpatrick asserts that environmental health planning is a crucial step in community development. With this position in mind, he discusses the essential planning criteria and then develops a comprehensive framework for the planning process. He then analyzes the environmental impact statements which were drawn up for ten new experimental communities. These statements prove to be inadequate when judged in terms of his proposed planning framework. He concludes that, in order to conserve scarce resources, the planning process must be improved.

Fox, Irving S., and Caldwell, Lynton K. RESEARCH ON POLICY AND ADMINISTRATION IN ENVIRONMENTAL QUALITY PROGRAMS. Environmental Studies, no. 4. Edited by Lynton K. Caldwell. Bloomington: Institute of Public Administration, Indiana University, 1967. 53 p. Paperbound.

The two authors examine the role of the political scientist in policy research. Fox proposes that such research should not only discover what may be, but, also given social needs and values, what should be. Two types of studies are involved: (1) engineering-economic, and (2) institutional. The most difficult research task is the judicious determination of research priorities. Caldwell differentiates research on environmental quality from natural resources research and suggests how research on environmental policy and administration might be strengthened.

Frenkiel, Francois N., and Goodall, David W., eds. SIMULATION MODELING OF ENVIRONMENTAL PROBLEMS. Scope Report no. 9. Chichester, Engl., and New York: John Wiley and Sons, 1978. xvi, 112 p. Paperbound. Bibliog.; Glossary.

This report stems from a SCOPE (Scientific Committee of Problems of Environment) Workshop on Simulation Modeling held at the

Holcomb Research Institute, Butler University, Indianapolis, 21-27
March 1976. Topics are purposes and applications of simulation
modelling in environmental problems and decision making, problems
of modelling for decision makers, case studies of simulation modelling
and national experience with modelling in environmental management, possible areas and priorities for improvements, and recommendations.

Friedlaender, Ann Fetter, ed. APPROACHES TO CONTROLLING AIR POL-
LUTION. Cambridge: MIT Press, 1978. x, 465 p.

This volume records the proceeding of a MIT-U.S. Bicentennial
Workshop and Conferences on Air Pollution and Administrative
Control held 2-3 December 1976. Seven papers were presented:
(1) "The Political Rationality of Innovation: The Clean Air Act
Amendments of 1970," H. Ingram; (2) "Judging the Impon-
derables of Environmental Policy: Judicial Review under the Clean
Air Act," R.B. Stewart; (3) "The Political Economy of Implementation: The Clean Air Act and Stationary Sources," M.J. Roberts
and S.O. Farrell; (4) "Regulatory Strategies for Pollution Control,"
A.M. Spence and N.L. Weitzman; (5) "Market Approaches to
the Measurement of the Benefits of Air Pollution Abatement,"
D.L. Rubenfeld; (6) "The Costs and Technology of Pollution Abatement," D.N. Dewees; and (7) "Government Policies toward Auto-
motive Emissions Control," E.S. Mills and L.J. White. Included
are invited comments and concluding comments.

Garvey, Gerald. ENERGY, ECOLOGY, ECONOMY. New York: W.W.
Norton and Co., 1972. 235 p.

Based on a three-year project conducted by the author for the
Princeton University Center of International Studies, this study of
the environmental impact of energy use in the United States is
intended to help supply a sound framework of relevant environmental concepts for building a national energy policy. The central
theme is that solution of problems in this field will require responses that are timely, informed by facts rather than by doctrines
either of free enterprise or of "eco-theology," and reliant on a
mix of technological and policy adjustments. Special attention
is devoted to coal, petroleum, and nuclear power, as each affects
air quality and water quality.

Gough, Beverly E., ed. WORLD ENVIRONMENTAL DIRECTORY. 4th ed.
Silver Spring, Md.: Business Publishers, 1980. cxxviii, 965 p. Indexes.

This edition contains eighty-two hundred listings and more than forty
thousand names of institutions and persons working in environmental
fields. For the United States, the listings include pollution control
manufacturers; professional services; federal and state government agencies; independent agencies and commissions; attorneys with environmental interests; professional (scientific), technical (trade) and public
interest organizations; universities and other educational institutions;

corporate environmental officials; state offices for air implementation plans; environmental libraries and periodical publications. There are also separate sections for international organizations; Africa; Asia; Australia; New Zealand; Europe; Middle America; North America; and South America.

Harvey, Brian, and Hallett, John D. ENVIRONMENT AND SOCIETY: AN INTRODUCTORY ANALYSIS. Cambridge: MIT Press, 1977. ix, 163 p. Paperbound. References.

Harvey and Hallett write about the environmental debate. Topics are ecological principles; interrelations among population, food, and resources; the environmental debate; environmental politics and economics; environmental policy; and the future of society.

Hey, Richard D., and Davies, Trevor D., eds. SCIENCE, TECHNOLOGY AND ENVIRONMENTAL MANAGEMENT. Westmead, Engl.: Saxon House and D.C. Heath; Lexington, Mass.: Lexington House and D.C. Heath, 1975. xvi, 297 p. Tables; Figures; Maps; References.

In order to protect and maintain environmental quality, scientists and technologists must join in the decision-making process of environmental management. This was the thrust of a symposium on Applied Environment Science held at the 1974 Annual Conference of the Institute of British Geographers, from which the present volume developed. The contributions are arranged under nine broad topics: introduction, countryside management, coast protection, river engineering, water resource management, rural water pollution, atmospheric pollution in rural areas, urban storm drainage, and techniques and applications of agroclimatology.

House, Peter William, and McLeod, John. LARGE-SCALE MODELS FOR POLICY EVALUATION. New York: John Wiley and Sons, 1977. xxi, 326 p. Appendixes; Figures; Tables; Bibliog.

House and McLeod address the application of large-scale models to evaluating environmental policy. They discuss background and terminology, data, methodology, verification, validation, documentation, use, implementation, and transfer.

International Bank for Reconstruction and Development. ENVIRONMENTAL, HEALTH, AND HUMAN ECOLOGIC CONSIDERATIONS IN ECONOMIC DEVELOPMENT PROJECTS. Washington, D.C.: World Bank, 1974. ix, 142 p. Paperbound. References.

For the use of developing countries planning modifications of the natural environment, such as dams, airports, irrigation systems, and industrial facilities, this handbook presents guidelines for project planning. Its purpose is to provide a checklist for detailed environmental considerations and standards, to be used in planning and appraising sixteen kinds of development projects (in agriculture, industry, transportation, and utilities). Also, public health services are discussed as related to construction projects in developing countries. There is a summary of existing environmental standards throughout the world.

James, David Edward; Jansen, Huib M.A.; and Opschoor, J.B. ECONOMIC APPROACHES TO ENVIRONMENTAL PROBLEMS: TECHNIQUES AND RESULTS OF EMPIRICAL ANALYSIS. Fundamental Aspects of Pollution Control and Environmental Science. Amsterdam: Elsevier Scientific Publishing Co., 1978. xi, 234 p. Appendixes; Bibliog.

The authors demonstrate how the analytical techniques of economics have been applied to environmental problems. Although prior knowledge of economics is helpful, it is not essential in using this book. The analytic techniques described include cost and benefit, monetary damage functions, project evaluation, general equilibrium assessment models, and input-output models. There is also a discussion of environmental policy.

Kelly, Donald R.; Stunkel, Kenneth R.; and Wescott, Richard R. THE ECONOMIC SUPERPOWERS AND THE ENVIRONMENT; THE UNITED STATES, THE SOVIET UNION, AND JAPAN. San Francisco: W.H. Freeman and Co., 1976. ix, 335 p.

The book deals with the environmental problems and the difficulties of developing mechanisms for managing those problems in three nations which are the leading producers, consumers, and polluters. Three separate national profiles are presented in a common framework which includes discussion of cultural and economic setting; scope and nature of problems such as population, energy, air and water pollution, solid wastes radioactive pollution, noise pollution, ecosystem deterioration, and environmental crisis and quality of life; awareness of problem; politics of environmental quality; and active program of environmental management. The authors are not optimistic about the long-term capabilities of these nations to cope with their problems.

Leive, David M. INTERNATIONAL REGULATORY REGIMES. CASE STUDIES IN HEALTH, METEOROLOGY, AND FOOD. 2 vols. Lexington Books. Lexington, Mass.: D.C. Heath and Co., 1976. xliv, 618 p.

Working under the auspices of the American Society for International Law, Leive carried out a comprehensive study of the development and implementation of the regulatory instruments of three UN specialized agencies. He chose to identify these instruments and the attendant legislative, administrative, and judicial procedures as "international regulatory regimes." Part 1 is devoted to regulatory activities of the World Health Organization, part 2, to the regulatory activities of the World Meteorological Organization, and part 3 to the Joint Food Standards Program of the Food and Agricultural Organization and the World Health Organization. In part 4, Leive compares and evaluates the three regulatory regimes and offers a number of recommendations for increasing their effectiveness.

McElrath, Dennis C.; Grant, Daniel R.; and Wengert, Norman. POLITICAL DYNAMICS OF ENVIRONMENTAL CONTROL. Environmental Studies, no. 1. Edited by Lynton K. Caldwell. Bloomington: Institute of Public Administration, University of Indiana, 1967. iv, 62 p. Paperbound.

> Three essays--"Public Response to Environmental Problems,"
> D.C. McElrath; "Carrots, Sticks and Political Consensus," D.R. Grant;
> and "Perennial Problems of Federal Coordination," N. Wengert--
> examine the political problems of formulating and implementing
> policies for environmental control.

McHarg, I.L. DESIGN WITH NATURE. Garden City, N.Y.: Natural History Press, 1969. viii, 197 p.

> McHarg demonstrates how it is possible to interrelate the resources
> of the land (physical features, minerals, soil, water, and plants)
> and the construction of town, cities, and recreational areas so as
> to minimize deleterious consequences both for the biosphere and
> man's health. He would call this exercice ecological planning
> and resource management.

Marquis, Ralph W., ed. ENVIRONMENTAL IMPROVEMENT (AIR, WATER, AND SOIL). Washington, D.C.: U.S. Department of Agriculture, Graduate School, 1966. ix, 105 p. Paperbound.

> Four public lectures given in May 1966 were sponsored by the
> Graduate School: (1) "Man and His Environment--Scope, Impact
> and Nature," R.J. Dubos; (2) "Environmental Improvement--
> Institutional and Governmental Aspects," E.S. Muskie; (3) "Control
> of Environment--Economic and Technological Prospects," J.T. Mid-
> dleton; and (4) "The Future of Environmental Improvement," S.D.
> Ripley. Reactions from invited speakers are included.

Mauss, Evelyn A., and Ullmann, John E., eds. "Conservation of Energy Resources." ANNALS OF THE NEW YORK ACADEMY OF SCIENCES 324 (22 April 1979): 1-83. Paperbound.

> This volume records a workshop conference held 15 October 1977.
> The papers and discussion focused on two broad areas: (1) basic
> problems and prospects, and (2) implementation of a national energy
> conservation program.

Mills, Edwin S. THE ECONOMICS OF ENVIRONMENTAL QUALITY. New York: W.W. Norton and Co., 1978. 304 p.

> In this undergraduate textbook, Mills assumes a familiarity with

microeconomic theory. The text is arranged in four parts. In part 1, the tools of economic analysis are discussed. Part 2 is devoted to the pollutants which cause degradation of environmental quality and applications of economic analysis. Mills examines the economic aspects of environmental policy in the United States in part 3, and international and global problems and policies in part 4. With each chapter, there are discussion questions, problems, and suggestions for further reading.

Moos, Rudolf, and Brownstein, Robert. ENVIRONMENT AND UTOPIA: A SYNTHESIS. New York: Plenum Press, 1977. ix, 284 p.

Moos and Brownstein survey the general conceptual and philosophical background for environmental, ecological, and utopian thoughts. They then present case studies of optimal communities--the Oneida community; Columbia, Maryland; Skinner's WALDEN II. In their final section, they discuss environmental and utopian perspectives and conclude that to achieve an ecological utopia, it must become a political issue of society.

National Research Council. Committee for Study of Environmental Manpower. MANPOWER FOR ENVIRONMENTAL POLLUTION CONTROL. Vol. 5. Analytical Studies for the U.S. Environmental Protection Agency. Washington, D.C.: National Academy of Sciences, 1977. xx, 427 p. Paperbound.

The members of the committee assembled information on the manpower needs for environmental pollution control and made projections for changes in manpower between 1974 and 1985. The topics addressed include rationale of environmental manpower planning and policy; role of manpower development in EPA: employment, demand, and supply of pollution control manpower; and quality of manpower. Five appendixes comprise the majority of the report: (1) legal authorities for manpower; (2) national data base; (3) federal employment; (4) state and local employment; and (5) employment in industrial and private sectors. The principal recommendation was that Congress should clarify its intent for environmental manpower development and provide EPA with a clear directive concerning its manpower and training authority.

National Research Council. Committee on Environmental Decision Making. DECISION MAKING IN THE ENVIRONMENTAL PROTECTION AGENCY. Vol. 2. Analytical Studies for the U.S. Environmental Protection Agency. Washington, D.C.: National Academy of Sciences, 1977. xvi, 249 p. Paperbound.

The committee studied the process of decision making in the Environmental Protection Agency. The principal focus of the study was the role of scientific and technical information in the agency's deliberations. Numerous recommendations were made for improving the decision-making process. These dealt with use of analyses in

decision making, barriers to implementing regulations, advice and
review from experts outside the agency, dependence on regulated
industries for data, scientific and technical research in support of
decision making, statutory deadlines on administrative actions, procedural steps in review of proposed regulations (e.g., interagency
review and public participation), and use of alternate strategies
for achieving goals.

National Research Council. Committee on Multimedium Approach to Municipal
Sludge Management. MULTIMEDIUM MANAGEMENT OF MUNICIPAL SLUDGE.
Vol. 9. Analytical Studies for the U.S. Environmental Protection Agency.
Washington, D.C.: National Academy of Sciences, 1978. xv, 187 p. Paper-
bound. References; Tables; Figures.

This report is a review of the options available for managing the
residuals of municipal wastewater treatment. It discusses the
processes by which sludge can be disposed of or reused. The options are compared in terms of their primary impacts, intermedium
effects, risk of environmental damage, technical reliability, costs,
and status in regard to environmental regulation. Findings are
drawn together to outline a general approach to decision making
on sludge management on a multimedium basis.

National Research Council. Committee on Pesticide Decision Making. PESTI-
CIDE DECISION MAKING. Vol. 7. Analytical Studies for the U.S. Environmental Protection Agency. Washington, D.C.: National Academy of Sciences,
1978. xiv, 109 p. Paperbound.

The principal concerns of the committee were the methods of data
acquisition and use by the Environmental Protection Agency in
making decisions regulating the application of pesticides. The
report includes a summary of recommendations and discussions of
regulatory authority and procedures, role of scientific information
in decision making (e.g., registration and reregistration of pesticides and assessment of risks and benefits), coordination and communication of information among federal and state agencies, manpower in regulatory activities and international impact of regulatory decisions.

National Research Council. Committee on Pollution. WASTE MANAGEMENT
AND CONTROL. Publication 1400. Washington, D.C.: National Academy
of Sciences, 1966. xii, 257 p. Paperbound.

This is an overview of pollution, in general and in relation to
legal, legislative, and institutional problems. Areas of inadequacy
are pointed out, together with possible improved approaches and
recommendations for remedial measures. Eight appendixes contain
the findings of study groups on specialized problems; pollution
processes in ecosystems; criteria instrumentation, and monitoring;
the transport system; the residue situation; pollution-abatement

technology; legal and public administration aspects; public policy and institutional arrangements; and analysis of pollution in the Delaware estuary.

National Research Council. Committee on Power Plant Siting. ENGINEERING FOR RESOLUTION OF THE ENERGY-ENVIRONMENT DILEMMA: A SUMMARY. Washington, D.C.: National Academy of Engineering, 1971. xii, 51 p. Paperbound.

The dilemma is the conflict between exploitation of resources to improve quality of living and conservation of resources. The document includes summary reports of four working groups on environmental protection: (1) power plant siting and air quality-engineering considerations; (2) water; (3) radiological aspects of power plants and their fuel cycles; and (4) aesthetics and land use; a group on systems approach to site selection, and a group on energy and economic growth. The conclusions and recommendations of the committee are presented.

National Research Council. Committee on Principles of Decision Making for Regulating Chemicals in the Environment. DECISION MAKING FOR REGULATING CHEMICALS IN THE ENVIRONMENT. Washington, D.C.: National Academy of Sciences, 1975. ix, 232 p. Paperbound.

Undertaken at the request of the Environmental Protection Agency, this study was intended to assess the state of the art of this type of decision making, to identify inadequacies in current methods, and to recommend ways to help regulatory agencies reach sound and equitable decisions for controlling chemicals in the environment. The report focuses primarily on industrial chemicals and on federal regulatory agencies. Its conclusions are in four areas: (1) the statutory and organizational basis for regulation; (2) openness and access to the decision-making process; (3) the availability of adequate and reliable information; and (4) the proper use of analysis. Eleven appendixes provide the working papers on which the report was developed, with other supplementary information.

National Research Council. Environmental Research Assessment Committee. RESEARCH AND DEVELOPMENT IN THE ENVIRONMENTAL PROTECTION AGENCY. Vol. 3. Analytical Studies for the U.S. Environmental Protection Agency. Washington, D.C.: National Academy of Sciences, 1977. xii, 99 p. Paperbound.

This is an examination of the process by which the Environmental Protection Agency utilizes scientific information in decision making. Two principal conclusions are reached: the agency should continue to perform and sponsor research; the agency's research program should both support decisions and anticipate future environmental problems.

National Research Council. Environmental Study Group. INSTITUTIONS FOR
EFFECTIVE MANAGEMENT OF THE ENVIRONMENT. Part 1. Washington,
D.C.: National Academy of Sciences, 1970. vii, 62 p. Paperbound.

> The topics discussed in this report to the Environmental Studies
> Board include Institute for Analytical Studies, education and the
> environment, monitoring the environment, national laboratory for
> environmental science, and federal organization for managing the
> environment. The study group made a series of recommendations
> relative to these topics.

National Research Council. Steering Committee for Analytical Studies. Commission on Natural Resources. PERSPECTIVES ON TECHNICAL INFORMATION
FOR ENVIRONMENTAL PROTECTION. Vol. 1. Analytical Studies for the
U.S. Environmental Protection Agency. Washington, D.C.: National Academy
of Sciences, 1977. xiii, 108 p. Paperbound. Index.

> The report provides an overview of a series of studies aimed at
> evaluating how the Environmental Protection Agency uses scientific
> information in decision making and in working with Congress and
> the public. Specific recommendations from four groups participating
> in the studies are included: (1) Committee on Environmental De-
> cision Making, (2) Environmental Research Assessment Committee,
> (3) Study Group on Environmental Monitoring, and (4) Committee
> for Study of Environmental Manpower.

OIL SPILL PREVENTION, CONTROL, AND COUNTERMEASURE PLAN REVIEW.
Houston: Pace Co., 1975. 378 p. Looseleaf. Appendixes; Glossary; Bibliog.

> This is an instructional manual for training Environmental Protection
> Agency inspectors charged with enforcing the federal regulations
> on oil pollution prevention and control, first made effective in
> January 1974. The manual was prepared by Pace Company under
> the sponsorship of Rice University, the University of Texas School
> of Public Health, and the EPA. The contents include a technical
> review of affected facilities both onshore and offshore (e.g., tank
> farms, drilling facilities, pipelines); areas of potential oil spills;
> oil spill prevention; oil spill countermeasures; and inspection pro-
> cedures.

Pearson, Charles, and Pryor, Anthony. ENVIRONMENT: NORTH AND SOUTH:
AN ECONOMIC INTERPRETATION. New York: John Wiley and Sons, 1978.
xxi, 355 p. Notes; Tables; Maps; References.

> In a monograph written for individuals other than professional
> economists, Pearson and Pryor explore the relationship between
> environmental degradation and development, asking whether eco-
> nomic development and preservation of the environment are com-
> patible or incompatible. They discuss concepts and issues, the
> environmental landscape, trade and investment impacts, environ-
> ment and development project appraisal, transnational pollution

and international common property resources, and agriculture and environment in developing countries. They conclude that development can be accomplished without necessarily causing environmental imbalances.

Pregel, Boris; Lasswell, Harold D.; and McHale, John, eds. "Environment and Society in Transition: World Priorities." ANNALS OF THE NEW YORK ACADEMY OF SCIENCES 261 (30 September 1975): 1-277. Paperbound.

"World Priorities" was the theme of the Second International Conference on Society and Environment sponsored by the American Division of the World Academy of Art and Science and the New York Academy of Sciences, 6-11 May 1974. The papers presented addressed several issues: a framework of world public order, the role of universities and the need for scientific and technical information, the problems of feeding the world's population, and a world energy policy. In addition, working groups prepared memoranda on these issues. Although there were differences of opinion, it was evident that the general issues addressed were ones of high priority.

Pregel, Boris; Lasswell, Harold D.; McHale, John; Mudd, Stuart; Armstrong, Fred G.; Korff, Serge; and Harte, Ben, eds. "Public Policy toward Environment 1973: A Review and Appraisal." ANNALS OF THE NEW YORK ACADEMY OF SCIENCES 216 (18 May 1973): 1-202. Paperbound.

The report, following up earlier recommendations (see Albertson and Barnett, p. 182), is a commentary on environmental policy. A series of reports was prepared covering such topics as pollution, weather modification, uses of resources, agricultural productivity, housing, population, health, education, and human genetics. Each examined the goals of public policy, positive and negative achievements, and alternate proposals. The consensus was that U.S. public policy toward the environment was disorganized and fragmentary. Energy, education, and population, in particular, needed serious attention from decision makers.

President's Science Advisory Committee. Environmental Pollution Panel. RESTORING THE QUALITY OF OUR ENVIRONMENT. Washington, D.C.: Government Printing Office for the White House, 1965. xii, 317 p. Paperbound.

The members of the panel and the members of several subpanels (soil contamination, health effects of environmental pollution, benchmark surveillance, atmospheric carbon dioxide, solid wastes, combined sewers, effects of chlorinating wastes, aquatic blooms, effects of pollutants on living organisms other than man, and improved pest control practices) studied environmental pollution, implications, and consequences for man and other living organisms. Major problems were identified and a series of recommendations were made relating to environmental management, research on environmental problems, and training.

Health Intervention Strategies

Romani, John H., and Caldwell, Lynton K. POLITICS, PROFESSIONALISM
AND THE ENVIRONMENT. Environmental Studies, no. 3. Edited by Lynton
K. Caldwell. Bloomington: Institute of Public Administration, Indiana Uni-
versity, 1967. 43 p. Paperbound.

> Two papers--"The Administration of Public Health Services,"
> J.H. Romani; and "The Application of Engineering Technology,"
> by L.K. Caldwell--deal with current public issues and provide an
> indication of why it is difficult to obtain a clear focus on envi-
> ronmental quality as an aspect of public policy.

Saarinen, Thomas F. ENVIRONMENTAL PLANNING. PERCEPTION AND
BEHAVIOR. Boston: Houghton Mifflin Co., 1976. xiii, 262 p. Paperbound.
Illus.

> Decision making in environmental planning depends very much on
> one's perception or conception of reality. This knowledge has,
> in recent years, stimulated much research. Saarinen has brought
> some of that work together in a book for beginning students in
> behavioral and social sciences, environmental studies, and human
> ecology. The perceptional space considered moves progressively
> from personal spaces and rooms, through architectural spaces, neigh-
> borhoods, cities, regions, and nations to the world.

Seneca, Joseph J., and Taussig, Michael K. ENVIRONMENTAL ECONOMICS.
2d ed. Englewood Cliffs, N.J.: Prentice-Hall, 1979. xiii, 399 p. References.

> Seneca and Taussig have extensively revised this edition from the
> first published in 1974. They assume that readers have had an
> introductory economic course and they treat environmental eco-
> nomics as a blend of economic theory, environmental facts, and
> social circumstances. There are five parts: (1) concepts of en-
> vironmental economics; (2) theory of environmental economics; (3)
> economics of environmental problems (e.g., water and air quality
> and quality of life); (4) mechanisms of environmental control; and
> (5) population, economic growth, and quality of life. Each chapter
> contains discussion questions and selected references. Chapter 2
> contains a technical treatment of efficiency in a private market
> economy.

Smithsonian Annual II. THE FITNESS OF MAN'S ENVIRONMENT. New York:
Harper and Row, 1968. 250 p. Paperbound.

> The volume comprises papers delivered at the Smithsonian Annual
> Symposium, 16-18 February 1967. The authors examine, from
> various angles, what is wrong with man's environment and search
> for solutions to the complex problems. The several essays deal
> with such topics as environmental ethics, values and ideals, stew-
> ardship of the earth, and problems of the city.

Teachem, Richard; McGarry, Michael; and Mora, Duncan, eds. WATER, WASTES AND HEALTH IN HOT CLIMATES. London: John Wiley and Sons, 1977. xvi, 399 p.

The editors have brought together a collection of original essays which provide innovative and provocative ideas concerning solutions to "the public health engineering crisis in developing countries." The contributions from twenty-two authors deal with health and water quality, water supplies for low-income communities, institutional development for water management, and sanitation. External forces, principally money and ideas, are seen as assisting the developing countries with their problems. This book aims to supply some of the ideas.

U.S. Department of Health, Education, and Welfare. A STRATEGY FOR A LIVABLE ENVIRONMENT. Washington, D.C.: Government Printing Office, 1967. xxi, 90 p. Paperbound.

This report to the secretary of Health, Education, and Welfare was prepared by a Task Force on Environmental Health and Related Problems. It was recommended that the department take action against the most serious existing problems and develop an environmental protection system to monitor environmental hazards and prevent them from causing damage. A priority list of action goals was drawn up and a strategy for achieving them was proposed as an Environmental Protection Act.

U.S. Environmental Protection Agency. THE ECONOMICS OF CLEAN WATER-- 1973. ANNUAL REPORT. January 1974. Serial no. 93-20. Washington, D.C.: Government Printing Office, 1974. x, 120 p. Paperbound. Tables; Figures.

This sixth in the series of Clean Water Reports to Congress has a broader scope than previous reports. It contains seven chapters which discuss the nature of and trends in water quality; the status of public sewerage services and the costs of municipal facilities to meet the 1977 standards; the costs of controlling industrial non-thermal pollution; the capacity of U.S. agriculture to meet food and fiber demand to the year 2000; an introduction to cost and benefit analysis; potential problems in implementing recent amendments to the Federal Water Pollution Control Act; summary and conclusions.

_____. U.S. DIRECTORY OF ENVIRONMENTAL SOURCES. 2d ed. Washington, D.C.: 1977. 739 p. Paperbound.

The directory includes 1,114 U.S. environmental organizations (sources) which have registered with U.S. International Environmental Referral Center. For each organization there is information on its address and phone number, its principal activity, a description of its program, sponsorship, and functions. The organizations are classified by principal activity, alphabetically, and geographically.

Vesilind, P. Aarne. ENVIRONMENTAL POLLUTION AND CONTROL. Ann Arbor, Mich.: Ann Arbor Science Publishers, 1975. 232 p. Paperbound. Glossary; Bibliog.

> Vesilind's book presents, in nontechnical terms, the engineering aspects of controlling the quality of air and water and managing pollution from solid wastes and noise. For each of these major topics, there are chapters dealing with the environmental problem, assessment techniques, and control procedures together with legal and economic consideration. The author also briefly discusses the environmental impact statement and environmental ethics.

Ward, Barbara, and Dubos, René. ONLY ONE EARTH: THE CARE AND MAINTENANCE OF A SMALL PLANET. New York: W.W. Norton and Co., 1972. ix, 225 p.

> This monograph comprises an unofficial report commissioned by the secretary-general of the United Nations Conference on the Human Environment which convened in Stockholm in the summer of 1972. The book was prepared with the assistance of a 152-member committee of corresponding consultants in fifty-eight countries. Topics examined are the planet's unity, the unities of science, the problems of technology, the problems of development, and strategies which might lead to a balanced biosphere and human survival. The authors achieve an objective overview of a complex set of human ecological problems.

Wright, Deil S. INTERGOVERNMENTAL ACTION ON ENVIRONMENTAL POLICY: THE ROLE OF THE UNITED STATES. Environmental Studies, no. 2. Edited by Lynton K. Caldwell. Bloomington: Institute of Public Administration, University of Indiana, 1967. 69 p. Paperbound.

> The public control of the environment, under the U.S. Constitution, is divided between the states and the federal government. In many cases, the states have failed to meet their responsibilities. Wright examines the reasons for these failures and suggests some mechanisms for more effective action at the state level within the context of intergovernmental relations. The traditional institutions, which will be around for some time to come, must accommodate to the new demands for the management of the quality of the environment.

D. HEALTH AND WELFARE

Abbott, Phillip C., et al. NUTRITION PROGRAM DEVELOPMENT IN INDONESIA. MIT International Nutrition Planning Program. Technical Report Series, no. 2. Cambridge: MIT, 1975. iii, 152 p. Paperbound. Appendixes.

> This report contains a response to the Indonesian government for advice concerning nutrition program identification, development

and implementation, and concurrent planning and evaluation to assure most efficient utilization of financial and human resources. Part 1 summarizes the findings and conclusions of the study team. In part 2, there is an extended discussion of nutrition programs in Indonesia together with background information, some of which is detailed in five appendixes.

Atherley, Gordon R.C. OCCUPATIONAL HEALTH AND SAFETY CONCEPTS: CHEMICAL AND PROCESSING HAZARDS. London: Applied Science Publishers, 1978. xii, 408 p. References; Bibliog.

For the reader with limited background in biology, this book provides a discussion of the biological and social aspects of occupational hazards for health and safety. Atherley discusses normal biological processes and mechanisms of defense as well as the pathological responses to hazard. These discussions are amplified with case histories and examples of exposure to hazardous chemicals and operations. The concluding chapter deals with preventive strategies.

Back, Kurt W., ed. IN SEARCH FOR COMMUNITY: ENCOUNTER GROUPS AND SOCIAL CHANGE. American Association for the Advancement of Science, Selected Symposium 4. Boulder, Colo.: Westview Press, 1978. xiii, 175 p. Tables; Bibliog.

The seven essays concern current efforts to deal with a problem of contemporary society: a frustrated longing for group membership, interaction, and emotional response. Various papers present an anthropological perspective; the historical setting; the changes in the science of psychology; and the workings and techniques of therapy groups, such as encounter groups and communes.

Bendick, Marc, Jr.; Campbell, Toby H.; Bawden, D. Lee; and Jones, Melvin. TOWARD EFFICIENCY AND EFFECTIVENESS IN THE WIC DELIVERY SYSTEM. Washington, D.C.: Urban Institute, 1976. iv, 219 p. Paperbound.

The authors report to the Food and Nutrition Service of the U.S. Department of Agriculture a contractual study of the Special Supplemental Food Program for Women, Infants, and Children (WIC) made in April 1975. Investigated were WIC participants, supplemental foods, benefits from nutrition education and medical care, costs of program, and operations of program. The authors compare alternative systems of food distribution; direct distribution, retail purchases, and home delivery, and conclude that no single system is superior in all aspects of the WIC program.

Brown, Bernard, ed. FOUND: LONG-TERM GAINS FROM EARLY INTERVENTION. American Association for the Advance of Science, Selected Symposium 8. Boulder, Colo.: Westview Press, 1978. xxi, 192 p. Tables; Figures; Bibliog.

The six papers were presented at a meeting of the AAAS held in
Denver in February 1977. The purpose was to examine the effectiveness of early intervention programs such as Project Head
Start, begun in 1965, in producing lasting gains in children's
intellectual development. In all, the papers describe ninety-six
major studies which report positive impacts from such programs.

Coe, Rodney M. SOCIOLOGY OF MEDICINE. 2d ed. New York: McGraw-
Hill Book Co., 1978. x, 437 p. Footnotes.

Reflecting current developments in medical sociology and health
care, this edition has been expanded from the 1970 edition. Coe
discusses the field of medical sociology and then examines four
principal topics: disease and the sick person, health practices
and practitioners, the hospital, and the cost and organization of
health care delivery.

Corwin, Edward A.H.L., ed. ECOLOGY OF HEALTH. New York: Commonwealth Fund, 1949. xiii, 196 p.

Working papers and discussions held at the Institute of Public
Health in April 1947 were part of the centennial celebration of
the New York Academy of Medicine. The presentations and discussions were edited into composites emphasizing topics on ecology
of health, social biology, and public health administration: genetics
and public health; maternal health and nutrition; animal and insect reservoirs of disease; climate, geography, and disease; realities
in preventive psychiatry; and trends in state and local health service. Three papers were published as originally presented: "The
Hospital Survey and Construction Act and Nation-Wide Health
Program," Haven Emerson; "The Preparation of Professional Workers
in the Field of Public Health," Charles Edward Armory Winslow; and
"Education of the Layman in Health Responsibilities," Franklin Bobbitt.

Davis, Karen, and Schoen, Cathy. HEALTH AND THE WAR ON POVERTY:
A TEN-YEAR APPRAISAL. Washington, D.C.: Brookings Institution, 1978.
xiv, 230 p. Appendix.

Davis and Schoen review basic issues of and linkages between
health and poverty and federal programs aimed at breaking the
link between low income and poor health. They examine the
performance of Medicaid, Medicare, the maternal and child health
program, and the comprehensive health centers between 1965 and
1975. Their recommendations focus on both these individual programs and public policy on comprehensive health care. In an
appendix, the authors discuss the methodological problems of measuring contributions of medical care to health.

Emery, Frederick Edmund, and Trist, E.L. TOWARDS A SOCIAL ECOLOGY:
CONTEXTUAL APPRECIATIONS OF THE FUTURE IN THE PRESENT. New York:
Plenum Press, 1973. xvi, 239 p. Appendix.

Emery and Trist discuss the social aspects of human ecology, emphasizing culture and social institutions. In part 1 by Emery, the theme is concepts and methods of planning for the future in terms of what is known today about sociotechnical organizations and their adaptability. In part 2 by Trist, these concepts and methods are applied to a consideration of some aspects of the transition to a postindustrial society, which the author suggests is already in progress. In the appendix, Emery and Trist discuss "The Socio-Technical System as a Source Concept."

Esser, Aristide H., and Greenbie, Barrie B., eds. DESIGN FOR COMMUNALITY AND PRIVACY. New York: Plenum Press, 1978. vii, 344 p.

Most of the papers were presented at a workshop entitled "Design for Communality and Privacy" held at the Sixth Annual Conference of the Environmental Design Research Association, Lawrence, Kansas, April 1975. The principal topics addressed by the contributing behavior scientists and designers included crowding, microecology (e.g., privacy and structures in interpersonal relations), residential design, and urban scale design. Each group of papers is preceded by an introductory note written by the editors.

FAO/WHO. Joint FAO/WHO Expert Committee on Nutrition. FOOD AND NUTRITION STRATEGIES IN NATIONAL DEVELOPMENT. Ninth Report. Technical Report Series, no. 584. Geneva: WHO, 1976. 64 p. Paperbound.

The members of the Expert Committee reviewed the then current food and nutrition situation and earlier approaches toward development of national nutrition policies. They then considered in some detail the role of food and nutrition planning, including program implementation and evaluation, in national development.

Fry, John A. A NEW APPROACH TO MEDICINE: PRINCIPLES AND PRIORITIES IN HEALTH CARE. Baltimore: University Park Press, 1978. viii, 154 p.

Fry examines the common problems and issues of primary health care. He wonders about the amount of care, the priorities and fair allocations, usefulness and uselessness of care, clinical freedom, public responsibilities, and control by planners and administrators, and searches for answers in the light of his experience with the national health system in Great Britain.

Gilbert, Neil, and Specht, Harry, eds. PLANNING FOR SOCIAL WELFARE: ISSUES, MODELS, AND TASKS. Englewood Cliffs, N.J.: Prentice-Hall, 1977. xiii, 398 p.

This is an anthology of articles by professional planners. The readings are organized under four major headings: (1) to plan or not to plan; (2) planning models: the analytic-interactional

continuum; (3) interactional tasks: perspectives on planning as a
sociopolitical process; and (4) analytical tasks: perspectives on planning as a technomethodological process.

György, Paul, and Kline, O.L., eds. MALNUTRITION IS A PROBLEM OF
ECOLOGY. Basel, Switz.: S. Karger, 1970. xi, 224 p. Paperbound.

This book consists of papers presented at a conference on worldwide
nutrition problems, sponsored by the International Union of Nutritional Sciences and held 1–7 October 1968, in Como, Italy. The
purposes of the conference were: to stimulate research in pilot
projects in various developing countries with the cooperation of
international experts; to place particular emphasis on all factors
emanating from the human ecosystem; to emphasize the role of
volunteers as irreplaceable catalysts in short-term ecological problems;
and to outline demonstration projects using volunteers.

Hardin, Garrett. THE LIMITS OF ALTRUISM: AN ECOLOGIST'S VIEW OF
SURVIVAL. Bloomington: Indiana University Press, 1977. 154 p.

Hardin examines the role of altruism in human survival. He first
asks, Does altruism exist? He then defines responsibility in social
systems, and discusses the ethical implications of carrying capacity,
the question of a significant posterity, the meaning of survival,
and brotherhood. Hardin concludes that altruism can be ruinous
when nations ignore inherent carrying capacity of the land. Because the human population is no longer under the control of other
species, survival under reasonable conditions will only be possible
if the practice of altruism is restricted.

HEALTH INFORMATION, PLANNING, AND MONITORING. Edited by Roy
M. Acheson, David J. Hall, and Lesely Aird. Seminars in Community Medicine,
vol. 2. London: Oxford University Press, 1976. xv, 189 p. Paperbound.
Bibliog.; Glossary.

Published under the auspices of the Centre for Extension Training
in Community Medicine, London School of Hygiene and Tropical
Medicine, the volume contains papers presented and their discussion at a seminar held April 1974. Five general topics were
addressed: (1) health information at a national level; (2) indicators of need, demand, and use; (3) information and central planning; (4) information and local planning; and (5) government statistics in monitoring health.

Hilton, Alice Mary, ed. AGAINST POLLUTION AND HUNGER. New York:
Halsted Press and John Wiley and Sons, 1974. xvi, 310 p.

This volume comprises the proceedings of a conference of the Society for Social Responsibility in Science held at University of
Trondheim, Oslo, in 1971. Topics include problems of hunger,
environmental pollution, and war; education; proposed solutions to
problems and action programs; and a social philosophy.

Howe, Barbara, and Smith, James E., Jr., eds. HEALTH CARE AND SOCIAL CLASS: A SELECTED BIBLIOGRAPHY. Occasional Papers, no. 3. Ithaca, N.Y.: Cornell University, Center for Urban Development Research, 1974. v, 166 p. Paperbound.

This bibliography is limited to literature of the United States published between 1950 and 1970. The focus is sociological and sociologically oriented health publications in journals rather than monographs, government publications, and dissertations. The annotations are arranged in five sections: (1) prevalence and incidence of illness; (2) social psychological aspects; (3) behavioral aspects, including expenditures; (4) structural aspects, including characteristics of system, physicians, and patients; and (5) general, e.g., methods and relevant bibliographies.

Kasschau, Patricia L. AGING AND SOCIAL POLICY: LEADERSHIP PLANNING. New York: Praeger Publishers, 1978. xxiii, 419 p. Appendix; Tables; Figures; References.

Kasschau reports the results of a five-year survey during which she conducted structured interviews with 316 legislators, agency administrators and program heads, supervisory service personnel, corporate personnel directors, union local presidents, and advocates for the aged to determine how decision making related to programs for the aged was accomplished. The topics include role of policy leadership planning, the climate of decision making, income maintenance, health care planning, housing, transportation, employment and retirement, pattern of information-seeking in decision making, and the effects of "senior power" on outcomes of social policy.

KEY ISSUES IN POPULATION AND FOOD POLICY: CAPON SPRINGS PUBLIC POLICY CONFERENCE NO. 2. Edited by Eliot Glassheim and Charles Cargille. Washington, D.C.: University Press of America, 1978. xvi, 432 p. Paperbound.

Participants in this conference, which was sponsored by the Population/Food Fund, included scholars from many disciplines (e.g., anthropology, economics, nutrition, agriculture, demography, philosophy, literature, and business administration); congressmen; government-agency personnel; farmers; laymen; and representatives of developing countries with firsthand experience of their food and population problems. Eighty-three papers are included on the general topics of overpopulation, world hunger and malnutrition, and population and food proposals.

Lalonde, Marc. A NEW PERSPECTIVE ON THE HEALTH OF CANADIANS. Ottawa: Government of Canada, 1974. 76 p. Paperbound. English and French versions bound together.

This book provides an analysis of the health problems of Canadians

and a strategy for dealing with those problems. The health field
concept proved to be a useful framework for analysis and planning. Under this concept, four elements were identified as causes
or underlying factors in sickness and death: human biology, environment, life-style, and health care organization.

Mabogunje, Akin L.; Hardoy, Jorge Enrique; and Misra, Rameshwar Prasad.
SHELTER PROVISION IN DEVELOPING COUNTRIES: THE INFLUENCE OF
STANDARDS AND CRITERIA. SCOPE Report 11. Chichester, Engl. and New
York: John Wiley and Sons, 1978. xii, 94 p. Paperbound.

The authors address the serious problem of providing shelter for
people in the rapidly urbanizing regions of Africa, Asia, and
Latin America. They find an absence of policy guidance and a
need for standards and criteria. They discuss sources and bases
for standards and criteria and approaches for setting and evaluating
standards.

McMullin, Ernan, ed. DEATH AND DECISION. American Association for
the Advancement of Science, Selected Symposium 18. Boulder, Colo.: Westview Press, 1978. xii, 154 p.

Based on a 1977 symposium of the AAAS, this book contains eight
papers dealing with dilemmas faced by the dying and by those who
care for them. The authors represent the fields of law, philosophy,
political economy, medicine, and psychiatry. A discussion is included of the "right to die" as recently authorized by state law
in California.

Moss, N. Henry, and Mayer, Jean, eds. "Food and Nutrition in Health and
Disease." ANNALS OF THE NEW YORK ACADEMY OF SCIENCES 300
(30 November 1977): 1-474. Paperbound.

The papers had been presented at a Bicentennial conference held
in Philadelphia 1-3 December 1976. The general topics discussed
included global problems in food production, food distribution and
food policy, and applications of technology; problems and solutions
in developing countries; clinical problems; and American nutriture
and nutrition.

National Research Council. Committee on Socioeconomic Effects of Earthquake
Predictions. A PROGRAM OF STUDIES ON THE SOCIOECONOMIC EFFECTS
OF EARTHQUAKE PREDICTIONS. Washington, D.C.: National Academy of
Sciences, 1978. x, 162 p. Paperbound. References.

Since scientifically credible earthquake predictions can soon be
made, the problems of the social consequences of use of this technology are considered. These consequences include five groups:
reactions of individuals and households; reactions of businesses and
effects on the regional economy; government issues; legal problems;

generation and dissemination of predictions. Three sets of research
recommendations are included, covering both theory and policy,
and listed in order of priority.

National Research Council. Panel on the Public Policy Implications of Earthquake Prediction. EARTHQUAKE PREDICTION AND PUBLIC POLICY. Washington, D.C.: National Academy of Sciences, 1975. ix, 142 p. Paperbound.

This report, the first in a new and unstudied field, is intended
for use by decision makers in governments and private agencies;
by leaders in business and other parts of the private sector; by
scientists and engineers concerned with handling disasters; and by
interested citizens. The panel's conclusions and recommendations
appear first in the report. The remaining chapters discuss the
socially significant characteristics of earthquake prediction; the
strategy for dealing with earthquake hazards on the basis of advance warning; guidelines for the release of predictions and warnings;
economic and legal issues involved; the problem of equity; political implications of earthquake prediction; and potentially constructive responses to earthquake warning.

Osborn, June E., ed. HISTORY, SCIENCE, AND POLITICS. INFLUENZA
IN AMERICA 1918-1976. New York: Prodist, 1977. 135 p. Appendix.

The contributions to this volume derive from a symposium held
during the meetings of the American Association for the History
of Medicine, Madison, Wisconsin, May 1977. There are four
papers: (1) "The Pandemic of 1918," A.W. Crosby, Jr.; (2)
"Precursors of the Scientific Decision-Making Process Leading to
the 1976 National Immunization Campaign," J.D. Millar and
J.E. Osborn; (3) "Immunization and Public Policy: A Short Political
History of the 1976 Swine Influenza Legislation," A.J. Viseltear;
and (4) "Epilogue--Cost and Benefits of the National Immunization
Program of 1976," J.E. Osborn. The legislative proceedings concerning the program are given in the appendix.

Roemer, Milton I. SOCIAL MEDICINE: THE ADVANCE OF ORGANIZED
HEALTH SERVICES IN AMERICA. New York: Springer Publishing Co., 1978.
x, 560 p.

This anthology on trends in American social medicine includes
thirty-eight articles published by Roemer in the 1960s and 1970s.
The articles are grouped under eight topics: (1) general organizing trends; (2) poverty and the problems of health care; (3)
health insurance and payment methods; (4) organized ambulatory
services; (5) hospital trends; (6) quality evaluation and regulation;
(7) health planning; and (8) prospects ahead. Each part and
chapter has a brief introductory comment.

Rogers, Beatrice Lorge, and Levinson, F. James. SUBSIDIZED FOOD CON-

SUMPTION SYSTEMS IN LOW INCOME COUNTRIES: THE PAKISTAN EX-
PERIENCE. Discussion Papers, no. 6. MIT International Nutrition Planning
Program. Cambridge: MIT Institute of Technology, Center for International
Studies, 1976. 30 p. Paperbound.

Rogers and Levinson examine the subsidized consumption system of
Pakistan, its political and economic feasibility, and its effectiveness for bringing about redistribution of food and income for the
poor. They review the role of food subsidies and report an analysis
of the food rationing system in Pakistan. The authors conclude
that, given the particular circumstances that prevailed in Pakistan,
the subsidized consumption program did achieve some redistribution
of income and an improvement in the dietary intake of the low
income groups.

Ross, Walter Sanford. THE LIFE/DEATH RATIO: BENEFITS AND RISKS IN
MODERN MEDICINES. New York: Reader's Digest Press and Thomas Y.
Crowell Co., 1977. xvii, 284 p.

Ross, a staff writer for READER'S DIGEST, discusses the regulation
of medicines. How are medicines (e.g., contraceptives, anti-
diabetic drugs, viricidal agents, immunosuppressive drugs, psycho-
tropic compounds, hormones, toxoids, and vaccines) developed and
tested, how are risks and benefits evaluated, and how is their
medical use regulated by federal agencies? He also focuses attention on the problems created by journalism, politicians and
consumer activists in the decision-making process.

Royal Society. TECHNOLOGIES FOR RURAL HEALTH. London: 1977. 187 p.

Papers delivered at a discussion held 9-10 December 1976 were
reprinted from PROCEEDINGS OF THE ROYAL SOCIETY OF LON-
DON, Series B, 199 (1977): 1-187. Among the topics discussed
were rural health and disease, agricultural productivity and its
health hazards, domestic water supplies, nutritional status of children, health planning, surgery and pediatrics, smallpox eradication,
immunization, rehydration in diarrheal diseases, family planning,
and organization and financing. Included in the latter two topics
were reports of experiments in rural health from Indonesia, Uganda,
and Bangladesh.

Sai, Fred T. HEALTH, NUTRITION AND POPULATION IN HUMAN SETTLE-
MENTS. Occasional Essay, no. 5. London: International Planned Parenthood
Federation, 1977. 32 p. Paperbound.

Sai focuses on the health programs of developing countries. He
maintains that realistic planning for human settlements and health
care services would alleviate many of the problems associated with
urbanization, maternal and child death, pollution, communicable
diseases, and occupational and industrial illnesses. There is an
extended consideration of health care services. Sai concludes

that the services should shift from an emphasis on hospital care to an emphasis on promotion and protection of health and on disease prevention.

SOCIOLOGY. Edited by Roy M. Acheson and Lesley Aird. Seminars in Community Medicine, vol. 1. London: Oxford University Press, 1976. xi, 166 p. Paperbound. Bibliog.; Glossary.

Published under the auspices of the Center for Extension Training in Community Medicine, London School of Hygiene and Tropical Medicine, this volume contains the papers presented and their discussion at a seminar held 17-18 October 1974. Six topics were addressed: (1) sociology in community medicine, (2) relationship between doctor and patient, (3) sociology and the aetiology of disease, (4) sociology and political science, (5) sociology and communication, and (6) sociology in the teaching of community medicine.

Sokolowska, Magdalena; Holowka, Jacek; and Ostrowska, Antonina, eds. HEALTH, MEDICINE, SOCIETY. Hingham, Mass.: D. Reidel Publishing Co., 1976. xi, 516 p.

This volume contains selected papers presented at the International Conference on the Sociology of Medicine, held in Warsaw, 20-25 August 1973. Participants included medical sociologists from the United States, Western Europe, and Eastern Europe. The book is in five parts, dealing with the following topics: health and society; the transformation of medical intervention; sociological insights into the health sciences; the health system; and teaching.

Thompson, Gene E., and Handelman, Ira. HEALTH DATA AND INFORMA-TION MANAGEMENT. Boston: Butterworth, 1978. viii, 310 p. References.

In this introductory textbook, the emphasis is on the problems and issues in health data and information management, particularly in the area of health care delivery. Among the topics addressed are accesses to data; the problem-oriented medical record; political and ethical problems; use of health statistics; planning for data collection, data management, and information systems management; and confidentiality, privacy, and security. Case histories illustrate each chapter.

U.S. Congress. Senate. Select Committee on Nutrition and Human Needs. DIETARY GOALS FOR THE UNITED STATES. 2d ed. 95th Cong., 1st sess. Washington, D.C.: Government Printing Office, Dec. 1977. v, 79 p. Paperbound.

This is a comprehensive statement on risk factors in the American diet. It offers the necessary plan of action to reach six basic goals for a better diet, including buying guides for consumers, and also recommends action within government and industry to maximize nutritional health. An accompanying volume of 869 pages, also paperbound, entitled DIETARY GOALS FOR THE UNITED STATES--SUPPLEMENTAL VIEWS, presents detailed testimony and scientific data from doctors, nutritionists, and other experts, including professional organizations and food industry sources.

Ville de Goyet, C. de; Seaman, J.; and Geijer, U. THE MANAGEMENT OF NUTRITIONAL EMERGENCIES IN LARGE POPULATIONS. Geneva: World Health Organization, 1978. 98 p. Paperbound. Tables.

This pamphlet gives guidelines for health personnel responsible for the field management of nutritional emergencies, especially mass starvation or widespread and severe malnutrition. It covers the major deficiency diseases; assessment and surveillance of nutritional status; food distribution, mass and supplementary feeding; therapeutic feeding; special foods; dealing with communicable diseases; camp administration, transportation, and food storage. Seven addenda give statistical tables concerned with food and nutrition, as well as sampling techniques and field tests.

Western Hemisphere Nutrition Congress V. Quebec, Canada, 1977. NUTRITION IN TRANSITION. Edited by Philip L. White and Nancy Selvey. Monroe, Wis.: American Medical Association, 1978. xvii, 426 p. References.

The proceedings include not only papers (in full) presented at twelve sessions, organized by subject, but also cover four research forums, giving these materials in abstract form. Some of the section topics are: evaluation of nutrition intervention programs; technological and nutritional aspects of fats; the metabolic basis of nutritional management; politics and realities of food safety and quality; protein conservation therapies during stress; nutritional modulation of behavior and brain function; nutritional adaptation to the environment; nutritional problems of Third World nations; international policies on food resources.

Wingo, Lowdon, and Evans, Alan, eds. PUBLIC ECONOMICS AND THE QUALITY OF LIFE. Baltimore, Md.: Johns Hopkins University Press, 1977. xv, 327 p. References.

At an International Resource Conference on Public Policy and the Quality of Life in Cities convened jointly by Resources for the Future, Washington, and Centre for Environmental Studies, London, 2-7 January 1975, in New Orleans, the participants examined the idea that quality of life might be a synonym for real consumption and its policy implications. Sixteen papers were presented: (1) "Can Public Policy Improve the Quality of Life?" A. Evans and L. Wingo; (2) "Objective, Subjective, and Collective Dimensions of the Quality of Life," L. Wingo; (3) "Variations in the Quality of Urban Life among Cities and Regions," I. Hoch; (4) "The Urban Disamenity Revisited," J.R. Meyer and R.A. Leone;

(5) "Problems of Measuring the Quality of City Environments,"
M. Whitbread; (6) "Local Government, the Property Tax, and
the Quality of Life: Some Findings on Progressivity," B.W. Hamilton;
(7) "Justifiable Government Intervention in Preserving the Quality
of Life," D.W. Pearce; (8) "The Quality of Life and the Limits
of Cost-Benefit Analysis," A.J. Culyer; (9) "Property Values and
the Benefits of Environmental Improvements: Theory and Measurement," A.M. Polinsky and D.L. Rubinfeld; (10) "Estimating Access
Values," P. Bohm; (11) "Neighborhood Externalities, Economic
Clubs and the Environment," A. Evans; (12) "The Treatment of
Externalities in National Income Statistics," M. Olson; (13) "Con-
ceptions of the Quality of Life in Theory and Practice," D. Don-
nison; (14) "Toward a New Civic Calculus," E.T. Haefele; (15)
"Measuring the Quality of Life of the Elderly," A. Williams; and
(16) "Reflections on the Quality of Working Life," H.C. Morton.
There is no subject index.

E. PREVENTIVE HEALTH MAINTENANCE

Kilbourne, Edwin D., and Smillie, Wilson G., eds. HUMAN ECOLOGY
AND PUBLIC HEALTH. 4th ed. London: Macmillan Co., 1969. xii, 462 p.

Like its previous editions published under the title PREVENTIVE
MEDICINE AND PUBLIC HEALTH, this book presents an integrated and cohesive discussion of the concepts underlying man's
approach to the prevention of disease and the preservation of
health. Contributors include fifteen experts in the fields of demography, human and microbial genetics, epidemiology, clinical
medicine, systems analysis, and health services administration.
The text consists of three parts, dealing with human ecology and
human disease; public health--problems and practice; and the administration of health services.

National Institute for Occupational Safety and Health. OCCUPATIONAL EX-
POSURE TO ORGANOTIN COMPOUNDS. DHEW (NIOSH) Publication, no.
77-115. Washington, D.C.: U.S. Department of Health, Education, and
Welfare, 1976. viii, 187 p. Paperbound. Appendixes.

This document contains recommendations for an occupational exposure standard for organotin compounds, based on research and
epidemiologic studies and on the development of sampling and
analytical methods. It is one of a series developed to apply to
workplace exposure to various substances, as applicable under the
Occupational Safety and Health Act of 1970. The text covers
biologic effects of exposure; environmental data and biologic
evaluation; work practices; research needs; and references. Three
appendixes supply sampling and analytical methods and a material
safety data sheet.

National Research Council. Safe Drinking Water Committee. DRINKING WATER AND HEALTH. Washington, D.C.: National Academy of Science, 1977. vi, 939 p. Paperbound. Bibliog.

> The study was undertaken to provide guidelines for drinking water regulations called for under Safe Drinking Water Act of 1974. The report includes discussions of safety and risk assessment of chemical contaminants, microbiology of drinking water, solid particles in suspension, inorganic solutes, organic solutes, and radioactivity.

Robbins, Lewis C., and Hall, Jack H. HOW TO PRACTICE PROSPECTIVE MEDICINE. Indianapolis: Methodist Hospital of Indiana, 1970. Reprint. 1974. 100 p. Paperbound.

> Prospective medicine is preventive. The physician evaluates individual's risks of developing disability or illness, and then works with him to reduce the risks. Robbins and Hall have prepared a manual for the general practitioner which describes in some detail how to perform a health risk appraisal and how to apply this evaluation to individual patients.

SYMPOSIUM ON HUMAN RIGHTS IN HEALTH, 1973. Ciba Foundation Symposium 23 (N.S.). Amsterdam: Associated Scientific Publishers, 1974. viii, 304 p.

> This symposium, held in London, 4-6 July 1973, dealt with four determinants of health as universal human rights: safe water to drink; sufficient food; protection against communicable disease; and access to means of controlling fertility. The twenty-eight contributors explored the practical implications--in terms of funding, human and material resources, and management needs--of adopting these four determinants as universal human rights. Also, they suggested ways in which people deprived of these necessities can obtain them for themselves or be helped with dignity to do so within the framework of their own cultures and of the prevailing economic realities.

Wolf, Stewart George; Bruhn, John G.; and Goodell, Helen. OCCUPATIONAL HEALTH AS HUMAN ECOLOGY. Springfield, Ill.: Charles C Thomas, 1978. xi, 115 p. References; Bibliog.

> The authors discuss various aspects of occupational health, such as history of occupational medicine; the role of the health care organization in the employees' coping with health hazards; means of insuring job satisfaction and productivity; pathophysiological effects of stress; and problems of aging and retirement. The relation of these topics to human ecology is implicit in their concept that human health and working capacity depend upon a complex interaction of genetic, environmental, sociocultural factors. The authors do not make linkage explicit.

ADDENDUM

This listing of recent materials in the field of human ecology was compiled by Stephanie L. Normann, director of library services, University of Texas Health Science Center in Houston.

The selection criteria for the books included in this addendum are: (1) those items the author had selected for review but had not yet written annotations, and (2) later published relevant materials. The arrangement of the items follows the table of contents of the text. To a certain extent, the imbalance in the numbers of items included in each of the various categories reflects current interests in the field. However, this is not meant to distort the emphasis of the general body of literature as described by Dr. Sargent or lessen the import of the historical material which highlights his text--rather it should suggest the increasing numbers of disciplines into which one must continue to delve in order to gain a full understanding of the discipline of human ecology.

II. B. MAN

ASSESSING CHEMICAL MUTAGENS: THE RISK TO HUMANS. Edited by Victor K. McElhany and Seymour Abrahamson. Banbury Report, no. 9. Cold Spring Harbor, N.Y.: Cold Spring Harbor Laboratory, 1979. xiii, 367 p.

Brusick, David. PRINCIPLES OF GENETIC TOXICOLOGY. New York: Plenum Press, 1980. xix, 279 p.

GOALS IN A GLOBAL COMMUNITY: THE ORIGINAL BACKGROUND PAPERS FOR GOALS FOR MANKIND, A REPORT TO THE CLUB OF ROME. 2 vols. Edited by Ervin Laszlo and Judah Bierman. New York: Pergamon Press, 1977.

   CONTENTS: Volume 1: STUDIES ON THE CONCEPTUAL FOUNDA-TIONS. Volume 2: THE INTERNATIONAL VALUES AND GOALS STUDIES.

THE EVOLUTIONARY SYNTHESIS: PERSPECTIVES ON THE UNIFICATION OF BIOLOGY. Edited by Ernst Mayr and William B. Provine. Cambridge, Mass.: Harvard University Press, 1980. xi, 487 p. Bibliog.

Guggenheim, Karl Y. NUTRITION AND NUTRITIONAL DISEASES: THE

EVOLUTION OF CONCEPTS. Lexington, Mass.: Collamore Press, 1981. xii, 378 p. Bibliog.

Roughgarden, Jonathan. THEORY OF POPULATION GENETICS AND EVOLU-TIONARY ECOLOGY: AN INTRODUCTION. New York: Macmillan, 1979. x, 634 p. Bibliog.

Wallace, Bruce. BASIC POPULATION GENETICS. New York: Columbia University Press, 1981. xii, 688 p. Bibliog.

Weiner, Joseph Sidney. PRACTICAL HUMAN BIOLOGY. London and New York: Academic Press, 1981. xv, 439 p. Bibliog.

> An update of the 1969 IBP Handbook No. 9, HUMAN BIOLOGY: A GUIDE TO FIELD METHODS, which was prepared for the Human Adaptability Section of the International Biological Programme (1964-74).

III. A. BIOLOGICAL

THE BIOLOGICAL ENVIRONMENT. General editors, John Lenihan and William W. Fletcher. Environment and Man, vol. 9. New York: Academic Press, 1979. 164 p. Bibliog.

DEVELOPMENTS IN ARID ZONE ECOLOGY AND ENVIRONMENTAL QUALITY. Edited by Hillel Shuval. Boston: Balaban International Science Services, 1981. xiii, 418 p. Bibliog.

III. B. BEHAVIORAL

Burton, Ian, et al. THE ENVIRONMENT AS HAZARD. New York: Oxford University Press, 1978. xvi, 240 p. Bibliog.

Greenwald, Howard P. SOCIAL PROBLEMS IN CANCER CONTROL. Cambridge, Mass.: Ballinger Publishing Co., 1980. xv, 293 p. Bibliog.

SEASONAL DIMENSIONS TO RURAL POVERTY. Edited by Robert Chambers et al. London: F. Pinter; Totowa, N.J.: Allanheld, Osmun, 1981. xvi, 259 p. Bibliog.

IV. MAN-ENVIRONMENT

Environmental Resources Limited. THE ENVIRONMENTAL IMPACT OF ENERGY STRATEGIES WITHIN THE EEC. Oxford and New York: Published for the

Commission of the European Communities, by Pergamon Press, 1980. xiii, 155 p. Bibliog.

Fisher, Anthony C. RESOURCE AND ENVIRONMENTAL ECONOMICS. New Rochelle, N.Y.: Cambridge University Press, 1981. 256 p. Bibliog.

Franke, Richard W., and Chasin, Barbara H. SEEDS OF FAMINE: ECOLOGI-CAL DESTRUCTION AND THE DEVELOPMENT DILEMMA IN THE WEST AFRI-CAN SAHEL. Montclair, N.J.: Allanheld, Osmun, 1980. xi, 266 p.

Giarini, Orio. DIALOGUE ON WEALTH AND WELFARE: AN ALTERNATIVE VIEW OF WORLD CAPITAL FORMATION: A REPORT TO THE CLUB OF ROME. Pergamon International Library of Science, Technology, Engineering, and Social Studies. Oxford and New York: Pergamon Press, 1980. xxv, 386 p. Bibliog.

Krebs, Charles J. ECOLOGY: THE EXPERIMENTAL ANALYSIS OF DISTRIBU-TION AND ABUNDANCE. 2d ed. New York: Harper and Row, 1978. xxv, 678 p. Bibliog.

Ridker, Ronald Gene, and Watson, William D. TO CHOOSE A FUTURE: RESOURCE AND ENVIRONMENTAL CONSEQUENCES OF ALTERNATIVE GROWTH PATHS. Baltimore, Md.: Published for Resources for the Future by the Johns Hopkins University Press, 1980. xv, 463 p.

SCARCITY AND GROWTH RECONSIDERED. Edited by V. Kerry Smith. Baltimore, Md.: Published for Resources for the Future by the Johns Hopkins University Press, 1979. xvi, 298 p. Bibliog.

U.S. National Committee for Geochemistry. Panel on the Trace Element Geochemistry of Coal Resource Development Related to Health. TRACE-ELEMENT GEOCHEMISTRY OF COAL RESOURCE DEVELOPMENT RELATED TO ENVIRONMENTAL QUALITY AND HEALTH. Washington, D.C.: National Academy of Sciences, 1980. xv, 153 p. Bibliog.

IV. A. AGRICULTURAL SYSTEMS

THE MAJOR PROBLEMS OF MAN AND ENVIRONMENT INTERACTIONS IN MOUNTAIN ECOSYSTEMS: A REVIEW. UNEP Report, no. 2 (1980). Nairobi, Kenya: UNEP, 1980. Reprint. New York: UNIPUB, 1980. 37 p.

IV. B. ENERGY

ATMOSPHERE-BIOSPHERE INTERACTIONS: TOWARD A BETTER UNDERSTAND-ING OF THE ECOLOGICAL CONSEQUENCES OF FOSSIL FUEL COMBUSTION:

A REPORT. Prepared by the Committee on the Atmosphere and the Biosphere, Board on Agriculture and Renewable Resources, Commission on Natural Resources, National Research Council. Washington, D.C.: National Academy Press, 1981. xvi, 263 p. Bibliog.

Balachandran, Sarojini, ed. ENERGY STATISTICS: A GUIDE TC INFORMATION SOURCES. Natural World Information Guide Series, vol. 1. Detroit: Gale Research Co., 1980. xii, 272 p.

Dunkerley, Joy. TRENDS IN ENERGY USE IN INDUSTRIAL SOCIETIES: AN OVERVIEW. Resources for the Future Research Paper, no. R-19. Washington, D.C.: Resources for the Future, 1980; distributed by the Johns Hopkins University Press. xiv, 149 p. Bibliog.

ENERGY DEVELOPMENT IN THE SOUTHWEST: PROBLEMS OF WATER, FISH AND WILDLIFE IN THE UPPER COLORADO RIVER BASIN. 2 vols. Edited by Walter O. Spofford et al. RFF Research Paper, no. R-18. Washington, D.C.: Resources for the Future, 1980.

RENEWABLE SOURCES OF ENERGY AND THE ENVIRONMENT. Edited by Essam el-Hinnawi and Asit K. Biswas. Natural Resources and the Environment Series, no. 6. Dublin, Ireland: Tycooly International Publishing, 1981. 219 p.

SELECTED STUDIES ON ENERGY: BACKGROUND PAPERS FOR ENERGY, THE NEXT TWENTY YEARS. Edited by Hans H. Landsberg. Cambridge, Mass.: Ballinger Publishing Co., 1980. xv, 439 p. Bibliog.

IV. C. WATER, WEATHER MODIFICATION, WEATHER CHANGE

CHEMISTRY AND BIOGEOCHEMISTRY OF ESTUARIES. Edited by Eric Olausson and Ingemar Cato. Chichester, Engl.; New York: Wiley, 1980. x, 452 p. Bibliog.

IV. D. LAND (CITIES, FARMS, MINING, RECREATION, WILDERNESS)

Schneider, Jan. WORLD PUBLIC ORDER OF THE ENVIRONMENT: TOWARDS AN INTERNATIONAL ECOLOGICAL LAW AND ORGANIZATION. Toronto and Buffalo: University of Toronto Press, 1979. xiv, 319 p. Bibliog.

V. A. GENERAL DETERIORATION OF THE ENVIRONMENT

American Chemical Society. Committee on Environmental Improvement. CLEANING FOR ENVIRONMENT, A CHEMICAL PERSPECTIVE: A REPORT. 2d ed. Washington, D.C.: 1978. ix, 457 p.

Dix, H[erbert]., M[ason]. ENVIRONMENTAL POLLUTION: ATMOSPHERE, LAND, WATER, AND NOISE. Institution of Environmental Sciences Series. Chichester, Engl.; New York: Wiley, 1981. x, 286 p.

ENVIRONMENTAL IMPACT DATA BOOK. Edited by Jack Golden et al. Ann Arbor, Mich.: Ann Arbor Science Publishers, 1979. xxi, 864 p.

Jørgensen, Sven Erik, and Johnsen, I. PRINCIPLES OF ENVIRONMENTAL SCIENCE AND TECHNOLOGY. Studies in Environmental Science, no. 14. Amsterdam and New York: Elsevier Scientific Publishing Co., 1981. xi, 516 p.

Rochester International Conference on Environmental Toxicity. 12th Conference, 1979. POLLUTED RAIN. Edited by Morton Miller et al. Environmental Science Research, vol. 17. New York: Plenum Press, 1980. xii, 502 p.

Ward, Diana Valiela. BIOLOGICAL ENVIRONMENTAL IMPACT STUDIES: THEORY AND METHODS. New York: Academic Press, 1978. viii, 157 p.

V. B. ENVIRONMENTAL POLLUTION

ASSESSING TOXIC EFFECTS OF ENVIRONMENTAL POLLUTANTS. Edited by Si Duk Lee and J. Brian Mudd. Ann Arbor, Mich.: Ann Arbor Science Publishers, 1979. x, 306 p.

THE BIOGEOCHEMISTRY OF MERCURY IN THE ENVIRONMENT. Edited by Jerome O. Nriagu. Topics in Environmental Health, vol. 3. Amsterdam and New York: Elsevier/North-Holland Biomedical Press, 1979. xv, 696 p.

CADMIUM IN THE ENVIRONMENT. 2 vols. Edited by Jerome O. Nriagu. Environmental Science and Technology. New York: Wiley, 1980-81.

COPPER IN THE ENVIRONMENT. 2 vols. Edited by Jerome O. Nriagu. Environmental Science and Technology. New York: Wiley, 1979.

   Contents: Part 1, Ecological cycling; part 2, Health effects.

ENVIRONMENTAL LEAD. Edited by Donald R. Lynam et al. Ecotoxicology and Environmental Quality Series. New York: Academic Press, 1981. xi, 358 p.

FEDERAL RESEARCH ON THE BIOLOGICAL AND HEALTH EFFECTS OF IONIZING RADIATION. Committee on Federal Research on the Biological and Health Effects of Ionizing Radiation, Division of Medical Sciences, Assembly of Life Sciences, National Research Council. Washington, D.C.: National Academy Press, 1981. xvii, 169 p. Bibliog.

Addendum

Hayes, Wayland J[ackson]., Jr. PESTICIDES STUDIED IN MAN. Baltimore: Williams and Wilkins Co., 1982. xiii, 672 p.

INTRODUCTION TO ENVIRONMENTAL TOXICOLOGY. Edited by Frank E. Guthrie and Jerome J. Perry. New York: Elsevier-New York, 1980. xxvii, 484 p. Bibliog.

Lippmann, Morton, and Schlesinger, Richard B. CHEMICAL CONTAMINATION IN THE HUMAN ENVIRONMENT. New York: Oxford University Press, 1979. vii, 456 p.

National Research Council. Committee on Lead in the Human Environment. LEAD IN THE HUMAN ENVIRONMENT. Washington, D.C.: National Academy Press, 1980. xxiii, 525 p.

NICKEL TOXICOLOGY. Edited by Stanley S. Brown and F. William Sunderman, Jr. London and New York: Academic Press, 1980. xx, 193 p.

   Proceedings of the second International Conference on Nickel Toxicology held 3-5 September 1980, in Swansea, Wales. Organized by the Subcommittee on Environmental and Occupational Toxicology of Nickel, Commission on Toxicology, International Union of Pure and Applied Chemistry, and the Association of Clinical Scientists.

Nijkamp, Peter. ENVIRONMENTAL POLICY ANALYSIS: OPERATIONAL METHODS AND MODELS. Chichester, Engl., and New York: J. Wiley, 1980. xvi, 283 p. Bibliog.

Ott, Wayne. ENVIRONMENTAL INDICES, THEORY AND PRACTICE. Ann Arbor, Mich.: Ann Arbor Science Publishers, 1978. xi, 371 p. Bibliog.

Ratcliffe, J.M. LEAD IN MAN AND THE ENVIRONMENT. Chichester, Engl.: Ellis Horwood; New York: Halsted Press, 1981. 240 p.

Santodonato, Joseph, et al. HEALTH AND ECOLOGICAL ASSESSMENT OF POLYNUCLEAR AROMATIC HYDROCARBONS. Edited by Si Duk Lee and Lester Grant. JOURNAL OF ENVIRONMENTAL PATHOLOGY AND TOXICOLOGY 5, no. 1. Park Forest South, Ill.: Pathotox Publishers, 1981. 364 p. Bibliog.

Tolley, George S., et al. ENVIRONMENTAL POLICY. Cambridge, Mass.: Ballinger Publishing Co., 1981. Bibliog.

   Contents: Vol. 1, ELEMENTS OF ENVIRONMENTAL ANALYSIS.

TRACE SUBSTANCES IN ENVIRONMENTAL HEALTH. Edited by Delbert D. Hemphill. Columbia: University of Missouri, 1967-- .

Proceedings of the University of Missouri's annual Conference on Trace Substances in Environmental Health.

THE USE OF BIOLOGICAL SPECIMENS FOR THE ASSESSMENT OF HUMAN EXPOSURE TO ENVIRONMENTAL POLLUTANTS. Edited by A. Berlin et al. The Hague and Boston: M. Nijhoff for the Commission of the European Communities, 1979. viii, 368 p.

Proceedings of the International Workshop at Luxembourg, 18-22 April 1977.

V. C. AIR POLLUTION

ATMOSPHERIC POLLUTION 1982. Proceedings of the 15th International Colloquium, UNESCO Building, Paris, France, May 4-7, 1982. Edited by Michel M. Benarie. Studies in Environmental Science, vol. 20. Amsterdam and New York: Elsevier Scientific Publishing Co., 1982.

ATMOSPHERIC POLLUTION 1978 and ATMOSPHERIC POLLUTION 1980 are the proceedings of the 13th and 14th international colloquia and appear as volumes 1 and 8 respectively of the series Studies in Environmental Science.

DENITRIFICATION, NITRIFICATION, AND ATMOSPHERIC NITROUS OXIDE. Edited by C.C. Delwiche. New York: Wiley, 1981. xi, 286 p. Bibliog.

Environmental Studies Board. Committee on Prevention of Significant Deterioration of Air Quality. ON PREVENTION OF SIGNIFICANT DETERIORATION OF AIR QUALITY. Washington, D.C.: National Academy Press, 1981. xxv, 141 p. Bibliog.

OHOLO Conference on Air Pollution and the Lung. 20th, Ma'alot, Israel, 1975. AIR POLLUTION AND THE LUNG. Edited by Ephraim F. Aharonson et al. New York: John Wiley and Sons, 1976. xii, 313 p. Bibliog.

The aim of this interdisciplinary conference was to promote inquiry into the problems of air pollution and its health hazards. Sessions were devoted to penetration and clearance of pollutants; interaction between inhaled pollutants and the lung; and methods for evaluation of air pollution effects.

V. D. WATER POLLUTION

Buikema, Arthur L., and Hendricks, Albert C. BENZENE, XYLENE, AND TOLUENE IN AQUATIC SYSTEMS: A REVIEW. Washington, D.C.: American Petroleum Institute, 1980. 69 p. Bibliog.

Addendum

DRINKING-WATER AND SANITATION, 1981-1990: A WAY TO HEALTH.
A WHO contribution to the international drinking water supply and sanitation
decade. Geneva: World Health Organization, 1981. 56 p.

International Symposium on the Analysis of Hydrocarbons and Halogenated
Hydrocarbons in the Acquatic Environment, McMaster University, 1978.
HYDROCARBONS AND HALOGENATED HYDROCARBONS IN THE AQUATIC
ENVIRONMENT. Edited by P.K. Afghan and D. Mackay, associated editors,
H.B. Braun et al. Environmental Science Research, vol. 16. New York:
Plenum Press, 1980. xiii, 588 p.

Laws, Edward A. AQUATIC POLLUTION, AN INTRODUCTORY TEXT.
Environmental Science and Technology. New York: Wiley, 1981. xii,
482 p. Bibliog.

Neff, Jerry M., and Anderson, Jack W. RESPONSE OF MARINE ANIMALS
TO PETROLEUM AND SPECIFIC PETROLEUM HYDROCARBONS. London:
Applied Science, 1981. x, 177 p. Bibliog.

Salvato, Joseph A. ENVIRONMENTAL ENGINEERING AND SANITATION.
3d ed. Environmental Science and Technology. New York: Wiley, 1982.
xxiv, 1,163 p. Bibliog.

WATER SUPPLY AND HEALTH: PROCEEDINGS OF AN INTERNATIONAL
SYMPOSIUM, NOORDWIJKERHOUT, THE NETHERLANDS, 27-29 AUGUST
1980. Edited by H. van Lelyveld and B.C.J. Zoeteman. Studies in Environmental Science, vol. 12. Amsterdam and New York: Elsevier Scientific
Publishing Co., 1981. 397 p. Bibliog.

V. F. AGRICULTURE AND FOOD

Benham, Harvey. MAN'S STRUGGLE FOR FOOD. Lanham, Md.: University
Press of America, 1981. xii, 496 p. Bibliog.

Caliendo, Mary Alice. NUTRITION AND THE WORLD FOOD CRISIS. New
York: Macmillan, 1979. viii, 368 p.

EDUCATION AND SAFE HANDLING IN PESTICIDE APPLICATION. Edited
by E.A.H. van Heemstra-Lequin and W.F. Tordoir. Studies in Environmental
Science, vol. 18. Amsterdam and New York: Elsevier Scientific Publishing
Co., 1981. 302 p. Bibliog.

> Proceedings of the Sixth International Workshop of the Scientific
> Committee on Pesticides of the International Association on Occu-
> pational Health, Buenos Aires and San Carlos de Bariloche,
> Argentina, 12-18 March 1981.

FOOD, CLIMATE, AND MAN. Edited by Margaret R. Biswas and Asit K. Biswas. Environmental Science and Technology. New York: Wiley, 1979. xxiii, 285 p. Bibliog.

HUMAN ECOLOGICAL ISSUES: A READER. Edited by Fergus M. Clydesdale and Frederick J. Francis. Dubuque, Iowa: Kendall/Hunt Publishing Co., 1980. vi, 302 p. Bibliog.

Hungate, Lois Simonds, and Sherman, Ralph W. FOOD AND ECONOMICS. Westport, Conn.: AVI Publishing Co., 1979. vii, 244 p.

V.G. POPULATION

RURAL AMERICA IN PASSAGE: STATISTICS FOR POLICY. Edited by Dorothy M. Gilford et al. Panel on Statistics for Rural Development Policy, Committee on National Statistics, Assembly of Behavioral and Social Sciences, National Research Council. Washington, D.C.: National Academy Press, 1981. ix, 592 p. Bibliog.

World Fertility Survey. BASIC DOCUMENTATION. No. 1-- . 1975-- . Voorburg, Netherlands: International Statistical Institute, 1975-- .

World Fertility Survey. SCIENTIFIC REPORTS. No. 1-- . 1977-- . Voorburg, Netherlands: International Statistical Institute, 1977-- .

World Fertility Survey. TECHNICAL BULLETINS. No. 1-- . 1976-- . Voorburg, Netherlands: International Statistical Institute, 1976-- .

WORLD FERTILITY SURVEY CONFERENCE 1980. 3 vols. Record of Proceedings, London, 7-11 July 1980. Voorburg, Netherlands: 1981.

VI. A. CHANGING PATTERNS OF ILLNESS AND DEATH

Levi, Lennart, ed. SOCIETY, STRESS AND DISEASE. WORKING LIFE, vol. 4. London: Oxford University Press, 1981. xvii, 370 p.

STRESSFUL LIFE EVENTS AND THEIR CONTEXTS. Edited by Barbara Snell Dohrenwend and Bruce P. Dohrenwend. Monographs in Psychosocial Epidemiology, vol. 2. New York: Prodist, 1981. xiii, 287 p.

STUDIES OF CHILDREN. Edited by Felton Earls. Monographs in Psychosocial Epidemiology, vol. 1. New York: Prodist, 1980. xiv, 185 p.

SYMPTOMS, ILLNESS BEHAVIOR, AND HELP-SEEKING. Edited by David
Mechanic. Monographs in Psychosocial Epidemiology, vol. 3. New York:
Prodist, 1982. xv, 157 p.

VI. B. HEALTH INDICATORS (HEALTH STATISTICS)

Bross, Irwin D. J. SCIENTIFIC STRATEGIES TO SAVE YOUR LIFE: A
STATISTICAL APPROACH TO PRIMARY PREVENTION. Statistics: Textbooks
and Monographs, vol. 35. New York: M. Dekker, 1981. v, 259 p.

MEDICAL CARE CHARTBOOK. 7th ed. Edited by Avedis Donabedian et al.
Washington, D.C.: AUPHA Press, 1980. xix, 420 p.

> Primarily tables and charts.

National Research Council. Committee on Food Consumption Patterns. ASSESS-
ING CHANGING FOOD CONSUMPTION PATTERNS. Washington, D.C.:
National Academy Press, 1981. 284 p. Bibliog.

NUTRITION AND GROWTH. Edited by Derrick B. Jelliffe and E.F. Patrice
Jelliffe. Human Nutrition, vol. 2. New York: Plenum Press, 1979. xx,
452 p. Bibliog.

VI. C. SOCIAL INDICATORS

AMERICA ENTERS THE EIGHTIES: SOME SOCIAL INDICATORS. Edited by
Conrad Taeuber. Annals of the American Academy of Political and Social
Science, vol. 453. Philadelphia: American Academy of Political and Social
Science, 1981. x, 308 p.

> This issue deals with a number of the salient statistical series
> which are presented in the report issued by the federal govern-
> ment entitled Social Indicators III.

Morris, Morris David. MEASURING THE CONDITION OF THE WORLD'S
POOR: THE PHYSICAL QUALITY OF LIFE INDEX. Pergamon Policy Studies.
New York: Published for the Overseas Development Council by Pergamon
Press, 1979. xiv, 176 p.

SOCIAL ACCOUNTING SYSTEMS: ESSAYS ON THE STATE OF THE ART.
Edited by F. Thomas Juster and Kenneth C. Land. Studies in Population.
New York: Academic Press, 1981. 479 p.

U.S. Bureau of the Census. SOCIAL INDICATORS III: SELECTED DATA ON
SOCIAL CONDITIONS AND TRENDS IN THE UNITED STATES. Washington,
D.C.: Government Printing Office, 1980. lx, 585 p. Bibliog.

Two previous editions prepared by U. S. Office of Management and Budget.

VII. A. ENVIRONMENTAL SURVEILLANCE AND MONITORING, IMPACT ANALYSIS

Baselt, Randall C. BIOLOGICAL MONITORING METHODS FOR INDUSTRIAL CHEMICALS. Davis, Calif.: Biomedical Publications, 1980. x, 301 p.

BIOLOGICAL MONITORING FOR ENVIRONMENTAL EFFECTS. Edited by Douglas L. Worf. Lexington, Mass.: Heath, 1980. xii, 227 p.

Workshop held at Raleigh, N.C., in May 1978 under the auspices of North Carolina State University and other bodies.

CHEMICAL MUTAGENESIS, HUMAN POPULATION MONITORING, AND GENETIC RISK ASSESSMENT. Proceedings of the International Symposium, held 14-16 October 1980, Ottawa, Canada. Edited by K.C. Bora et al. Progress in Mutation Research, vol. 3. Amsterdam and New York: Elsevier Biomedical Press, 1982. xxiv, 364 p.

Clark, Brian D., et al. ENVIRONMENTAL IMPACT ASSESSMENT: A BIBLIOGRAPHY WITH ABSTRACTS. New York: Bowker, 1980. vi, 516 p.

ENVIRONMENTAL IMPACT ASSESSMENT: PRINCIPLES AND PROCEDURES. Edited by R. E. Munn. 2d ed. SCOPE Report, No. 5. Chichester, Engl. and New York: Published on behalf of the Scientific Committee on Problems of the Environment of the International Council of Scientific Unions by Wiley, 1979. 189 p.

Environmental Studies Board. Committee to Review Methods for Ecotoxicology. TESTING FOR EFFECTS OF CHEMICALS ON ECOSYSTEMS: A REPORT. Washington, D.C.: National Academy Press, 1981. xv, 103 p. Bibliog.

_____. WORKING PAPERS PREPARED AS BACKGROUND FOR TESTING FOR EFFECTS OF CHEMICALS ON ECOSYSTEMS. Washington, D C.: National Academy Press, 1981. vii, 257 p. Bibliog.

GUIDELINES FOR ASSESSING INDUSTRIAL ENVIRONMENTAL IMPACT AND ENVIRONMENTAL CRITERIA FOR THE SITING OF INDUSTRY. Industry and Environment Office, United Nations Environment Programme. UNEP--Industry and Environment Guidelines Series, vol. 1. Paris: UNEP, 1980. xv, 105 p.

GUIDELINES FOR STUDIES OF HUMAN POPULATIONS EXPOSED TO MUTA-GENIC AND REPRODUCTIVE HAZARDS. Proceedings of Conference held 26-27 January 1981 in Washington, D.C., sponsored by Center for Disease

Control et al. Edited by Arthur D. Bloom; associate editor, Natalie W. Paul.
White Plains, N.Y.: March of Dimes Birth Defects Foundation, 1981. xiv,
163 p.

Jain, R[avinder].K[umar]., et al. ENVIRONMENTAL IMPACT ANALYSIS: A
NEW DIMENSION IN DECISION MAKING. 2d ed. Van Nostrand Reinhold
Environmental Engineering Series. New York: Van Nostrand Reinhold Co.,
1980. 393 p. Bibliog.

Monson, Richard R. OCCUPATIONAL EPIDEMIOLOGY. Boca Raton, Fla.:
CRC Press, 1980. 219 p.

National Research Council. Committee on Measurement and Control of
Respirable Dust. MEASUREMENT AND CONTROL OF RESPIRABLE DUST IN
MINES. Washington, D.C.: National Academy of Sciences, 1980. ix, 405 p.

OCCUPATIONAL HEALTH AND SAFETY MANAGEMENT. Edited by S.S.
Chissick and R. Derricott. Chichester, Engl. and New York: J. Wiley, 1981.
xv, 705 p.

Rochester International Conference on Environmental Toxicity (13th, 1980,
University of Rochester). MEASUREMENT OF RISKS. Edited by George G.
Berg and H. David Maillie. Environmental Science Research, vol. 21. New
York: Plenum, 1981. x, 550 p.

Selikoff, Irving J. A SURVEY OF THE GENERAL POPULATION OF MICHI-
GAN FOR HEALTH EFFECTS OF POLYBROMINATEDBIPHENYL EXPOSURE.
Report to the Michigan Department of Public Health, 30 September 1979.
New York: Mount Sinai School of Medicine of the City University of New
York, 1979. iv, 73 p., 8 p.

Symposium on Pollution and Physiology of Marine Organisms (1980, Milford,
Conn.). BIOLOGICAL MONITORING OF MARINE POLLUTANTS. Proceedings
of a Symposium on Pollution and Physiology of Marine Organisms, held in
Milford, Connecticut, 7-9 November 1980. Edited by F. John Vernberg
et al. New York: Academic Press, 1981. xii, 559 p.

VII. B. RESOURCE MANAGEMENT

U.S. Council on Environmental Quality. THE GLOBAL 2000 REPORT TO
THE PRESIDENT--ENTERING THE TWENTY-FIRST CENTURY: A REPORT.
3 vols. Washington, D.C.: Government Printing Office, 1980-81. Reprinted 1980-81 by Pergamon Press with a few additions.

ENERGY AND ENVIRONMENT IN THE DEVELOPING COUNTRIES. Edited by Manas Chatterji. Chichester, Engl. and New York: J. Wiley and Sons, 1981. xii, 357 p. Bibliog.

Selected papers presented at the International Conference on Energy and Environment in the Developing Countries held at the Indian Institute of Management, Bangalore, India, 11-14 January 1979.

EVALUATION FOR VILLAGE WATER SUPPLY PLANNING. Edited by Sandy Cairncross et al. Chichester, Engl. and New York: Published in association with International Reference Centre for Community Water Supply by J. Wiley, 1980. xviii, 179 p. Bibliog.

FOOD AND NUTRITION POLICY IN A CHANGING WORLD. Edited by Jean Mayer and Johanna Dwyer. New York: Oxford University Press, 1979. xii, 300 p. Bibliog.

FOOD POLITICS: THE REGIONAL CONFLICT. Edited by David N. Balaam and Michael Carey. Montclair, N.J.: Allanheld, Osmun, 1981. 246 p.

Gabor, Dennis, et al. BEYOND THE AGE OF WASTE: A REPORT TO THE CLUB OF ROME. Pergamon International Library of Science, Technology, Engineering and Social Studies. Oxford, Engl. and New York: Pergamon Press, 1978. xviii, 237 p. Bibliog.

GROUNDWATER MANAGEMENT, THE USE OF NUMERICAL MODELS. Edited by Yehuda Bachmat et al. Water Resources Monograph, vol. 5. Washington, D.C.: American Geophysical Union, 1980. viii, 127 p.

Ives, Jane H. INTERNATIONAL OCCUPATIONAL SAFETY AND HEALTH RESOURCE CATALOGUE. New York: Praeger, 1981. x, 311 p.

Murdoch, William W. THE POVERTY OF NATIONS: THE POLITICAL ECONOMY OF HUNGER AND POPULATION. Baltimore: Johns Hopkins University Press, 1980. xv, 382 p.

NUTRITION INTERVENTION IN DEVELOPING COUNTRIES: AN OVERVIEW. Prepared by the Harvard Institute for International Development. Cambridge, Mass.: Oelgeschlager, Gunn & Hain, 1981. xviii, 227 p. Bibliog.

NUTRITION POLICY IN TRANSITION. Edited by Jurgen Schmandt et al. Lexington, Mass.: Lexington Books, 1980. xxv, 289 p.

TRADE AND ENVIRONMENT: A THEORETICAL ENQUIRY. Edited by H. Siebert et al. Studies in Environmental Science, vol. 6. Amsterdam: Elsevier Scientific Publishing Co.; New York: Elsevier/North Holland, 1980. x, 355 p. Bibliog.

United Nations Environment Programme. THE ENVIRONMENTAL IMPACTS OF PRODUCTION AND USE OF ENERGY: AN ASSESSMENT. Natural Resources and the Environment Series, vol. 1. Dublin: Published for the United Nations Environment Programme by the Tycooly Press, 1981. 322 p.

VII. C. ENVIRONMENTAL MANAGEMENT

ADAPTIVE ENVIRONMENTAL ASSESSMENT AND MANAGEMENT. Edited by C. S. Holling. International Series on Applied Systems Analysis, vol. 3. Laxenburg, Austria: International Institute for Applied Systems Analysis; Chichester, Engl., and New York: Wiley, 1978. xviii, 377 p. Bibliog.

Cottrell, Alan Howard. ENVIRONMENTAL ECONOMICS: AN INTRODUC-TION FOR STUDENTS OF THE RESOURCE AND ENVIRONMENTAL SCIENCES. Resource and Environmental Sciences Series. New York: Wiley, 1978. 66 p.

Dasgupta, Partha S., and Heal, G.M. ECONOMIC THEORY AND EXHAUSTIBLE RESOURCES. Cambridge Economic Handbooks. Welwyn, Hertfordshire, Engl.: Nisbet; Cambridge: Cambridge University Press, 1979. xiv, 501 p. Bibliog.

ECONOMICS OF THE ENVIRONMENT. Edited by John Lenihan and William W. Fletcher. Environment and Man, vol. 10. New York: Academic Press, 1979. xii, 193 p.

IARC MONOGRAPHS ON THE EVALUATION OF THE CARCINOGENIC RISK OF CHEMICALS TO HUMANS. Lyon: International Agency for Research on Cancer.

Selected Titles:

SOME INORGANIC SUBSTANCES, CHLORINATED HYDRO-CARBONS, AROMATIC AMINES, N-NITROSO COMPOUNDS, AND NATURAL PRODUCTS. Vol. 1, 1972. 184 p.

SOME INORGANIC AND ORGANOMETALLIC COMPOUNDS. Vol. 2, 1973. 181 p.

SOME ORGANOCHLORINE PESTICIDES. Vol. 5, 1974. 241 p.

SOME NATURALLY OCCURRING SUBSTANCES. Vol. 10, 1976. 353 p.

CADMIUM, NICKEL, SOME EPOXIDES, MISCELLANEOUS INDUSTRIAL CHEMICALS AND GENERAL CONSIDERATIONS ON VOLATILE ANAESTHETICS. Vol. 11, 1976. 306 p.

ASBESTOS. Vol. 14, 1977. 106 p. Bibliog.

SOME FUMIGANTS, THE HERBICIDES 2,4-D AND 2,4,5-T, CHLORINATED DIBENZODIOXINS AND MISCELLANEOUS INDUSTRIAL CHEMICALS. Vol. 15, 1977. 354 p.

SOME AROMATIC AMINES AND RELATED NITRO COMPOUNDS--
HAIR DYES, COLOURING AGENTS AND MISCELLANEOUS IN-
DUSTRIAL CHEMICALS. Vol. 16, 1978. 400 p.

SOME N-NITROSO COMPOUNDS. Vol. 17, 1978. 365 p.

POLYCHLORINATED BIPHENYLS AND POLYBROMINATED
BIPHENYLS. Vol. 18, 1978. 140 p. Bibliog.

SOME HALOGENATED HYDROCARBONS. Vol. 20, 1979.
609 p.

CHEMICALS AND INDUSTRIAL PROCESSES ASSOCIATED WITH
CANCER IN HUMANS. IARC Monographs Supplement 1, 1979.
xi, 71 p.

SOME METALS AND METALLIC COMPOUNDS. Vol. 23, 1980.
438 p.

SOME PHARMACEUTICAL DRUGS. Vol. 24, 1980. 337 p.

WOOD, LEATHER AND SOME ASSOCIATED INDUSTRIES. Vol.
25, 1980. 412 p.

SOME AROMATIC AMINES, ANTHRAQUINONES AND NITROSO
COMPOUNDS, AND INORGANIC FLUORIDES USED IN DRINKING-
WATER AND DENTAL PREPARATIONS. Vol. 27, 1982. 341 p.

Kneese, Allen V., and Bower, Blair T. ENVIRONMENTAL QUALITY AND
RESIDUALS MANAGEMENT: REPORT OF A RESEARCH ON ECONOMIC,
TECHNOLOGICAL, AND INSTITUTIONAL ASPECTS. Baltimore: Published
for Resources for the Future by the Johns Hopkins University Press, 1979.
xiv, 337 p. Bibliog.

Pineo, Charles S., et al. ENVIRONMENTAL SANITATION AND INTEGRATED
HEALTH DELIVERY PROGRAMS. Monograph Series, American Public Health
Association International Health Programs, no. 4. Washington, D.C.: Ameri-
can Public Health Association International Health Programs, 1981. 82 p.

Purdom, Paul Walton, et al. HEALTH PLANNING RELATED TO ENVIRON-
MENTAL FACTORS: PRELIMINARY TECHNICAL GUIDELINES. Health Planning Methods and Technology Series, no. 18. Hyattsville, Md.: U.S. Health
Resources Administration, Bureau of Health Planning, National Technical Information Service, 1980. x, 159 p.

RADIOACTIVE WASTE MANAGEMENT AT THE SAVANNAH RIVER PLANT.
National Research Council, Panel on Savannah River Waste, Board on Radio-
active Waste Management, Commission on Natural Resources. Washington,
D.C.: National Academy Press, 1981. xii, 68 p.

U.S. National Committee for Geochemistry. Panel on the Geochemistry of
Water in Relation to Cardiovascular Disease. GEOCHEMISTRY OF WATER

IN RELATION TO CARDIOVASCULAR DISEASE. Washington, D.C.: National Academy of Sciences, 1979. xiii, 98 p.

VII. D. HEALTH AND WELFARE

Donabedian, Avedis. THE DEFINITION OF QUALITY AND APPROACHES TO ITS ASSESSMENT. Explorations in Quality Assessment and Monitoring, vol. 1. Ann Arbor, Mich.: Health Administration Press, 1980. xiii, 163 p.

FEDERAL HEALTH PROGRAMS: PROBLEMS AND PROSPECTS. Edited by Stuart H. Altman and Harvey M. Sapolsky. Lexington, Mass.: Lexington Books, 1981. 248 p. Bibliog.

Manning, Willard G., et al. THE STATUS OF HEALTH IN DEMAND ESTI-MATION: BEYOND EXCELLENT, GOOD, FAIR AND POOR. Santa Monica, Calif.: Rand Corp., 1981. ix, 64 p.

NATIONAL DECISION-MAKING FOR PRIMARY HEALTH CARE: A STUDY. UNICEF/WHO Joint Committee on Health Policy. Geneva: World Health Organization, 1981. 69 p.

Raffel, Marshall W. THE U.S. HEALTH SYSTEM: ORIGINS AND FUNCTIONS. New York: Wiley, 1980. ix, 639 p.

WORLD NUTRITION AND NUTRITION EDUCATION. Edited by H.M. Sinclair and G.R. Howat. Oxford and New York: Oxford University Press; Paris: UNESCO, 1980. xx, 226 p.

Wilson, Florence A., and Neuhauser, Duncan. HEALTH SERVICES IN THE UNITED STATES. 2d ed. Cambridge, Mass.: Ballinger Publishing Co., 1982. Rev. ed. of: HEALTH SERVICES IN THE UNITED STATES. Edited by Duncan Neuhauser and Florence A. Wilson. 1973. xvi, 339 p.

VII. E. PREVENTIVE HEALTH MAINTENANCE

CONCEPTS OF HEALTH AND DISEASE: INTERDISCIPLINARY PERSPECTIVES. Edited by Arthur L. Caplan et al. Reading, Mass.: Addison-Wesley Publishing Co., 1981. xxxi, 756 p.

Green, Lawrence W., and Anderson, C.L. COMMUNITY HEALTH. 4th ed. St. Louis: C.V. Mosby Co., 1982. xiv, 620 p.

Hall, Jack H., and Zwemer, Jack D. PROSPECTIVE MEDICINE. 2d ed.

Health Hazard Appraisal, vol. 3. Indianapolis: Dept. of Medical Education, Methodist Hospital of Indiana, 1979. xiii, 300 p. First ed. by Lewis C. Robbins and Jack H. Hall published in 1970 under title: HOW TO PRACTICE PROSPECTIVE MEDICINE.

Institute of Medicine. HEALTHY PEOPLE: THE SURGEON GENERAL'S REPORT ON HEALTH PROMOTION AND DISEASE PREVENTION. BACK-GROUND PAPERS: REPORT TO THE SURGEON GENERAL ON HEALTH PROMOTION AND DISEASE PREVENTION. Washington, D.C.: Government Printing Office, 1979. viii, 484 p.

Institute of Medicine. Division of Health Promotion and Disease Prevention. PERSPECTIVES ON HEALTH PROMOTION AND DISEASE PREVENTION. Washington: National Academy of Sciences, 1978. xvi, 244 p.

National Research Council. Safe Drinking Water Committee. DRINKING WATER AND HEALTH. Vols. 2-3. Washington, D.C.: National Academy Press, 1980.

> Volumes 2 and 3 contain data and background documentation which supplement the 1977 DRINKING WATER AND HEALTH: SUMMARY REPORT of this National Research Council Committee.

PREVENTION. Washington, D.C.: Public Health Service, Office of Disease Prevention and Health Promotion, 1981-- .

> Annual extension of two Surgeon General's reports: HEALTHY PEOPLE and PROMOTING HEALTH/PREVENTING DISEASE: OBJECTIVES FOR THE NATION.

PREVENTIVE AND COMMUNITY MEDICINE. Edited by Duncan W. Clark and Brian MacMahon. 2d ed. Boston: Little, Brown, 1981. xi, 794 p.

PREVENTIVE NUTRITION AND SOCIETY. Edited by M.R. Turner. London and New York: Academic Press, 1981. xii, 228 p.

PROMOTING HEALTH/PREVENTING DISEASE: OBJECTIVES FOR THE NATION. U.S. Public Health Service. Washington, D.C.: Government Printing Office, 1980. 102 p.

PUBLIC HEALTH AND PREVENTIVE MEDICINE. Edited by John M. Last. 11th ed. New York: Appleton-Century-Crofts, 1980. xxv, 1,926 p.

> At head of title: Maxcy-Rosenau. 10th edition edited by Philip E. Sartwell, has title: PREVENTIVE MEDICINE AND PUBLIC HEALTH.

Addendum

Rand Corporation. MODEL FOR HEALTH AND METHODOLOGY. Edited by John E. Ware, Jr. et al. Conceptualization and Measurement of Health for Adults in the Health Insurance Study, vol. 1. Santa Monica, Calif.: 1980. xv, 49 p.

U.S. Council on Environmental Quality. Toxic Substances Strategy Committee. TOXIC CHEMICALS AND PUBLIC PROTECTION: A REPORT TO THE PRESIDENT. Washington, D.C.: Government Printing Office, 1980. xlii, 187 p.

U.S. Department of Health, Education, and Welfare. MODEL STANDARDS FOR COMMUNITY PREVENTIVE HEALTH SERVICES: A REPORT TO THE U.S. CONGRESS. Washington, D.C.: 1979. 110 p.

> A collaborative project of the U.S. Conference of City Health Officers; National Association of County Health Officials; Association of State and Territorial Health Officials; American Public Health Association; and Center for Disease Control, Public Health Service, Department of Health, Education, and Welfare.

U.S. Public Health Service. Office of the Surgeon General. HEALTHY PEOPLE: THE SURGEON GENERAL'S REPORT ON HEALTH PROMOTION AND DISEASE PREVENTION, 1979. Rockville, Md.: Government Printing Office, 1979. 250 p.

JOURNALS

The primary literature in human ecology ranges across the many disciplines which contribute to the subject. The listing below attempts to reference each of these disciplines, however, in order to limit the number of titles, preference was given to society and association sponsored literature. Further restrictions include monographic series which were itemized in the main text of this volume as individual titles and current awareness materials, i.e., newsletters that were considered too specialized.

ADVANCES IN ENVIRONMENTAL SCIENCE AND TECHNOLOGY. New York: Wiley, 1971-- . Irreg. Continues: ADVANCES IN ENVIRONMENTAL SCIENCES, 1969.

ADVANCES IN MODERN HUMAN NUTRITION. Park Forest South, Ill.: Pathotox, 1980-- . Irreg.

ADVANCES IN MODERN TOXICOLOGY. Washington, D.C., and New York: Hemisphere; distributed by Halsted Press, 1976-- . Irreg.

AMBIO: A JOURNAL OF THE HUMAN ENVIRONMENT, RESEARCH AND MANAGEMENT. Stockholm: Royal Swedish Academy of Sciences, distributed by Pergamon Press, Elmsford, N.Y., 1972-- . Bimonthly.

AMERICAN ANTHROPOLOGIST. Washington, D.C.: American Anthropological Association, 1888-- . Quarterly.

AMERICAN INDUSTRIAL HYGIENE ASSOCIATION JOURNAL. Akron: American Industrial Hygiene Association, 1958-- . Monthly. Continues: AMERICAN INDUSTRIAL HYGIENE ASSOCIATION QUARTERLY, 1946-57.

AMERICAN JOURNAL OF CLINICAL NUTRITION. Bethesda, Md.: American Society of Clinical Nutrition, 1952-- . Monthly.

AMERICAN JOURNAL OF EPIDEMIOLOGY. (Sponsored by the Society for

Epidemiologic Research) Baltimore, Md.: School of Hygiene and Public Health of the Johns Hopkins University, 1921-- . Monthly.

AMERICAN JOURNAL OF HUMAN GENETICS. (American Society of Human Genetics) Chicago: University of Chicago Press, 1949-- . Bimonthly.

AMERICAN JOURNAL OF INDUSTRIAL MEDICINE. New York: Liss, 1980-- 4 issues per year.

AMERICAN JOURNAL OF PUBLIC HEALTH. Washington, D.C.: American Public Health Association, 1911-- . Monthly. 1928-70 published with THE NATION'S HEALTH under title AMERICAN JOURNAL OF PUBLIC HEALTH AND THE NATION'S HEALTH.

AMERICAN NATURALIST. (American Society of Naturalists) Chicago: University of Chicago Press, 1867-- . Monthly.

AMERICAN REVIEW OF RESPIRATORY DISEASES: CLINICAL AND LABORATORY STUDIES OF TUBERCULOSIS AND RESPIRATORY DISEASES. New York: American Thoracic Society, Medical Section of the American Lung Association, 1917-- . Monthly.

AMERICAN SCIENTIST. (Issued in cooperation with the Scientific Research Society of America) New Haven, Conn.: Sigma Xi, 1942-- . Bimonthly. Continues: SIGMA XI QUARTERLY, 1913-42.

ANNALS OF HUMAN BIOLOGY. (Society for the Study of Human Biology) London: Taylor and Francis, 1974-- . Bimonthly.

ANNALS OF OCCUPATIONAL HYGIENE. (British Occupational Hygiene Society) Oxford and New York: Pergamon, 1958-- . Quarterly.

ARCHIVES OF ENVIRONMENTAL CONTAMINATION AND TOXICOLOGY. New York: Springer Verlag, 1972-- . Quarterly.

ARCHIVES OF ENVIRONMENTAL HEALTH. Washington, D.C.: Heldref, 1960-- . Bimonthly. Continues: ARCHIVES OF INDUSTRIAL HEALTH, 1955-60, which superceded A.M.A. ARCHIVES OF INDUSTRIAL MEDICINE AND OCCUPATIONAL MEDICINE, 1950-54.

ATMOSPHERIC ENVIRONMENT: AN INTERNATIONAL JOURNAL. Elmsford, N.Y.: Pergamon, 1966-- . Monthly.

AVIATION, SPACE AND ENVIRONMENTAL MEDICINE. Washington, D.C.: Aerospace Medical Association, 1975-- . Monthly. Continues: AEROSPACE MEDICINE, 1962-74.

BIOSCIENCE. Arlington, Va.: American Institute of Biological Sciences, 1951-- . Monthly.

BRITISH JOURNAL OF INDUSTRIAL MEDICINE. London: British Medical Association, 1944-- . Quarterly.

BULLETIN OF ENVIRONMENTAL CONTAMINATION AND TOXICOLOGY. New York: Springer-Verlag, 1966-- . Monthly.

BULLETIN OF THE ATOMIC SCIENTISTS; SCIENCE AND PUBLIC AFFAIRS. Chicago: Educational Foundation for Nuclear Science, 1974-- . Monthly. Continues: SCIENCE AND PUBLIC AFFAIRS, 1970-74.

CHEMOSPHERE. Elmsford, N.Y.: Pergamon, 1972-- . Monthly.

CRC CRITICAL REVIEWS IN ENVIRONMENTAL CONTROL. West Palm Beach, Fla.: CRC Press, 1970-- . Quarterly.

CURRENT ANTHROPOLOGY. (Sponsored by the Wenner-Gren Foundation for Anthropological Research) Chicago: University of Chicago Press, 1960-- . Bimonthly.

DEMOGRAPHY. Chicago: Population Association of America, 1964-- . Quarterly.

EHP; ENVIRONMENTAL HEALTH PERSPECTIVES. Research Triangle Park, N.C.: U.S. National Institute of Environmental Health Sciences; Washington, D.C.: Government Printing Office, 1972-- . Quarterly.

ES&T, ENVIRONMENTAL SCIENCE & TECHNOLOGY. Washington, D.C.: American Chemical Society, 1978-- . Monthly. Continues: ENVIRONMENTAL SCIENCE & TECHNOLOGY, 1967-77.

ECOLOGY: ALL FORMS OF LIFE IN RELATION TO THE ENVIRONMENT. (Ecological Society of America) Durham, N.C.: Duke University Press, 1920-- . Bimonthly.

ECOLOGY OF FOOD AND NUTRITION. London: Gordon and Breach, 1971-- . 8 issues per year.

ECOTOXICOLOGY AND ENVIRONMENTAL SAFETY. (International Academy of Environmental Safety) New York: Academic Press, 1977-- . Quarterly. Continues: ENVIRONMENTAL QUALITY AND SAFETY, 1972-76.

EKISTICS. Athens: Athens Center for Ekistics of the Athens Technological Organization, 1958-- . 10 issues per year.

ENVIRONMENT. Washington, D.C.: Heldref Publications, 1969-- . 10 issues per year. Continues: SCIENTIST AND CITIZEN, 1958-68.

ENVIRONMENTAL MANAGEMENT: AN INTERNATIONAL JOURNAL FOR DECISION MAKERS AND SCIENTISTS. New York: Springer-Verlag, 1977-- . Bimonthly.

ENVIRONMENTAL QUALITY AND SAFETY: CHEMISTRY, TOXICOLOGY AND TECHNOLOGY. Stuttgart: Georg Thieme Verlag, 1972-- . Irregular.

ENVIRONMENTAL RESEARCH. New York: Academic, 1967-- . Bimonthly.

ENVIRONMENT INTERNATIONAL: A JOURNAL OF SCIENCE TECHNOLOGY, HEALTH MONITORING AND POLICY. Oxford and New York: Pergamon Press, 1978-- . Monthly.

ENVIRONMENT REPORTER. Washington, D.C.: Bureau of National Affairs, 1970-- . (Looseleaf) Weekly. Issued in parts: CURRENT DEVELOPMENTS. DECISIONS, FEDERAL LAWS. FEDERAL REGULATIONS. STATE AIR LAWS. STATE SOLID WASTE-LAND USE. STATE WATER LAWS.

FEDERATION PROCEEDINGS. Bethesda, Md.: Federation of American Societies for Experimental Biology, 1942-- . Monthly.

HABITAT INTERNATIONAL. New York: Pergamon Press, 1977-- . Bimonthly. Continues: HABITAT, 1976-77.

HEALTH PHYSICS. (Health Physics Society) New York: Pergamon Press, 1958-- . Monthly.

HEALTH VALUES; ACHIEVING HIGH LEVEL WELLNESS. Thorofare, N.J.: C. B. Slack, 1977-- . Bimonthly.

HUMAN ECOLOGY; AN INTERDISCIPLINARY JOURNAL. New York: Plenum, 1972-- . Quarterly.

INTERNATIONAL ARCHIVES OF OCCUPATIONAL AND ENVIRONMENTAL HEALTH. Berlin and New York: Springer-Verlag, 1975-- . Quarterly. Continues: INTERNATIONAL ARCHIVES OF OCCUPATIONAL HEALTH, 1970-75. This title superceded INTERNATIONALES ARCHIV FUER GEWERBEPATHOLOGIE UND GEWERBEHYGIENE, 1962-68.

INTERNATIONAL JOURNAL OF BIOMETEOROLOGY. (International Society of Biometeorology) Amsterdam: Swets and Zeitlinger, 1957-- . 4 issues per year.

JOURNAL OF APPLIED TOXICOLOGY. (Genetic Toxicology Association)
Philadelphia: Heyden and Son, 1981-- . Bimonthly.

JOURNAL OF BIOGEOGRAPHY. Oxford, Engl.: Blackwell Scientific Publications, 1974-- . Bimonthly.

JOURNAL OF CHRONIC DISEASES. New York: Pergamon Press, 1955-- . Monthly.

JOURNAL OF ENVIRONMENTAL ECONOMICS AND MANAGEMENT. New York: Academic Press, 1974-- . Quarterly.

JOURNAL OF ENVIRONMENTAL HEALTH. Denver: National Environmental Health Association, 1938-- . Bimonthly. Continues: SANITARIAN'S JOURNAL OF ENVIRONMENTAL HEALTH, 1962-63, and SANITARIAN, 1958-62, issued by National Association of Sanitarians.

JOURNAL OF ENVIRONMENTAL MANAGEMENT. London and New York: Academic Press, 1973-- . Bimonthly.

JOURNAL OF ENVIRONMENTAL PATHOLOGY AND TOXICOLOGY. Park Forest South, Ill.: Pathotox Publishers, 1977-- .

JOURNAL OF ENVIRONMENTAL QUALITY. Madison, Wis.: Published cooperatively by American Society of Agronomy, Crop Science Society of America, and Soil Science Society of America, 1972-- . Quarterly.

JOURNAL OF EPIDEMIOLOGY AND COMMUNITY HEALTH. London: British Medical Association, 1979-- . Quarterly. Continues: EPIDEMIOLOGY AND COMMUNITY HEALTH, 1979. Formerly: BRITISH JOURNAL OF PREVENTIVE AND SOCIAL MEDICINE, 1953-77; BRITISH JOURNAL OF SOCIAL MEDICINE, 1947-52.

JOURNAL OF HEALTH AND SOCIAL BEHAVIOR. Washington, D.C.: American Sociological Association, 1967-- . Quarterly. Continues: JOURNAL OF HEALTH AND HUMAN BEHAVIOR, 1960-67.

JOURNAL OF HEALTH POLITICS, POLICY AND LAW. Durham, N.C.: Duke University Press, 1976-- . Quarterly.

JOURNAL OF NUTRITION. Bethesda, Md.: American Institute of Nutrition, 1928-- . Bimonthly.

JOURNAL OF PUBLIC HEALTH POLICY. South Burlington, Vt.: Journal of Public Health Policy, 1980-- . Quarterly.

JOURNAL OF THE AIR POLLUTION CONTROL ASSOCIATION. Louisville, Ky.: Air Pollution Control Association, 1951-- . Quarterly.

JOURNAL OF THE ATMOSPHERIC SCIENCES. Boston: American Meteorological Society, 1944-- . Monthly.

JOURNAL OF TOXICOLOGY AND ENVIRONMENTAL HEALTH. Washington, D.C.: Hemisphere Publishing Corp., 1975-- . 9 issues per year.

MAN AND MEDICINE. New York: Man and Medicine, 1975-- . Quarterly.

MEDICAL ANTHROPOLOGY. Pleasantville, N.Y.: Redgrave Publishing Co., 1977-- . Quarterly.

MEDICAL CARE. (American Public Health Association, Medical Care Section, 1967--) Philadelphia: Lippincott, 1963-- . Monthly.

MONTHLY VITAL STATISTICS REPORT. Hyattsville, Md.: U.S. Public Health Service, Health Resources Administration, National Center for Health Statistics; Washington, D.C., Government Printing Office, 1952-- .

MORBIDITY AND MORTALITY WEEKLY REPORT. Atlanta, Ga.: Centers for Disease Control; Washington, D.C.: Government Printing Office, 1952-- .

NATURE. London: Macmillan Journals Ltd., 1869-- . Biweekly.

NUTRITION REVIEWS. Washington, D.C.: Nutrition Foundation, 1942-- . Monthly.

OCCUPATIONAL HEALTH. London: Balliere Tindall, 1949-- . Monthly.

OCCUPATIONAL HEALTH & SAFETY. Waco, Texas: Medical Publications, 1976-- . Monthly.

POPULATION AND DEVELOPMENT REVIEW. New York: Population Council, 1975-- . Quarterly.

POPULATION STUDIES. (Population Investigation Committee) London: University Press, 1947-- . 3 issues per year.

PREVENTIVE MEDICINE. (American Health Foundation) New York: Academic Press, 1972-- . Bimonthly.

PUBLIC HEALTH. (Society of Community Medicine) London and New York: Academic Press, 1888-- . Bimonthly. Formerly: SOCIETY OF MEDICAL OF-FICERS OF HEALTH. TRANSACTIONS.

PUBLIC HEALTH IN EUROPE. Copenhagen: Regional Office for Europe, World Health Organization, 1972-- . Irregular.

RADIATION RESEARCH. (Radiation Research Society) New York: Academic Press, 1954-- . Monthly.

REGULATORY TOXICOLOGY AND PHARMACOLOGY. New York: Academic Press, 1981-- . Quarterly.

REMOTE SENSING OF ENVIRONMENT. New York: American Elsevier Publishing Co., 1969-- . Bimonthly.

RISK ANALYSIS. (Society for Risk Analysis) New York: Plenum Press, 1981-- . Quarterly.

SCANDINAVIAN JOURNAL OF SOCIAL MEDICINE. (Scandinavian Association for Social Medicine) Stockholm: Almqvist and Wiksell, 1973-- . 4 issues per year.

SCANDINAVIAN JOURNAL OF WORK, ENVIRONMENT & HEALTH. Stockholm: National Board of Occupational Safety and Health, 1975-- . Quarterly.

SCIENCE. Washington, D.C.: American Association for the Advancement of Science, 1880-- . Weekly.

SOCIAL INDICATORS RESEARCH. Dordrecht, Holland, and Boston: Reidel Publishing Co., 1974-- . 4 issues per year.

SOCIAL SCIENCE & MEDICINE. Oxford, Engl.: Pergamon Press, 1967-- . Semimonthly. Issued in 6 parts, individually subtitled, 1978-81.

SOCIOLOGY OF HEALTH & ILLNESS. Boston: Routledge and Kegan Paul, 1979-- . Quarterly.

SYSTEMS ANALYSIS AND SIMULATION IN ECOLOGY. New York: Academic Press, 1971-- . Annual.

THEORETICAL POPULATION BIOLOGY. New York: Academic Press, 1970-- . Bimonthly.

Journals

TOXICOLOGY AND APPLIED PHARMACOLOGY. (Society of Toxicology) New York: Academic Press, 1959-- . Monthly.

WATER POLLUTION CONTROL FEDERATION JOURNAL. Washington, D.C.: Water Pollution Control Federation, 1928-- . Monthly.

WATER RESEARCH. (International Association on Water Pollution Research) Oxford and New York: Pergamon Press, 1967-- . Monthly.

WATER RESOURCES BULLETIN. Minneapolis: American Water Resources Association, 1965-- . Bimonthly.

WATER RESOURCES RESEARCH. Washington, D.C.: American Geophysical Union, 1965-- . Bimonthly.

WORLD HEALTH FORUM. Geneva: World Health Organization, 1980-- . Quarterly.

ABSTRACTS AND INDEXES

Because of the multidisciplinary nature of human ecology the list of primary sources is indeed extensive. One way to cut through the abundance of literature is to search the abstracting and indexing tools for the particular topical aspect of interest to you. The titles listed below will yield very good results with either manual or automated (on-line) bibliographic searching.

ABSTRACTS ON HEALTH EFFECTS OF ENVIRONMENTAL POLLUTANTS. Philadelphia: BioSciences Information Service of Biological Abstracts, 1972-- . Monthly.

CHEMICAL ABSTRACTS. Columbus, Ohio: Chemical Abstracts Service, 1907-- . Weekly. Index cumulated annually and every ten years 1907-56; every five years 1957-- .

CUMULATED INDEX MEDICUS. Rockville, Md.: National Library of Medicine; Washington, D.C.: Government Printing Office, 1960-- . Also issued monthly as INDEX MEDICUS.

DIRECTORY OF PUBLISHED PROCEEDINGS. SERIES SEMT: SCIENCE/ENGI-NEERING/MEDICINE/TECHNOLOGY. Harrison, N.Y.: InterDok, 1967-- . Monthly with annual cumulations. Continues: DIRECTORY OF PUBLISHED PROCEEDINGS, 1965-67.

EPA PUBLICATIONS BIBLIOGRAPHY QUARTERLY ABSTRACTS BULLETIN. Washington, D.C.: U.S. Environmental Protection Agency (available through the National Technical Information Service, Springfield, Va.), 1977-- . Quarterly. Continues: EPA REPORTS BIBLIOGRAPHY, 1977-- . Cumulation 1970/76 issued separately as EPA CUMULATIVE BIBLIOGRAPHY.

ENVIRONMENTAL PERIODICAL BIBLIOGRAPHY: INDEXED ARTICLE TITLES. Santa Barbara, Calif.: International Academy at Santa Barbara, Environmental Studies Institute, 1973-- . Bimonthly. Continues: ENVIRONMENTAL PERI-ODICALS, 1972.

EXCERPTA MEDICA. SECTION 17: PUBLIC HEALTH, SOCIAL MEDICINE AND HYGIENE. Amsterdam: Excerpta Medica Foundation, 1955-- . 2 volumes per year, 10 issues per volume.

EXCERPTA MEDICA. SECTION 35. OCCUPATIONAL HEALTH AND INDUSTRIAL MEDICINE. Amsterdam: Excerpta Medica Foundation, 1971-- . 10 issues per year.

EXCERPTA MEDICA. SECTION 46. ENVIRONMENTAL HEALTH AND POLLUTION CONTROL. Amsterdam: Excerpta Medica Foundation, 1972-- . 10 issues per year.

INTERNATIONAL BIBLIOGRAPHY, INFORMATION, DOCUMENTATION. IBID. New York: Bowker and Unipub, 1973-- . Quarterly.

MEDOC: A COMPUTERIZED INDEX TO U.S. GOVERNMENT DOCUMENTS IN THE MEDICAL AND HEALTH SCIENCES. Salt Lake City: Spencer S. Eccles Medical Sciences Library, University of Utah, 1968-- . Quarterly.

POLLUTION ABSTRACTS. La Jolla, Calif.: Pollution Abstracts, 1970/71-- . Annual.

AUTHOR INDEX

This index includes all authors, editors, compilers, translators, and other contributors to works cited in the text. References are to page numbers and alphabetization is letter by letter.

Author Index

Author Index

Author Index

Author Index

Author Index

Author Index

TITLE INDEX

This index includes all titles of books cited in the text. In some cases titles have been shortened. References are to page numbers and alphabetization is letter by letter.

Title Index

Title Index

SUBJECT INDEX

This index is alphabetized letter by letter.   Underlined page numbers refer to main entries within a subject.

influence of the potato on social-
economic-political conditions
in 52
Iron, as a health hazard 105-6
Irrigation 63, 93, 127, 132
salinization resulting from 133
silting of systems for 134
Islands, physical and biological
features of 7

J

Japan
employment problems in 136
environmental problems and quality
in 97, 102-3, 191
food production in 66, 136
mortality statistics of 156
national nutrition planning in 169
natural resources of 59
population problems of 140
statistical information on 59
use of social indicators in 158-59

K

Kepone, health hazards of 121

L

Lakes
eutrophication of 126, 128
exploitation of 29
man-made 125, 128, 131, 132,
187
Land tenure, agricultural production
and 63
Land use 82, 94, 97, 102, 171,
177, 186
aesthetics and 195
among the Tzotzil Indians 83
climate and 51
conflicts between agriculture and
wildlife in 85-86
effect of the "Green Revolution"
on 133, 136
environmental remote sensing
applied to 162, 167
pollution and 110
rural 91, 187

transportation planning in 169
urban 85, 88, 91
See also Reclamation of land
Latin America
increasing agricultural production
in 180
population policy in 140
See also South America; names of
Latin American countries
(e.g., Brazil)
Law, as an adaptive phenomenon 50
Lead, as a health hazard 101,
106-7, 108, 217
Leisure 4, 180
social indicators in measuring 159
Leptospirosis, man-made lakes and
132
Life-styles
health problems and 206
population levels and 140
resource conservation and 181
See also Quality of Life
Literature 4
Low-income groups
food intake among Pakistani 63
medical beliefs among 36
Lung cancer. See Cancer; Respiratory
diseases

M

Madagascar, state information in 6
Magic, as an adaptive phenomenon
50
Malaria
man-made lakes and 132
pesticide problems in control of
131
Malaysia, ecological considerations in
development of 5
Malnutrition. See Nutrition
Manganese, as a health hazard 113
Maoris, effect of gunpowder on
warfare of 53
Marine environments. See Oceans;
Shorelines; Water resources
Maring (New Guinea people), popu-
lation pressure and war
among 53

Subject Index

Subject Index

P

Pacific Ocean area, influence of man on 7
Pakistan
 relationship between income and food intake in 63
 social information and development in 158
 subsidized food consumption system in 207-8
Paleoecology, human 34
Parks and reserves, African 91
Pellagara, social history of 134, 136
Peru, child growth and development in 46
Pest control and pesticides 28, 64, 86, 96, 102, 120, 127, 128, 129-31, 132, 133, 175, 185, 220
 health implications of 182, 218, 226
 monitoring and regulation of pesticides 164, 194
 properties of pesticides 91, 92
 in tropical areas 173
 See also DDT; Herbicides
Petroleum 179
 pollution and 96, 119, 120, 122, 220
 monitoring of 165-66
 prevention and control 196
Phenoxy acids, health hazards of 108
Phillipine Islands, food and employment problems of 136
Philosophy 4
Phylogeny 31-32
Physical activity, health and 156-57
Plant breeding, genetics and epidemics related to 134, 135
Political scientists, role in environmental policy research 188
Politics and the environment 12, 49, 91, 97, 183, 190, 191, 192, 193
 in agricultural technology 61
 in energy resource choice 68, 174
 in food and hunger problems 137, 179, 225

 in health care delivery 174
 in nutrition 181
 population and 139, 225
 in resource management 178, 183
 in urban planning 172
 in weather modification 78
 See also Government
Polybrominated biphenyls, health hazards of 224
Population 5, 6, 7, 12, 13, 24, 28, 29, 33, 36, 37-39, 45, 47, 58, 59, 90, 92, 95, 96, 97, 98, 138-40, 146, 175, 190, 191, 197, 198, 205
 of Africa 96
 control and growth of 35, 36, 58, 60, 102, 133, 138, 179
  ethical considerations in 173
  global approaches to 169
 in developing countries 20, 140, 179
 food production, hunger, and 60-61, 63, 93, 98, 133, 134, 135-36, 137, 138, 145, 171, 175, 176
 forecasts and projections of 91, 171
 genetics and 30
 geography of 88
 human behavior and 51
 influence on health 149
 of Japan 140
 politics of 139, 225
 structure of 4
 warfare as a reaction to problems of 53
 See also Crowding
Potatoes, history and social influence of 52
Poverty 81, 99, 181, 225
 culture of 84
 the "Green Revolution" and 133
 health and 202
 hunger and 175
 rural 214
Power (social science), genetics of 46
Power resources. See Energy resources

288

Privacy 203
Project Head Start. See Head Start
    program
Protein 94, 210
    alternative sources of 137
    development of products high in
      65
    fish as a source of 178
Psychiatry, preventive 202
Psychology
    abnormal 33
    of adaptive strategies 50
    changes in the science of 201
    of crowding and urbanization 143
    ecological and environmental 28,
      52
Psychosomatic disease, social causes
    of 148-49
Psychotherapy 201
Public health. See Health, com-
    munity and public
Public utilities
    in developing countries 190
    plant siting considerations of 195
    weather modification and 79
    See also Electric power production

Q

Quality of life 149, 191, 195,
    198
    ecological implications for 94-95,
      99
    index of measurement of 222
    population levels and 140
    proposals for improving 168
    urban 210-11
    See also Life-styles

R

Race 30, 31, 47
    biological problems of 33
    concept of 32
    human variations within 35
    social problems and 90
    See also Ethnicity
Radiation; radioactivity 6, 71, 93,
    102, 120, 191, 195

biological and health problems of
    36, 104-5, 109, 182, 185,
    217
    environmental monitoring of 164
    human intake of 32
    management of radioactive waste
      177-78, 227
    See also Solar radiation
Range land, exploitation of 29.
    See also Grasslands
Reclamation of land 86-87
Recreation 97, 177, 180
    climate and 51
    monitoring of environments serving
      163
    shoreline 102
    water pollution and 124
    weather modification and 79
Recycling operations 58, 174, 177
Regionalism 7
Regional planning 29, 187
Religion 35
    as an adaptive phenomenon 50
    attitudes toward 95
    nature and 92
Reproduction 5, 33, 37, 92. See
    also Fertility
Resettlement
    resulting from dam and lake build-
      ing 132
    social consequences of 126
Resource management. See Natural
    resources and resource
    management
Respiratory diseases
    environmental factors in 111, 219
    mining industries and 224
    See also Bronchitis
Retardation. See Mental retardation
Retirement 205
Revolutions. See Riots and revolu-
    tions
Riots and revolutions, influence of
    hunger on 52
Rivers; river basins
    development of 20, 58
    ecology of 78
    river engineering 190
    See also names of rivers (e.g.,
    Hudson River)
Rural areas 4, 177, 221